D1593995

The Damascus Chronicle of the Crusades

Extracted and Translated from the Chronicle of Ibn Al-Qalānisī

H. A. R. Gibb

DOVER PUBLICATIONS, INC.
Mineola, New York

Bibliographical Note

This Dover edition, first published in 2002, is an unabridged republication of the work first published by Luzac & Co., London, in 1932.

Library of Congress Cataloging-in-Publication Data

Ibn al-Qalanisi, Abu Ya'lá Hamzah ibn Asad, d. 1160.
[Dhayl tarikh Dimashq. English. Selections]
The Damascus chronicle of the Crusades / extracted and translated from the Chronicle of Ibn Al-Qalanisi [by] H.A.R. Gibb.
p. cm.
Originally published: London : Luzac, 1932, in series: University of London historical series.
Includes bibliographical indexes.
ISBN 0-486-42519-3 (pbk.)
1. Crusades. 2. Damascus (Syria)–History. I. Gibb, H. A. R. (Hamilton Alexander Rosskeen), Sir, 1895–1971. II. Title.

D152 .I25213 2002
956.91'4402–dc21

2002031543

Manufactured in the United States of America
Dover Publications, Inc., 31 East 2nd Street, Mineola, N.Y. 11501
42519302

CONTENTS

INTRODUCTION

The Damascus Chronicle

THE absence of contemporary Arabic records of the First Crusade and its immediate sequel has been generally remarked by historians, though it is recognized that Ibn al-Athīr and the subsequent Arabic compilers must have utilized contemporary materials for their work. Some years ago, however, one of the Arabic manuscripts preserved in the Bodleian Library (Hunt. 125) was found to contain the supposedly lost " Continuation of the Chronicle of Damascus" of Ibn al-Qalānisī, a work which is frequently quoted by later writers, but which was thought to deal with a period posterior to the Second Crusade. Examination of the manuscript showed that more than two-thirds of the book was devoted to the history of the first sixty years of the Crusades, and the late H. F. Amedroz, recognizing its importance, edited and published the text in 1908, together with a summary of contents, notes, and extracts from other unpublished sources. Owing to lack of a translation the recovery of this chronicle seems to have passed unnoticed by European historians, and the extracts contained in the present volume constitute the first attempt to make it accessible to Western scholarship.

Of the author of the " Damascus Chronicle " scarcely anything can be gathered from the work itself. Fortunately, however, brief but sufficient particulars of his life are to be found both in the biographical dictionary of famous men of Damascus compiled by his younger contemporary Ibn 'Asākir, and in the pages of several later historians, thanks to their pious custom of closing the annals of each year with short obituaries of notable men deceased in its course.

Hamza son of Asad, known as Abū Ya 'lā, belonged to an old-established and respected family of Damascus, which boasted descent from the Arab tribe of Tamīm and bore the surname of al-Qalānisī (" the Hatter "). Like most upperclass citizens, he was well educated in literature, theology and law, and went into public service as a secretary in the Correspondence Bureau or Chancery (*Dīwan al-Rasā'il*), of which, apparently, he rose to be head (*'amīd*). In addition, he twice held the highest civil office in the city, that of *ra'īs* or Mayor, though the exact functions attached to this office are not quite clear to us. The same post was held also by his nephew in later years (A.H. 548 ; Arabic text p. 325). He died on Friday 7th First Rabī' 555 (18th March, 1160), over ninety years of age, his elder brother Muhammad having predeceased him in January, 1145 at the age of eighty-four (both, of course, reckoned in lunar years). He was therefore, already of mature age when the First Crusade burst upon Syria and though he does not appear to have taken any part in the actual fighting, his Chronicle is of exceptional interest as presenting a contemporary account of the fortunes of the Crusaders, in so far as they were known at Damascus, from the beginning of the Crusades down to the year of his death.

Apart from his poems, many of which he quotes, the Chronicle seems to be the only literary work undertaken by Ibn al-Qalānisī. The composition and title of the book, " Continuation of the Chronicle of Damascus " (*Dhail* or *Mudhayyal Ta'rīkh Dimashq*), show that it was intended as a supplement to an earlier Chronicle, the work of the famous historian Hilāl b. al-Muhassin al-Sābi', from the point where it was interrupted by the death of its author in A.H. 448 (1056). On the other hand, whereas Hilāl's Chronicle was universal in its scope, Ibn al-Qalānisī's continuation (together with the extracts from the earlier work which he prefaced to it) is centred on the city of Damascus and treats only incidentally of events in other regions.

It was, in all probability, the facilities offered to him by his official connections which led him to this undertaking, since the entire period with which he deals was covered by the lives of his father and himself. The information which he gives is derived from oral and written reports, sometimes taken down from the lips of actual participants. It is perhaps remarkable that he should so seldom quote documents, though many of his narratives doubtless give the gist of documentary materials. Most of them were apparently written down at the time when they were received and subjected to revision afterwards, as is evident from many indications in the text, such as the frequent use of the present tense, especially in the later sections. One obvious advantage of his work in consequence is the accuracy of his chronology of events. For the rest, he himself explains his methods of compilation in an excursus under date A.H. 540 (Arabic text p. 283) :

> I have completed the narrative of events set forth in this chronicle, and I have arranged them in order and taken precautions against error and rashness of judgment and careless slips in the materials which I have transcribed from the mouths of trustworthy persons and have transmitted after exerting myself to make the fullest investigations so as to verify them, down to this blessed year 540. Since the year 535 and down to this point I had been engaged with matters which distracted my mind from making the fullest enquiries into those current events which required to be set down in this book, and from seeking out the truth concerning them and all the attendant circumstances. Consequently I left a blank space after the events of each year, in order to insert therein those narratives and events the truth of which was ascertained.

The importance of the " Damascus Chronicle " for the history of the early Crusades is evident from the fact that it formed one of the primary sources of all subsequent Arabic historians. It was extensively quoted by Sibt ibn al-Jawzī and Ibn al-Athīr in their general histories and by Abū Shāma in his biographical work on Nūr al-Dīn, as well as by numerous later writers. As the works of all these compilers have been translated and utilized by modern historians of the Crusades, there is little of its contents that is entirely new. By itself also, it presents a one-sided view of the Crusades, since the interest of the writer was concentrated on Damascus, and he therefore devotes much more attention to the neighbouring kingdom of Jerusalem than to the struggle of the northern Crusading states with the principalities of Aleppo and Mosul. For this aspect of the Crusades it is necessary to supplement his history by the "Aleppo Chronicle" of Kamāl al-Dīn,[1] who, though he occasionally quotes Ibn al-Qalānisī verbatim, based his narrative on independent local sources.[2]

Nevertheless the original work of Ibn al-Qalānisī still retains so much material not utilized by the later compilers, and so many features of its own, that it will form an indispensable source for all future students of the early Crusades. It makes it possible, for example, to trace for the first time the hardening of Muslim feeling against the Crusaders, and the stages by which the mutual jealousies of the Muslim princes were overborne by the rising temper of the people, which came to expression in the reign of Nūr al-Dīn and culminated in the great *revanche* under Saladin. In the writings of the generation contemporary with Saladin and even of one who, like Usāma ibn Munqidh, lived through the earlier period but wrote his *Memoirs* late in life, this development is obscured. It is this fact which justifies the inclusion in these selections of what would other-

[1] French translations of the part of this work dealing with the early Crusades may be found : (a) in the *Receuil*, Hist. Or., III ; (b) by de Sacy in Röhricht's *Beiträge zur Geschichte der Kreuzzüge*, Vol. I (1874) ; (c) by Defrémery in *Mélanges d'histoire orientale*, Paris, 1854.

[2] Kamāl al-Dīn's contemporary authority for the history of the early Crusades was probably " The History of the Franks who came forth to the Land of Islam " (*Siratu'l-Ifranji'l-khārijīna'ilā bilādi'l-'islāmi*) of Hamdān b. 'Abd al-Rahīm of al-Athārib, d. 1159 (referred to by Ibn Muyassar, *Annales d'Egypte*, ed. H. Massé (Cairo, 1919), p. 70, 6-7).

wise seem to be the excessive space given up to the record of the internal history of Damascus and its relations with other Muslim states. In addition to this, there are many episodes in regard to which the " Damascus Chronicle " presents new material. Outstanding instances will be found in the lively accounts of the siege of Tyre in the winter of 1111–1112 below (pp. 121-5) and of the early activities of the "Assassins" (pp. 187 ff). The close relations which, as Ibn al-Qalānisī shows, still existed between Damascus and the Fātimid court in Egypt also enabled him to give fairly full accounts of the sporadic Egyptian activities against the Crusaders. Moreover, the later chroniclers usually abridged his narratives very considerably, and in so doing omitted many details which are of value to the modern historian. One of the details thus omitted was the day of the week, which Ibn al-Qalānisī is generally careful to insert along with his dates, and which, by supplying a check upon the errors of copyists, is of special importance in determining the exact chronology.

On the other hand, the " Damascus Chronicle " presents difficulties of its own, particularly in regard to the language and style. In true diplomatic fashion Ibn al-Qalānisī frequently covers up his meaning with a mass of verbiage and vague phrases which make it difficult to gather the precise significance of his words. To the modern student this difficulty is enhanced by the peculiarities of his vocabulary. Many usages of words are apparently peculiar to the Syrian style of his time, and while the *Memoirs* of Usāma ibn Munqidh, the only other Syrian author of this period whose work is still extant, occasionally throw some light upon them, in most cases their meaning can only be inferred from the context. A number of these Arabic words and phrases are quoted in the foot-notes, in the hope that others may correct the interpretation given in the text if it should prove to be faulty. Moreover, the reconstruction of a text from a single manuscript presents, as is well known, dangers in all languages, and in none more than in Arabic. Many readings are obviously corrupt, and the extracts from the '' Chronicle '' in later works give singularly little assistance in their correction, as most of the passages concerned have been omitted by the compilers. If undue liberties appear to have been taken with the text in consequence, it can only be pleaded that without such emendations it gave either no sense or an obviously wrong sense, and that where they could be tested by comparison with the excerpts given by later writers they have generally been found to be justified.

Since this version is primarily intended as a textbook for students, it has been the aim of the translator to render the Arabic text as literally as possible, neither adding to nor subtracting from the author's own words and arrangement. For the same reason, the annotation has been kept down to a minimum, and no attempt has been made to correlate the narratives with those of the other Arabic chronicles and the western sources. Those who are most familiar with the pitfalls in the way of a first translation of an Arabic text will probably be the most ready to look with an indulgent eye upon its imperfections, and any corrections or observations which they may be kind enough to communicate will be welcomed.

SYRIA AT THE TIME OF THE FIRST CRUSADE

That the First Crusade owed its success in large measure to the weakness of the opposition which it encountered is a fact accepted by all modern historians. The complexity of the political situation in Syria at the end of the eleventh century and during the early decades of the twelfth, a complexity verging almost upon anarchy, is an element of the first importance in the history of the Crusades. Not only did it render the task of the invaders much less formidable than it would have been a few years earlier, but it also contributed greatly to the acquiescence of the Syrian princes in the establishment of the Crusading states, since the resulting political divisions followed on the whole traditional lines. The full appreciation of these circumstances naturally presents difficulties to the modern student, especially if he is unfamiliar with the background of oriental history against which the drama of the Crusades was staged, and a detailed analysis of conditions in Syria at this period forms a necessary preliminary to the study of the Arabic sources.

There were at this time six distinct forces which were in conflict with one another in Syria. These were : (1) the Fātimid empire ; (2) the local Arab tribes and princes ; (3) the Saljūqid Turkmen princes ; (4) the Turkish military officers, or *amirs* ; (5) the independent or non-Saljūqid

Turkmen tribes ; (6) the general body of the population. It will probably be more helpful to deal with each of these elements separately than to follow a strictly chronological order of events.

(1) The Fātimid Caliphate, which had established itself in North-West Africa in 909, and in 972 transferred its seat to Egypt, constituted a deliberate challenge to the religious headship of the Islamic world claimed by the 'Abbāsid Caliphs of Baghdād. In order to press home their claim in Baghdād itself, it was necessary for them to hold Syria, and ever since their capture of Egypt they had made this their chief object, with the aid first of Berber troops from their African provinces and subsequently of Turkish slave-armies. In Syria, however, they encountered a bitter resistance, less on grounds of religious dogma [1] than from the ambition of the Arab Syrian princes to maintain their independence. Between 1038 and 1058 their authority was at length made effective throughout all Syria (with the exception of Antioch, held by the Greeks) and was recognized also in Western Mesopotamia ; in the latter year their suzerainty was acknowledged even at Baghdād, thanks to the temporary success of a rebellious vassal of the 'Abbāsid government. From this moment, however, their power steadily declined, more especially after a prolonged economic and military crisis in Egypt (1062–1073)

[1] The esoteric Shi'ite doctrine of the Fāṭimids was for private consumption ; the official practice of their Empire differed little from that of the orthodox Sunnīs, and in religious matters they were as a rule most tolerant. The main point at issue was political, i.e., the right of the house of 'Alī to the Caliphate as against the right of the house of 'Abbās.

deprived them of the means of maintaining their authority. Aleppo was finally lost in 1060, Tripoli and Tyre fell into the hands of local rulers, the governors in Damascus could not maintain themselves in face of military indiscipline, and the appearance of the Turkmen armies in Syria in 1070 led to the definitive loss not only of Damascus, but of the greater part of Palestine (including Jerusalem) as well.

The misrule of the first Turkmen general caused a general revulsion of popular feeling in favour of the Fātimids, but the opportunity was not followed up by effective military action. Sporadic expeditions were made into the interior, but they produced no results. On the other hand, the Egyptians were still powerful on sea, and thus succeeded in recovering (1089) the coast towns as far north as Jubail, and in holding them until the advent of the Crusaders. It will be seen from the pages of Ibn al-Qalānisī that, apart from the recapture of Jerusalem in 1098 and a few expeditions into southern Palestine during the rule of the great Armenian wazīr al-Afdal, the share of the Fātimid state in the war operations in Syria was almost entirely confined to naval activities. In subsequent years the Fātimid armies were distracted by bitter internal feuds, and formed a greater danger to their rulers than to their enemies.

Nevertheless, it would be a serious mistake to assume that the influence of the Fātimids in Syria was entirely dissipated by their misfortunes and growing weakness. Our narratives show clearly that they still had a strong following both in the chief cities and in the outer districts, and that even the Saljūqid princes and their successors found it expedient to court their favour. The definite breach between the Fātimids and the Muslim princes of Syria seems to have come about only in the time and at the instance of Nūr al-Dīn.

(2) The main opposition to the Fātimids in their attempts to establish their rule in Syria was offered by the shaikhs of semi-nomadic Arab tribes, who had created small principalities for themselves in, or taken possession of, various parts of the country. Transjordan and the western fringes of the Syrian desert were held by the tribe of Tayy, which was a perpetual thorn in their side in Palestine and remained to play a minor part in the history of the Crusades. Of greater political importance were the tribes of Mesopotamia, particularly the confederations of 'Uqail and Kilāb. The latter, under the leadership of the house of Mirdās, after half a century of struggle in northern Syria, finally succeeded in capturing Aleppo in 1060, only to lose it in 1079 to their 'Uqailid rivals, who were at that time supporting the cause of the Saljūqids. The momentary expansion of the 'Uqailid dominions from Aleppo to Mosul, however, brought them in turn into conflict with the Saljūqid prince of Syria. In the upshot they were decimated and expelled from Aleppo and their Mesopotamian holdings, but two branches succeeded in maintaining themselves at Qal 'at Ja 'bar and on the Middle Euphrates until the time of Zankī and Nūr al-Dīn.

It was not only the heads of great tribal groups, however, who succeeded in creating principalities for their own benefit in Syrian territory. At the time of the First Crusade several important cities and fortresses were in the hands of local Arab rulers, who were able to maintain their independence by virtue of supple diplomacy and the dissensions of their more powerful neighbours. On the breakdown of the Fātimid government in 1070 the qādī of Tyre, Ibn Abī 'Aqīl, made himself independent, and held the city until it was recovered by the Egyptians in 1089. The qādī of Tripoli, Hasan ibn 'Ammār, who revolted in the same year, was more fortunate, and Tripoli remained in the hands of successive members of the same family until its capture by the Crusaders.[1] One of them, in 1080, even extended his rule to Jabala at the expense of the Greeks. It is noteworthy that neither in Tyre nor in Tripoli was the spiritual suzerainty of the Fātimid Caliph rejected, though the rulers of both sought the aid of the Turkmen invaders against Fātimid attempts at the reconquest of their cities, and Ibn 'Ammār at Tripoli claimed to possess a regular diploma of investiture from the Saljūqid sultan at Baghdād.

A still more remarkable Arab principality was founded at Shaizar in 1081 by one 'Alī ibn Munqidh, who bought the town and its citadel in that year from its Christian bishop. The tolerant policy which he pursued towards his Christian subjects stood his family in good stead, and the princes of Shaizar frequently figure in the annals of northern Syria until the entire family perished

[1] On the history of this family see "Inscription d'un Prince de Tripoli de la dynastie des Banū 'Ammār," by G. Wiet, in *Mémorial Henri Basset* (Paris, 1928), 279-284.

in the ruins of the citadel during the earthquakes of 1157. Usāma ibn Munqidh, the writer of those vivacious Memoirs [1] which throw such a flood of light on the social history of the Crusading period, was a great-grandson of ʿAlī. An adventurer of much less reputable character, Khalaf ibn Mulā ʿib, also succeeded in carving out an independent principality. He was originally established in Hims in 1082 by the ʿUqailid prince of Aleppo, in order to form a buffer between himself and the Saljūqid prince at Damascus, but was ejected thence in 1090, and from Afāmiya, whither he had betaken himself, in 1091. After some years of imprisonment in Isfahān he retired to Egypt, and was restored in 1096 or 1097 to Afāmiya by the Fātimid Caliph, to whom the inhabitants of the town, in revolt against the Saljūqids, had sent a deputation to ask for a governor. The subsequent fate of Khalaf will be found in the extracts translated from Ibn al-Qalānisī.

(3) The eleventh century witnessed an extensive migration of Turkmen tribes, known generally as the Ghuzz, from the borders of the Asiatic steppe-lands across Western Asia. The Saljūqids were chieftains of one of these tribes, who succeeded in building up a strong military power, with which they established their authority successively in Khurāsān, Persia, ʿIrāq, Armenia, and Anatolia. As strictly orthodox Sunnīs, they constituted themselves the champions of the ʿAbbasid Caliphs of

[1] See *An Arab-Syrian Gentleman and Warrior in the Period of the Crusades*, translated by Philip K. Hitti, Columbia Univ. Press, 1929.

Baghdād, and were in consequence declared enemies of the Fātimid Caliphs of Cairo. The first Ghuzz bands appeared in Syria shortly before 1070. In that year one of their leaders, Atsiz, seized Palestine on behalf of the Saljūqid Sultan Alp-Arslān, who in the same year made the 'Uqailid prince of Aleppo his vassal. In 1075, Atsiz captured Damascus from the leader of the Berber garrison, but was defeated in the following year in an attack upon the outposts of Egypt— to the great joy of the Damascenes, who detested his tyranny.

The failure of Atsiz may have been in part responsible for the decision of Alp-Arslān's successor, Malikshāh, to dispatch his brother Tutush into Syria with a Saljūqid army in 1077, at the same time investing him with the possession of "everything which he could conquer in Syria." Tutush had little difficulty in seizing Damascus and recovering Palestine from the Fātimids, but Aleppo resisted his assaults. Indeed, Malikshāh twice intervened in person in order, it would almost seem, to protect Aleppo against his brother. On the first occasion the 'Uqailid prince had attempted to form an alliance with the Fātimids against Tutush ; Malikshāh thereupon occupied the city at the close of 1082, but restored it to the 'Uqailid as his vassal. Two years later, the Saljūqid Sultan of Anatolia, Sulaimān ibn Qutulmish, invaded northern Syria, recovered Antioch, and subsequently killed the 'Uqailid in battle, but failed to capture Aleppo. A conflict then broke out (1086) between Sulaimān and Tutush, in the course of which Sulaimān was killed and Tutush seized

Aleppo. Malikshāh again intervened, occupied Aleppo, Antioch and al-Ruhā (Edessa), and handed them over as fiefs to Turkish generals, Aleppo falling to the share of Āq-Sunqur, the father of Zankī.

During the next few years these generals loyally seconded the efforts of Tutush to extend the Saljūqid dominions in Syria and to overthrow the power of the 'Uqailids in Mesopotamia and Diyār-Bakr. Meanwhile, Malikshāh had died (November 1092) and was succeeded as Sultan by his son Barkyāruq. But Tutush coveted the imperial title for himself and marched into Khurāsān. His first attempt was, however, frustrated by the decision of Āq-Sunqur of Aleppo and several of his fellow generals to support Barkyāruq, and he was forced to retire to Syria in order to deal with them. In May, 1094, he routed the combined forces of Aleppo, al-Ruhā, and Mosul, executed Āq-Sunqur and his allies, seized their cities, and once again marched into Khurāsān. For a few months he was publicly proclaimed as Sultan, until Barkyāruq resumed the offensive and on 26th February, 1095, routed his forces near Rayy (Teheran). Tutush himself perished on the field, at the hands, it is said, of the troops of Āq-Sunqur. It was this battle which decided the fate of the First Crusade. Had the Crusaders been met with the combined resources of the unitary kingdom built up by Tutush, history would certainly have been rewritten ; as it was, his hard-won Syrian possessions were again disintegrated by the rivalries of his sons Rudwān and Duqāq and the jealousy and self-seeking of his former generals.

(4) In the course of the tenth century the old bureaucratic administration of the Caliphate and the states which arose on its ruins had gradually given way to a military system of government. The governors of cities and provinces were selected from amongst the military commanders or *amirs*, who were in most cases Turkish ex-slaves, and these governors not only enjoyed almost unfettered control of their " fiefs " but also maintained standing armies of Turkish slaves of their own. The temptation to assert their independence was enhanced by the arbitrary manner in which their overlords were accustomed to revoke their commands, despoil them of their possessions, and even execute them on mere suspicion. The accession of a weak ruler or a dispute regarding the succession was consequently the signal for the disruption of a kingdom into a number of petty principalities, the rulers of which, mere " robber barons," unceasingly engaged in warfare with one another until order was restored by the sword of the strongest. Not infrequently an amīr betook himself with his private troops to some remote district and forcibly seized possession of it, maintaining himself until he was either dislodged or granted a formal diploma of investiture.

The Saljūqids did not introduce any material change into this system, if such a term can be applied to it. Their own imperial organization consisted of a loose association of kingdoms under different members of the Saljūqid house (" kings "), each of whom owed allegiance to the head of the family or " Great Saljūq " in Persia and Baghdād, who bore the title of " Sultān." The subordinate

Turkish governors were even required to maintain standing armies as a condition of holding their grants. This organization worked well enough under the first three sultans, but from the death of Malikshāh in 1092 the old weakness began to reassert itself, and in various parts of the empire (and nowhere more than in Syria) the rival ambitions of generals and princes produced a s:ate of constant warfare. It has already been seen that Tutush was faced with a rising of the governors in northern Syria, and though he was successful in putting it down for the moment, the spirit of revolt reappeared on his death. After the execution of Āq-Sunqur, the most powerful of the governors was Yāghī-Siyān, who had been appointed to Antioch about 1090, and whose dominions had subsequently been extended (apparently by Tutush) to Manbij and Tell-Bāshir. From the moment of the occupation of Aleppo by Rudwān, son of Tutush, Yāghī Siyān was engaged in open hostilities with him, and his example was not long in finding imitators.

Another factor which contributed to the rise of independent Turkish principalities was the Atābegate, an institution peculiar to the Saljūqids. We have seen that in the Saljūqid theory of administration each province was governed by a member of the ruling house. To each of these princes there was attached a Turkish general, who bore the title *Atābek*, or " tutor," and who was responsible for their military education and the government of their provinces. Since the Atābek stood in a paternal relationship to the Saljūqid " king " he enjoyed an authority far above that of, the ordinary generals ; it seems also to have been the custom for the Atābek to receive in marriage the mother of his charge and to give one of his daughters in marriage to him. In accordance with the usual practice Tutush assigned the amīr Janāh al-Dawla al-Husain as atābek to his son Rudwān and the amīr Zahīr al-Dīn Tughtagīn as atābek to Duqāq. After the defeat and death of Tutush, when Rudwān occupied Aleppo and claimed possession of Syria, Janāh al-Dawla assumed control of his territories without question. Duqāq, the second son of Tutush, also retired to Aleppo, but escaped to Damascus on the secret invitation of its governor and set up his rule there. Meanwhile Tughtagīn was in captivity in Persia, having been taken prisoner at the battle of Rayy, but on his release shortly afterwards he at once proceeded to Damascus, and resumed his position as Atābek with the assistance of his wife, Duqāq's mother, the energetic and intriguing princess Safwat al-Mulk.

With the decline of Saljūqid solidarity, it was inevitable that in due course the Atābeks should substitute their own dynasties for those of their protégés. Yet this did not imply, as might be expected, a definite breach with their suzerains, the Great Saljūqs. On the contrary, they continued to maintain a strictly correct attitude of subordination to the Sultans, who, on their part, accepted the course of events with surprisingly little protest. The Atābegate became a mere form ; when, for example, it was decided in 1127 to appoint Zankī to the province of Mosul, he was officially assigned as Atābek to two of the Sultan's younger sons, but they neither took, nor were expected to take, any part whatever in the government of the province. Tughtagīn's elimination, therefore, of the Saljūqid "kings" of Damascus after the death of Duqāq was wholly in accordance with the practice of the time.

(5) Together with the local Arab princes, the Saljūqids and their Atābeks, and the Turkish amīrs, a fresh element of political unsettlement was introduced by the Ghuzz in Mesopotamia and Diyār-Bakr. The influx of these nomadic Turkmens, who lived by horse-breeding and plunder, was itself a perpetual source of disturbances, which were accentuated by the impatience of restraint and political ambitions of their chiefs. Such a person was Atsiz, the precursor of the Saljūqids in Syria, but the power of Malikshāh and Tutush held them in check for a time, and many, at least, of the chiefs served in the Saljūqid armies. The dissolution of the kingdom created by Tutush restored their freedom, and within two or three years several of them succeeded in founding independent principalities.

Of these Turkmen chieftains the most prominent in Syrian affairs were Il-Ghāzī and Sukmān, the sons of Ortuq, a Turkmen officer who had been appointed by Tutush to the governorship of Jerusalem. Il-Ghāzī succeeded to his father's position, while his brothers dispersed to seek their fortune elsewhere. Sukmān at first allied himself with Rudwān in the struggle against Duqāq, and was rewarded with the possession of Ma'arrat al-Nu'mān, but after the capture of Jerusalem by the Fātimid troops in 1098 he attempted to establish himself in al-Ruhā. Subsequently he founded a more permanent principality in Hisn Kaifā, and also captured Mārdīn, which was however transferred to Il-Ghāzī about 1108, and a second Ortuqid dynasty established there. Il-Ghāzī's son Sulaimān had already made himself independent at Samosata before the advent of the Crusaders, and other members of the family founded ephemeral principalities during this period. Another Turkmen chief, Ināl, revolted against Duqāq about 1096, seized Āmid, and founded a dynasty there, which afterwards allied itself by marriage with the Ortuqids of Mārdīn.

(6) Amidst all these struggles of rival princes, chiefs, and generals, little place seems to be left for the initiative of the people themselves. But while in many parts of the Islamic world, notably in Egypt and 'Iraq, they had ceased to count in political matters, in Syria, on the other hand, they had retained something of their martial qualities and still exercised an important influence on the course of events. The power of the Fātimids, the Saljūqids, and the Turkish generals, it is true, rested upon their slave armies, but the existence of such native principalities as that of the Banū Munqidh at Shaizar was possible only by reason of the support which they received from the local population. Even in the chief cities, however, especially in Aleppo and Damascus, the military strength of the citizens was sufficient to hold the autocratic tendencies of their governors in check. The Turkish rulers on the whole feared their

martial spirit, and were more inclined to adopt repressive measures against it than to direct it into healthy channels. The natural consequence was that the *ahdāth* or armed citizen bands tended to become an undisciplined mob rather than a disciplined force, and under the Fātimids the population of Damascus was notorious for insubordination to its governors. In the defence of their homes against the Crusaders, the civil population proved themselves to possess military qualities which with better support would certainly have been more effective in stemming the tide of conquest. It must not be overlooked that political vicissitudes and the ravages of war affected the citizen population no less than the helpless agriculturists. Sibt b. al-Jawzī informs us that the convulsions attending the dissolution of the Fātimid administration and the misrule of Atsiz produced such economic distress that in 1075 the population of Damascus had shrunk from half a million to three thousand. On the other hand, the enlightened administration and commercial policy of Āq-Sunqur brought a sudden revival of prosperity to Aleppo, and under Tughtagīn Damascus also recovered with striking rapidity from the effects of the former misrule.

It is, however, less in the cities and in the rich agricultural lands of Syria that the strength of the popular movements can be discerned, than in the mountainous backbone which divides the interior from the coast. The ranges of Lebanon and its northward extension, the *Jabal Summāq* of the Arabs, were not only the home of the Maronite Christians, but also the refuge of rebels and schismatics, in which they were able to build up powerful organizations which defied all the forces of the Muslim princes. During the two centuries preceding the Crusades, two offshoots of the Shī 'a sect, which in some of its earlier aspects bore the character of a popular revolutionary movement, had succeeded in establishing themselves in these fastnesses. To the north, in the Jabal Summāq, were the Nusairīs ; in the south, round Mount Hermon, were the settlements of their bitter foes, the Darazīs or Drūz ; in between lay the mass of the Christian Maronites. The interposition of these independent, and often hostile, groups added to the difficulties of communication between the coast and the interior, and did much to prevent the possibility of common action. Moreover, their military organizations had recently been strengthened to meet the assaults of the Saljūqids, to whom, as orthodox Muslims and empire-builders, their heresy and their independence were equally obnoxious. On the appearance of the Crusaders, they adopted different policies. Of the Nusairīs little is known, beyond the fact that large numbers of them were massacred by the Franks. The Drūz threw in their lot wholeheartedly with the Muslims. The Maronites naturally sided with the Crusaders, and many of them fought in their ranks.

In addition to Nusairīs and Drūz, a third Shi 'ite movement, also revolutionary in character, was in process of organization in northern Syria at the moment of the First Crusade. This was the celebrated Bātinī movement, a schismatic offshoot of the Fātimids, the adherents of which were popularly known as the Assassins. It was not until some years later that their public activities began, but there is justification for mentioning them at this point in the evidence which their movement affords of the continued existence of political activity amongst the general population, and especially of a strong sentiment of hostility to the Turkish governors and the other local princes.

Finally, the population of Syria was not at all uniform in composition, or even in language. The great bulk of both the settled and nomadic population doubtless consisted of Arabs and Arabicized elements, who spoke Arabic. Amongst these are to be included large numbers of the native Christian inhabitants in the north, belonging to the Greek, Nestorian, and Jacobite churches. The Maronites, who appear to have still used Syriac to a considerable extent, formed probably the largest minority. In addition to these and the Turkish-speaking Turkmen immigrants, there were also large communities of Kurds and especially of Armenians, settled mainly in the north. In the foothills of the Taurus and on the banks of the Euphrates both Kurds and Armenians had succeeded in founding several baronies and even more extensive principalities, which were, however, disappearing before the onslaught of the Turkmens. In several, if not most, of the northern cities, Armenians formed the majority of the populations, and it does not appear that the treatment which they received was in any way worse than that meted out to the other subjects.

The foregoing analysis of the situation in Syria throws a clearer light upon the events which immediately preceded the arrival of the first Crusaders. The central fact of the situation was the hostility between the two sons of Tutush, Rudwān and Duqāq. Rudwān had acted as viceroy for his father in Syria during the campaigns of Tutush in Mesopotamia and Khurāsān, whereas Duqāq appears to have received Diyār-Bakr as his fief. When the news arrived of the battle of Rayy, Rudwān was on his way to join Tutush with reinforcements from Syria, and he at once retired to Aleppo, with the object of securing his inheritance as king of Syria. Before he was able to complete his measures, Duqāq also arrived at Aleppo, and on a secret invitation from the governor of Damascus escaped from his brother's supervision and took possession of Damascus, while still retaining his earlier fiefs in Diyār-Bakr and Mesopotamia. Rudwān naturally prepared to assert his rights by force, and both princes, seeking for allies in the impending struggle, turned in the first place to the Turkish generals and Turkmen chiefs. The most powerful of these was Yāghī Siyān of Antioch, who would probably have supported Rudwān had it not been for a strong personal antipathy which he felt against Janāh al-Dawla, Rudwān's atābek. He thus became the natural ally of Duqāq, who was joined also by Il-Ghāzī, the governor of Jerusalem. Rudwān now turned for assistance to Il-Ghāzi's brother Sukmān (then at Sarūj) with his Turkmens, and to the Arab tribe of Kilāb.

Hostilities were begun in 1096 with a successful attack by Rudwān and his allies on the eastern possessions of Yāghī Siyān. Duqāq and Il-Ghāzī appear to have gone to the assistance of Yāghī-Siyān, and in their absence Rudwān laid siege to Damascus. The attempt was foiled by the inhabitants, but Rudwān devastated a great part of the province before withdrawing to Antioch. Meanwhile a temporary estrangement between Duqāq and Il-Ghāzī and the imprisonment of the latter had given Sukmān an opportunity to take possession of Jerusalem. In the following year (1097), Duqāq and Yāghī-Siyān took the offensive and recaptured some towns in Northern Syria. About the same time Il-Ghāzī returned to Jerusalem and Sukmān rejoined Rudwān, who with his assistance and that of Il-Ghāzī's son, who had made himself lord of Samosata, drove them back. Shortly afterwards, Rudwān fell out with his atābek, Janāh al-Dawla, who quitted Aleppo with all his forces and seized Hims. Yāghī Siyān at once offered his services to Rudwān and constituted himself his atābek, giving him his daughter in marriage. Immediate preparations were made for a campaign against Hims and Damascus. At the same time, an embassy from Egypt reached Aleppo, and the opportunity was seized by Rudwān to propose a joint attack upon Damascus, on his undertaking to acknowledge the spiritual suzerainty of the Fātimid Caliph. This project was, however, dropped on the remonstrances of Yāghī Siyān and Sukmān, and the three allies advanced with their forces to Shaizar. At this juncture news reached them of the arrival of the Franks on the northern borders of Syria. The report threw them into confusion and the expedition was abandoned, but instead of keeping together in face of the new enemy the army broke up. Rudwān hastily retired to Aleppo, while Yāghī Siyān set out for Antioch in order to defend it against the Franks. Even at this stage Sukmān appears to have given no thought to the defence of Syria against the Crusaders. His ambition was wholly directed to the conquest of Diyār-Bakr, the governors of which had made themselves independent of Duqāq, and he even attempted to persuade Yāghī Siyān and Rudwān to march thither and pay no heed to the Frankish invaders. When his appeals failed, he set out in company with Yāghī Siyān, but subsequently rejoined Rudwān. Yāghī Siyān was thus left to face the first onset of the Crusading armies with none but his own forces and what piecemeal assistance he could obtain by appeals to the other princes.

The Armies of the Muslim States

Few students of the Crusades will need to be reminded that the Muslim nation-in-arms had long since ceased to be. The old militia organization, when every man on the tribal registers received a pension from the public treasury and was required to hold himself permanently in readiness for military expeditions, had gradually been modified by the creation of standing armies, and during the ninth century the military basis of the majority of eastern Islamic states was profoundly altered. The nucleus of their forces was henceforth formed by a corps of salaried guards, composed for the most part of slaves who had been bought, levied as tribute, or inherited by the ruling prince ; these guards constituted a standing army, the cost of which was the first charge upon the revenues of the state. The majority were Turks from Central Asia, but their numbers were augmented by Slavs transported from Eastern Europe, and by Greeks and other captives from Anatolia, Armenia, and Georgia. They were organized in regiments, one of which constituted the private guard and furnished the personnel for ceremonial duties. All of them were mounted, and were especially skilled in shooting the bow on horseback ; for close fighting they were armed with lances and swords.

This standing army of mounted guards was termed the *'askar ;* the individual trooper was called an *'askarī* or *ghulām* (" boy," whence probably the " Angulani " of the *Gesta Francorum*). There appears to have been a regular system of promotion according to length of service, each rank being distinguished by some feature of dress. The commander of a regiment was entitled *amīr* (often, but incorrectly, translated " prince "), and the higher officers or the commander-in-chief *hājib* (" chamberlain "). The commanders were usually selected from the ruler's private guard, and frequently held important court offices in addition to their military commands. The officers who rose to these high stations were permitted, even expected, to purchase and maintain private troops of their own slaves, which were enrolled on their master's death in the general body of the *'askar*, usually as a separate regiment, called by the name of their former owner.

The principal amīrs of course required large sums

for the upkeep of their private troops, and for this purpose each was allotted the whole or part of the revenues of a specified district, of which he became the governor and for the defence of which he was responsible in the first instance. This is a " fief " (*iqtā'*) in the Islamic sense ; the term is too convenient to be avoided, but the sharp distinction between such " fiefs " and a true feudal system should be borne in mind. The gradual weakening of the bureaucracy, which had at first controlled the financial administration of the imperial provinces and maintained a check upon the military governors, gave the latter practically a free hand in the administration of their " fiefs." The natural results of this system were chronic misgovernment and endless rivalries between the amīrs for the privilege of milking the most productive districts, in addition to the standing encouragement which, as we have seen, it gave to rebellion and the foundation of independent principalities. There were few rulers, however illustrious, who were not harassed by repeated attempts of the kind on the part of their amīrs. The weakness of the Saljūqid Sultanate in particular, and its failure to support the Syrian princes against the Crusaders both at the outset and in after years, is explained by its constant fear of and preoccupation with such revolts in all parts of its dominions.

The numerical strength of the 'askar naturally varied with the power and resources of the ruler, and the Arabic sources supply no figures for those of the Syrian princes at the time of the First Crusade. It is certain, however, that those of Rudwān and Duqāq, the leading princes in Syria, cannot have exceeded a few thousands each, and those of the lesser rulers were correspondingly smaller. The 2,000 *optimi milites* with which a western source [1] credits Yāghī Siyān were probably his 'askar. The smallness of these figures is borne out by the continued existence of such petty principalities as that of Shaizar, whose lords disposed of only a few hundred men, and by the extravagant expressions employed by Ibn al-Qalānisī in respect of forces which numbered at most some four or five thousand. The Atābeks of Mesopotamia, on the other hand, possessed much stronger standing armies, and the predominant part which they took in the subsequent history of the Crusades was in large measure, doubtless, due to this fact.

Although the core of the 'askar was formed by the slave troops, its numbers were frequently supplemented by bodies of mercenaries in the stricter sense. Regiments of Dailamites, natives of the mountainous regions south-west of the Caspian Sea, were to be found in the service of most princes, and Armenians served in the 'askars of at least Damascus and Egypt. In Syria, also, we hear of freemen enrolling in the 'askar and receiving, like the regular troopers, a *dīwān* or assignment of pay from a stipulated head of revenue.[2] On many occasions the standing 'askars of the princes were reinforced by Turkmen tribesmen, who were likewise mounted archers, and are

---

[1] Raimund of Agiles (Migne, Vol. CLV), 598 D : " 2,000 *optimi milites,* 4,000–5,000 *milites gregarii,* 10,000 *pedites.*"   On the latter two classes see below.

[2] e.g., Usāma ibn Munqidh, who served successively in the 'askars of Zankī, Damascus, Egypt, and Nūr al-Dīn.   See also his story of the negotiations between Rudwān b. al-Walakhshī and Mu 'īn al-Dīn Unur (ed. Hitti, 30–31 ; *An Arab-Syrian Gentleman,* 56–57).

commonly referred to as an 'askar. When we are told that the standing army of the Saljūqid sultan Malikshāh numbered 400,000 men, we must take this figure to include the Turkmens under his command in addition to the very large guard of Turkish slaves (about 46,000 men) which he maintained. The Turkmens, however, in spite of their individual bravery and warlike qualities, lacked the stability and discipline of the regular troops, and often proved dangerous allies. The Kurdish tribesmen also supplied auxiliary cavalry forces, and in addition large numbers of Kurds were enrolled in the regular 'askars.

The greater part of the ordinary fighting amongst the Syrian princes and between them and the Crusaders was waged by the 'askars alone, with a certain number of camp-followers. On more important occasions a second line of troops was called up.[1] The name given to these troops, *jund* (plural *ajnād*), is the same as that by which the old Arab militia had formerly been called. This militia system had in fact persisted in Syria and Mesopotamia down to a much later date than elsewhere in the East, owing to the continuance of the Arab tribal organizations and to the unceasing conflict with the Byzantines, but it would probably be erroneous to identify the *ajnād* of the eleventh century completely with the former militia. It is fairly clear from the Syrian sources, however, that they were still territorial troops of a militia type, in contrast to the 'askarīs. The military forces of

[1] Cf. e.g., Ibn al-Qalānisī (Arabic text), 132, 6–7 : *indāfa 'ilaihim* [i.e. *al-'askarīya*] *jamā 'atun mina'l-'ajnādi.* These are probably the *milites gregarii* of Raimund of Agiles.

the smaller Arab principalities, the Drūz, and other local organizations were composed entirely of such territorial troops ; the princes of Shaizar, for example, had only a small 'askar. From the narratives of Usāma we learn that their *ajnād* consisted mainly of Arabs of various local tribes, together with incomers from the Maghrib (northwest Africa) and a certain number of Kurds.[1] It may therefore be assumed that the *ajnād* of Damascus and the other Syrian cities were composed of similar elements, at least in part. For the 'askar system in its turn also led to the formation of a force of territorial reserves, likewise called *ajnād*, consisting of such troops as were not permanently mobilized and were maintained by grants of land. As these territorial reserves are attested for Egypt in the twelfth century,[2] they may also have existed in Syria at the time of the early Crusades. Whether the nomadic Arab tribesmen were normally reckoned amongst the *ajnād* is open to doubt ; they probably formed an independent *jund*, corresponding to the 'askar of the Turkmens.

The troops who constituted the *ajnād* were, like the 'askarīs, mounted, and it was this, rather than any difference of organization, which distinguished them from the third line of troops, the footsoldiers. On the other hand, the *ajnād* were not as a rule archers, but fought with the spear and sword. The footmen were composed of various elements : town levies, countrymen pressed into service, volunteers seeking the temporal and spiritual rewards of participation in the Holy War, camp-

[1] Ed. Hitti, 38, 13 ; 46, 11 ; 48, 3 from foot ; 49, 12 ; 70, 2, etc.
[2] Cf. Ibn al-Qalānisī, p. 331, last line.

followers of all races and religions. Their military training and discipline was, like their equipment, at the mercy of chance, and though their courage need not be called in question their military value was generally small. Their part in the conduct of operations seems to have been limited to such subsidiary functions as the construction of military works and defences, mining operations during sieges, the protection of camps and garrisoning of fortresses and citadels.

The armour worn by the Muslim knights ordinarily consisted of a coat of mail, generally with a skirt, and a round helmet with back flap but no visor, along with which they carried a light circular shield. Light-armed horsemen wore leather jerkins or quilted coats in place of coats of mail. During the course of the Crusades various features of the Frankish armour, such as visors, vambraces, etc., were adopted by the Muslims. The horses appear generally to have been unprotected. The principal weapons of the Muslim horsemen were the bow, the lance and the sword. Their light and comparatively short lances put them at first at a disadvantage in combat with the Franks, but this was met by binding two lance-shafts together [1] and subsequently by the adoption of the heavy Frankish lance. The bulk of the armour and of the weapons was kept, when not in use, in the arsenal of the ruler, situated in his citadel and under the charge of one of the most trusted officers of his 'askar. When orders were issued to the 'askar to make ready for an expedition, such equipment as was required was issued

[1] Usāma, ed. Hitti, 101, 11-12 (*An Arab-Syrian Gentleman*, 131).

to the troops, and was replaced in store on their return. The *ajnād* were sometimes supplied from the arsenal also, but they were apparently expected to provide their own weapons as well as their own horses. Additional stores of weapons and armour were carried in the baggage train. The infantry also provided their own weapons, such as bows, swords, daggers, or at the least sharp stakes hardened by fire and used as javelins or spears.

On campaign the 'askar was accompanied by a large baggage-train, generally carried on camels and mules, which necessitated slow movements as a rule. Details as to commissariat are lacking, but it is evident that some sort of organization existed for the transport of provisions and forage, and that indiscriminate foraging, at least in friendly territory, was disapproved of. The difficulty of obtaining adequate local supplies, on the other hand, was one reason why campaigns were rarely undertaken during the winter, and even at other times of the year they were usually limited to rapid excursions, occupying no more than two or three months at a time. The Crusaders appear to have set the example of constructing special camps for the prosecution of winter campaigns.

The usual mode of attack was to take up a position opposite the enemy and to engage first in an archery duel. When the enemy showed signs of weakness, the cavalry charged with their lances and engaged in hand-to-hand fighting with the sword. To charge on an unbroken line seems generally to have been avoided, as well as undue precipitancy in engaging the enemy. The Arab cavalry maintained their traditional tactics of advancing and wheeling in simulated flight before reaching the opposing line, then when the enemy started in pursuit, wheeling round again at a prearranged point and charging upon them. The Crusaders are often criticized for excessive caution, but their " famous charge " was universally feared. The infantry played little part in the actual battle ; the fortunes of the day were decided by the cavalry charge, and the infantry of the defeated force were ruthlessly cut down, and taken prisoner by the victorious horsemen.

Prior to the advent of the Crusaders the technique of fortification and of siege operations was relatively simple. As a rule an attempt was made first to capture the town or fortress by direct assault, and preferably by surprise. If this failed, the attacking army often retired without more ado, or merely beleaguered the place in the hope of starving it into surrender. The principal siege weapon was the mangonel, sometimes supplemented by the battering ram, the use of both being ultimately derived from the Romans. A more effective method of breaching was to run a sap under a tower or part of the wall, and by lighting a fire beneath it cause the ground to cave in and bring down the superstructure. These methods, however, were of little avail against a citadel built upon rock, especially when its foundations, as was often the case in Syria, were of solid antique masonry, and a determined governor could generally hold out against attacks for an indefinite time. No little part of the success of the Crusaders was indeed due to their more thorough siege methods and the solidity of their fortifications.

PART I

From 1097 to 1132

A.H. 490

(19th December, 1096, to 8th December, 1097)

In this year there began to arrive a succession of reports that the armies of the Franks had appeared from the direction of the sea of Constantinople with forces not to be reckoned for multitude. As these reports followed one upon the other, and spread from mouth to mouth far and wide, the people grew anxious and disturbed in mind. The king, Dā'ud b. Sulaimān b. Qutulmish,[1] whose dominions lay nearest to them, having received confirmation of these statements, set about collecting forces, raising levies, and carrying out the obligation of Holy War. He also summoned as many of the Turkmens [2] as he could to give him assistance and support against them, and a large number of them joined him along with the 'askar [3] of his brother. His confidence having

---

[1] Qilij Arslān I, Saljūqid Sultan of Rūm (Anatolia).

[2] i.e., free members of the nomadic Turkish tribes which had migrated into Western Asia, as distinct from the Turks, i.e., Turkish slaves purchased for military service.

[3] The word 'askar, usually rendered "army " or " military forces " is retained in this translation when it is employed in its technical sense, to denote the standing army of mounted archers maintained by each ruler and governor, and composed for the most part of Turkish, Caucasian, and Slavonic slaves and freedmen.

been strengthened thereby, and his offensive power
rendered formidable, he marched out to the fords,
tracks, and roads by which the Franks must pass,
and showed no mercy to all of them who fell into
his hands. When he had thus killed a great
number, they turned their forces against him,
defeated him, and scattered his army, killing many
and taking many captive, and plundered and
enslaved. The Turkmens, having lost most of
their horses, took to flight. The King of the Greeks
bought a great many of those whom they had
enslaved, and had them transported to Constantinople. When the news was received of this
shameful calamity to the cause of Islām, the
anxiety of the people became acute and their fear
and alarm increased. The date of this battle was
the 20th of Rajab (4th July, 1097).

In the middle of Sha'bān (end of July) the
amīr Yāghī Siyān, lord of Antioch, accompanied
by the amīr Sukmān b. Ortuq [1] and the amīr
Karbuqā [lord of Mosul], set out with his 'askar
towards Antioch, on receipt of news that the
Franks were approaching it and had occupied
al-Balāna. Yāghī Siyān therefore hastened to
Antioch, and dispatched his son to al-Malik
Duqāq at Damascus, to Janāh al-Dawla at Hims,
and to all the other cities and districts, appealing
for aid and support, and inciting them to hasten
to the Holy War, while he set about fortifying
Antioch and expelling its Christian population.
On the 2nd of Shawwāl (12th September) the
Frankish armies descended on Baghrās and de-
veloped their attack upon the territories of Antioch,

---

[1] On the Ortuqids see the genealogical table below p. 168.

whereupon those who were in the castles and forts adjacent to Antioch revolted and killed their garrisons except for a few who were able to escape from them. The people of Artāh did likewise, and called for reinforcements from the Franks. During Sha'bān a comet appeared in the West ; it continued to rise for a space of about twenty days, and then disappeared.

Meanwhile, a large detachment of the Frankish army, numbering about thirty thousand men, had left the main body and set about ravaging the other districts, in the course of which they came to al-Bāra and slaughtered about fifty men there. Now the 'askar of Damascus had reached the neighbourhood of Shaizar, on their way to support Yāghī Siyān, and when this detachment made its descent on al-Bāra, they moved out against it. After a succession of charges by each side, in which a number of their men were killed, the Franks returned to al-Rūj, and thence proceeded towards Antioch. Oil, salt, and other necessaries became dear and unprocurable in Antioch, but so much was smuggled into the city that they became cheap again. The Franks dug a trench between their position and the city, owing to the frequent sallies made against them by the army of Antioch.

Now the Franks, on their first appearance, had made a covenant with the king of the Greeks, and had promised him that they would deliver over to him the first city which they should capture. They then captured Nicæa, and it was the first place they captured, but they did not carry out their word to him on that occasion, and refused to deliver it up to him according to the stipulation.

Subsequently they captured on their way several frontier fortresses and passes.

A.H. 491

(9th December, 1097, to 27th November, 1098)

At the end of First Jumādā (beginning of June, 1098) the report arrived that certain of the men of Antioch among the armourers in the train of the amīr Yāghī Siyān had entered into a conspiracy against Antioch and had come to an agreement with the Franks to deliver the city up to them, because of some ill-usage and confiscations which they had formerly suffered at his hands. They found an opportunity of seizing one of the city bastions adjoining the Jabal, which they sold to the Franks, and thence admitted them into the city during the night. At daybreak they raised the battle cry, whereupon Yāghī Siyān took to flight and went out with a large body, but not one person amongst them escaped to safety. When he reached the neighbourhood of Armanāz, an estate near Ma 'arrat Masrīn, he fell from his horse to the ground. One of his companions raised him up and remounted him, but he could not maintain his balance on the back of the horse, and after falling repeatedly he died. As for Antioch, the number of men, women and children, killed, taken prisoner, and enslaved from its population is beyond computation. About three thousand men fled to the citadel and fortified themselves in it, and some few escaped for whom God had decreed escape.

In Sha'bān (July) news was received that al-Afdal, the commander-in-chief (amīr al-juyūsh), had come up from Egypt to Syria at the head of a strong 'askar. He encamped before Jerusalem, where at that time were the two amīrs Sukmān and Il-Ghāzī, sons of Ortuq, together with a number of their kinsmen and followers and a large body of Turks, and sent letters to them, demanding that they should surrender Jerusalem to him without warfare or shedding of blood. When they refused his demand, he opened an attack on the town, and having set up mangonels against it, which effected a breach in the wall, he captured it and received the surrender of the Sanctuary of David [1] from Sukmān. On his entry into it, he shewed kindness and generosity to the two amīrs, and set both them and their supporters free. They arrived in Damascus during the first ten days of Shawwāl (September), and al-Afdal returned with his 'askar to Egypt.

In this year also the Franks set out with all their forces to Ma'arrat al-Nu'mān, and having encamped over against it on 29th Dhu'l-Hijja (27th November), they opened an attack on the town and brought up a tower and scaling-ladders against it.

Now after the Franks had captured the city of Antioch through the devices of the armourer, who was an Armenian named Fīrūz,[2] on the eve of Friday, 1st Rajab (night of Thursday 3rd June), and a series of reports were received confirming this news, the armies of Syria assembled in un-

---

[1] The Citadel of Jerusalem.   [2] In the text Nairūz.

countable force and proceeded to the province of Antioch, in order to inflict a crushing blow upon the armies of the Franks. They besieged the Franks until their supplies of food were exhausted and they were reduced to eating carrion ; but thereafter the Franks, though they were in the extremity of weakness, advanced in battle order against the armies of Islām, which were at the height of strength and numbers, and they broke the ranks of the Muslims and scattered their multitudes. The lords of the pedigree steeds [1] were put to flight, and the sword was unsheathed upon the footsoldiers who had volunteered for the cause of God, who had girt themselves for the Holy War, and were vehement in their desire to strike a blow for the Faith and for the protection of the Muslims. This befel on Tuesday, the [twenty] sixth of Rajab, in this year (29th June, 1098).

A.H. 492

(28th November, 1098, to 16th November, 1099)

In Muharram of this year (December, 1098), the Franks made an assault on the wall of Ma'arrat al-Nu'mān from the east and north. They pushed up the tower until it rested against the wall, and as it was higher, they deprived the Muslims of the shelter of the wall. The fighting raged round this point until sunset on 14th Muharram (11th December), when the Franks scaled the wall, and the townsfolk were driven off it and took to flight.

[1] Literally " of the short-haired and swift-paced."

Prior to this, messengers had repeatedly come to them from the Franks with proposals for a settlement by negotiation and the surrender of the city, promising in return security for their lives and property, and the establishment of a [Frankish] governor amongst them, but dissension among the citizens and the fore-ordained decree of God prevented acceptance of these terms. So they captured the city after the hour of the sunset prayer, and a great number from both sides were killed in it. The townsfolk fled to the houses of al-Ma 'arra, to defend themselves in them, and the Franks, after promising them safety, dealt treacherously with them. They erected crosses over the town, exacted indemnities from the townsfolk, and did not carry out any of the terms upon which they had agreed, but plundered everything that they found, and demanded of the people sums which they could not pay. On Thursday 17th Safar (13th January, 1099) they set out for Kafr Tāb.

Thereafter they proceeded towards Jerusalem, at the end of Rajab (middle of June) of this year, and the people fled in panic from their abodes before them. They descended first upon al-Ramla, and captured it after the ripening of the crops. Thence they marched to Jerusalem, the inhabitants of which they engaged and blockaded, and having set up the tower against the city they brought it forward to the wall. At length news reached them that al-Afdal was on his way from Egypt with a mighty army to engage in the Holy War against them, and to destroy them, and to succour and protect the city against them. They therefore attacked the city with increased vigour,

and prolonged the battle that day until the day-
light faded, then withdrew from it, after promising
the inhabitants to renew the attack upon them on
the morrow. The townsfolk descended from the
wall at sunset, whereupon the Franks renewed
their assault upon it, climbed up the tower, and
gained a footing on the city wall. The defenders
were driven down, and the Franks stormed the
town and gained possession of it. A number of the
townsfolk fled to the sanctuary [of David], and a
great host were killed. The Jews assembled in the
synagogue, and the Franks burned it over their
heads. The sanctuary was surrendered to them
on guarantee of safety on the 22nd of Sha 'bān
(14th July) of this year, and they destroyed the
shrines and the tomb of Abraham. Al-Afdal
arrived with the Egyptian armies, but found himself forestalled, and having been reinforced by the
troops from the Sāhil,[1] encamped outside Ascalon
on 14th Ramadān (4th August), to await the
arrival of the fleet by sea and of the Arab levies.
The army of the Franks advanced against him
and attacked him in great force. The Egyptian
army was thrown back towards Ascalon, al-Afdal
himself taking refuge in the city. The swords of
the Franks were given mastery over the Muslims,
and death was meted out to the footmen, volunteers, and townsfolk, about ten thousand souls,
and the camp was plundered. Al-Afdal set out for
Egypt with his officers, and the Franks besieged
Ascalon, until at length the townsmen agreed to
pay them twenty thousand dinars as protection

[1] The Sāhil was the general name given to the coastal plain and the
maritime towns, from Ascalon to Bairūt.

money, and to deliver this sum to them forthwith. They therefore set about collecting this amount from the inhabitants of the town, but it befel that a quarrel broke out between the [Frankish] leaders, and they retired without having received any of the money. It is said that the number of the people of Ascalon who were killed in this campaign—that is to say of the witnesses,[1] men of substance, merchants, and youths, exclusive of the regular levies—amounted to two thousand seven hundred souls.

A.H. 493

(*17th November*, 1099, *to* *5th November*, 1100)

Al-Malik Shams al-Mulūk Duqāq, son of Tāj al-Dawla, set out from Damascus for Diyār Bakr with his 'askar in order to recover possession of it from a governor who had forcibly seized it. He reached al-Rahba by the desert route and thence entered Diyār Bakr, where he occupied Mayyā-fāriqīn, and established a garrison in it for its protection and defence.

In Rajab of this year (May-June, 1100), Bohemond,[2] King of the Franks and lord of Antioch, marched out to the fortress of Afāmiya (Apamea), and besieged it. He remained there for some days and laid waste its crops, when he received news of the

---

[1] i.e., the respectable citizens, men of unblemished character, whose witness was accepted in a court of law.
[2] In the text *Bimand* or *Baimand*.

arrival at Malatiya of al-Dānishmand [1] with the
'askar of Qilij Arslān b. Sulaimān b. Qutulmish.
On learning of this, Bohemond returned to Antioch,
and having collected his forces, marched against
the Muslim army. But God Most High succoured
the Muslims against him, and they killed a great
host of his party and he himself was taken captive
together with a few of his companions. Messengers
were dispatched to his lieutenants at Antioch,
demanding the surrender of the city, in the second
decade of the month of Safar in the year 494.[2]

In this year also, reports arrived that the water
in the wells had sunk at a number of places in the
northern districts, and likewise the springs in
most of the forts, and the water was low and prices
were high in those parts.

A.H. 494

(6th November, 1100, to 25th October, 1101)

In this year, the amīr Sukmān b. Ortuq collected
a great host of Turkmens, and marched with them
against the Franks of al-Ruhā (Edessa) and Sarūj,
in the month of First Rabī' (January, 1101). He
captured Sarūj, and was joined by a large body
[of volunteers], while the Franks also collected
their forces. When the two armies met, the
Muslims were on the point of victory over them,
but it happened that a party of the Turkmens

[1] Gumushtagīn b. Dānishmand, ruling prince of Sīwās.
[2] The text has 493, which is obviously a slip, 11th-20th Safar
494 corresponds to 16th-25th December, 1100.

fled and Sukmān lost heart and retired. The Franks then advanced to Sarūj, recaptured it, and killed and enslaved its inhabitants, except those of them who escaped by flight.

In this year also, Godfrey,[1] lord of Jerusalem, appeared before the fortified port of 'Akkā and made an assault upon it, but he was struck by an arrow and killed. Prior to this he had rebuilt Yāfā (Jaffa) and given it in charge to Tancred.[2] When Godfrey was killed, his brother Baldwin the count,[3] lord of al-Ruhā, set out for Jerusalem with a body of five hundred knights and footmen. On hearing the report of his passage, Shams al-Mulūk Duqāq gathered his forces and moved out against him, together with the amīr Janāh al-Dawla, lord of Hims, and they met him near the port of Bairūt. Janāh al-Dawla pressed forward towards him with his 'askar, and he defeated him and killed some of his companions.[4]

In this year the Franks captured Haifā, on the sea coast, by assault, and Arsūf by capitulation, and they drove its inhabitants out of it. At the end of Rajab also (end of May) they captured Qaisarīya by assault, with the assistance of the Genoese, killed its population, and plundered everything in it.

In Sha 'bān of this year (June, 1101), the qādī Ibn Sulaiha, who had made himself master of the fortified port of Jabala, wrote to Zahīr al-Dīn

[1] Kundufrī.
[2] Tankrī.
[3] Baghdawīn al-Qomis.
[4] The pronouns in the text do not clearly specify which side was victorious.

Atābek,[1] requesting him to select and send a trustworthy officer, that he might hand over to him the fortress of Jabala, and himself retire with all his property to Damascus, and that he would convey him thence to Baghdād with an escort, and under guarantee of safe conduct, protection, and honourable treatment. The Atābek consented to this proposal, and promised to carry his desire into effect, and deputed as governor of the port his son, the amīr Tāj al-Mulūk Būrī. The king Shams al-Mulūk Duqāq was at the time absent from Damascus in Diyār Bakr, and he returned thence and entered Damascus on 1st Shawwāl (30th July). The arrangements were confirmed according to Ibn Sulaiha's request, and Tāj al-Mulūk set out with his train for Jabala, and took it over.

Ibn Sulaiha departed thence and arrived at Damascus with his followers, goods and effects, baggage and riding-beasts, and all that he possed of money, movable property, and estate. He was received with honour and richly entertained, and after a stay of some days at Damascus was conveyed to Baghdād with everything that he possessed by a strong detachment of troops. When he arrived, it came about that some person denounced him and gave such a report of his riches to the Sultan at Baghdād,[2] that he was plundered

---

[1] The amīr Tughtagīn, at this time atābek (regent and commander-in-chief) of al-Malik Duqāq at Damascus. In the Saljūqid system, the title of Sultān was reserved for the head of each line ; vassal Saljūqid princes were entitled *king* (malik) and non-Saljūqid generals who exercised effective power in the name of the latter received the title of *atabek* (" tutor ").

[2] The Saljūqid Barkyāruq, son of Malikshāh, or perhaps his brother Ghiyāth al-Dīn Muhammad, governor of Baghdād.

and all that he possessed fell into the Sultan's hands.

As for Tāj al-Mulūk, when he took possession of the fortress of Jabala and he and his followers were firmly established there, they ill-treated its people and behaved evilly towards them, and acted contrary to the approved custom of justice and fair dealing. The townsfolk therefore sent a complaint of their condition under the misfortune that had befallen them to the Qāḍī Fakhr al-Mulk, Abū 'Alī 'Ammār b. Muhammad b. 'Ammār, who had seized the fortified port of Tarābulus (Tripolis), on account of the proximity of Tarābulus to their town. He promised to assist them to attain their object, and to send them support, and dispatched to them a considerable force from his 'askar, which entered the town and, having joined with its people against the Turks, defeated and drove them out, and took possession of it. They captured Tāj al-Mulūk and carried him to Tarābulus where Fakhr al-Mulk received him honourably, treated him kindly, and sent him back to Damascus, together with a letter to his father informing him of the state of affairs and presenting his excuses to him for what had happened.

In this year also a great army came up from Egypt with the amīr Sa'd al-Dawla known as al-Qawāmisī, and arrived at Ascalon at the beginning of Ramadān (early July) to prosecute the Holy War against the Franks. He remained where he was until Dhu'l-Hijja (beg. 27th September), when he advanced from Ascalon. A thousand knights and ten thousand footsoldiers of the Franks marched against him. When the two armies joined battle, the right and left wings of the Muslims were broken and pursued, but the commander Sa 'd al-Dawla held his ground in the centre with a small body of his 'askar. The Franks charged against him, and he strove to maintain his ground, but his predestined fate outstripped him, for his horse stumbled with him and he fell from it to the ground and gained the prize of martyrdom on the spot (God's mercy upon him). Then the Muslims wheeled against the Franks, urging one another to avenge his loss upon them and sacrificing their lives in the charge against them, and drove them back to Yāfā, slaying and taking captive and plundering. Thus the issue turned in favour of the Muslims and only a small number of them were killed.

A.H. 495

(26th October, 1101, to 14th October, 1102)

In this year reports were brought to the effect that the peoples of Khurāsān, 'Irāq, and Syria were in a state of constant bickering and hatred, wars and disorder, and fear of one another, because their rulers neglected them and were distracted from the task of governing them by their dissensions and mutual warfare.

In this year also the Count of al-Ruhā,[1] the commander of the Franks, arrived with his God-forsaken troops at the fortified port of Bairūt, and encamped over against it, in the hope of capturing

---

[1] *Qomis ar-Ruha*, i.e., Baldwin I.

it. He remained before it for a long time, attacking and besieging the town, but his ambition could not be realised, and he raised the siege and departed.

Letters arrived from Fakhr al-Mulk Ibn 'Ammār, lord of Tarābulus, beseeching aid in driving back the son of St. Gilles,[1] who had descended with his army of Franks on Tarābulus, and asking for the assistance of the 'askar of Damascus. His request was granted, and the 'askar set off towards him. The amīr Janāh al-Dawla, lord of Hims, was summoned also, and he too arrived with his 'askar. Their armies united and marched in brave force in the direction of Antartūs (Tortosa). The Franks hastened towards them with their host and levies, and the two armies approached one another and engaged in battle there. The army of the Muslims was shattered by the army of the infidels, and a great number of them were killed. Those who escaped retreated to Damascus and Hims, after suffering considerable losses, and arrived on 23rd Latter Jumādā (14th April, 1102).

In this year also the Egyptian armies came up from Egypt to assist the governors of the Sāhil in those fortified ports which still remained in their hands against the besieging parties of the Franks. They reached Ascalon in Rajab (April-May), and when Baldwin, Count of Jerusalem, learned of their arrival, he marched against them with his force of Franks, consisting of about seven hundred knights and footmen, picked men. With these he charged on the Egyptian army, but God gave the

[1] *Ibn Sanjīl*

victory to the Egyptians against his broken faction, and they killed most of his knights and footsoldiers. He himself fled to Ramla with three followers. The Egyptians pursued and surrounded him, but he disguised himself and succeeded in eluding their vigilance, made for Yāfā, and got away from them. During the pursuit, he had hidden in a brake of canes, which was set on fire, and the fire singed part of his body, but he escaped from it and reached Yāfā. His companions were put to the sword, and all his men and champions who were captured in Ramla were killed or made prisoner, and carried off to Egypt at the end of Rajab. At this time, some Frankish vessels arrived, about forty in all, laden with men and goods, and it was reported that they had been storm-tossed and driven about by changing winds, so that most of them were lost and only a few were saved.

A.H. 496

(15th October, 1102, to 4th October, 1103)

In this year the king Shams al-Mulūk Duqāq and Zahīr al-Dīn Atābek left Damascus with the 'askar, and making for al-Rahba, encamped before it and blockaded its inhabitants, cutting off all means of provisioning from them. The blockade caused such distress that the resident in the town was compelled to sue for quarter for himself and the inhabitants. They were promised safety and the town was delivered up to the king after severe fighting and prolonged warfare in Latter Jumādā

(March, 1103). He placed a garrison in it and appointed a reliable officer to guard it, and having settled the affairs of its inhabitants, he set out thence on Friday the 22nd of the same month (3rd April) on his return journey to Damascus.

In this year also news was received from Hims that its lord, the amīr Janāh al-Dawla Husain Atābek on descending from the citadel to the mosque for the Friday prayer, surrounded by his principal officers with full armour, and occupying his place of prayer, according to custom, was set upon by three Persians belonging to the Bātinīya. They were accompanied by a shaikh, to whom they owed allegiance and obedience,[1] and all of them were dressed in the garb of ascetics. When the shaikh gave the signal they attacked the amīr with their knives and killed both him and a number of his officers. There were in the mosque at the time ten Sūfīs, Persians and others ; they were suspected of complicity in the crime, and were straightway executed in cold blood, every man of them, although they were innocent. The people of Hims were greatly perturbed at this event, and at once dispersed in panic. Most of the Turks amongst the inhabitants fled to Damascus, and everything fell into confusion. The townsfolk then wrote to the king Shams al-Mulūk at Damascus, begging him to send an officer to take over the town and be responsible for its defence, before the news reached the Franks and their

[1] In Sibṭ b. al-Jawzi's transcript (*R.H.C.*, III, 526) " they began to pray for him and to exhort him," in Jewett's edition (4, 1) " and to examine him."

covetous desires extended to it. The king Shams al-Mulūk and Zahīr al-Dīn Atābek thereupon set out with the 'askar from Damascus, reached Hims, took possession of it, and occupied the citadel. At the same time the Franks arrived at Hims and encamped at al-Rastan,[1] with the intention of cutting off and besieging the town, but on learning what had taken place, they kept at a discreet distance and eventually withdrew.

Now the person known as al-Hakīm al-Munajjim the Bātinī,[2] a number of the entourage of the king Fakhr al-Mulūk Rudwān, lord of Aleppo, was the first to profess the doctrines of the Bātinīya in Aleppo and Syria, and it was he who commissioned the three men to kill Janāh al-Dawla at Hims. The news of his death arrived fourteen days after this event.

After Shams al-Mulūk had established a garrison in Hims and set its affairs in order and returned to Damascus on 1st Ramadān (8th June), the Egyptian armies came up from Egypt by land, and the fleet by sea, under the command of Sharaf, the son of al-Afdal Shāhinshāh, who wrote asking that the 'askar of Damascus might be sent to co-operate in the Holy War and to give its aid to the Muslim cities and populations. A favourable reply was sent to his request, but the despatch of the army was prevented by certain circumstances which arose and accidents which intervened. The fleet arrived and made an attack on Yāfā at the

[1] The ancient Arethusa, lying midway between Hamāh and Hims.
[2] Al-Hakīm al-Munajjim, lit. the physician-astrologer. The Bātinīya or Esoteric sect is the extreme Shi'ite sect generally known in Europe as the Assassins.

end of Shawwāl (ended 5th August), but after some days both fleet and troops were distributed along the coast. Prices had risen in the coast towns and their supplies of food had run short, but they were relieved by the grain which arrived with the fleet and prices fell again. Nevertheless, the Franks continued to attack them without intermission.

In Dhu'l-Qa'da of this year (August) reports arrived from various sources that Qilij Arslān b. Sulaimān b. Qutulmish had come out from the land of Rūm (Anatolia) on an expedition against Antioch, and had reached the neighbourhood of Mar 'ash. A disagreement and dispute broke out between him and the amīr al-Dānishmand, lord of Malatiya, which made it necessary for him to turn back against him and inflict upon him a severe punishment. When he returned after scattering the army of al-Dānishmand and putting his men to the sword, it is said that he arrived in Syria and sent his envoy to Aleppo, asking that permission might be given to the merchants to supply his 'askar with stores and provisions and all the requirements of the troops and levies. The people were gladdened by this and joyfully spread the news of it.

A.H. 497

(5th October, 1103, to 22nd September, 1104)

In Rajab of this year (began 30th March) reports were received that a Frankish fleet coming from their country, laden with merchants, troops, and

pilgrims, amongst others, had arrived at the
roadstead of al-Lādhiqīya (Laodicea). It was
said that St. Gilles, who was then besieging
Tarābulus, called them in to blockade Tarābulus
and assist him to gain possession of it, and that
they came in response to his invitation and joined
him in the siege and blockade of the city, but
withdrew after a few days' fighting. They then
made a descent on the fortified port of Jubail,
attacked and blockaded it, and gained possession
of it by capitulation, but when they had taken
possession, they dealt treacherously with its people
and did not observe the promises of security which
they had given to them, but confiscated their
property, and deprived them of all their possessions
and money by penalties and various torments.

News arrived that the amīrs Sukmān b. Ortuq
and Jikirmish, lord of Mosul, had joined forces
and made a solemn agreement with one another to
prosecute the Holy War against the Franks, the
enemies of God, and to devote their entire strength
and means to active warfare with them. At the
beginning of Sha'bān (began 29th April) they
encamped at Ra's al-'Ain. Thereupon Bohemond
and Tancred marched with their armies from the
district of Antioch towards al-Ruhā to assist its
lord against these two amīrs. When they approached the Muslim army which was attacking
ar-Ruhā, each of the two forces prepared to meet
the other. The battle took place on 9th Sha'bān
(7th May) ; God gave victory to the Muslims over
their enemy, and they put them to flight, and did
great execution amongst them. Their numbers

exceeded ten thousand horse and foot, exclusive
of baggage-train and campfollowers. Bohemond
and Tancred fled with a small following. This was
a great and unexampled victory for the Muslims; it
discouraged the Franks, diminished their numbers
and broke their power of offence, while the hearts
of the Muslims were strengthened, and their zeal
for the victory of the Faith and the war against the
heretics was whetted and sharpened. The people
joyfully noised abroad the good news of the victory
over them, and became assured of their destruction
and the turning of fortune against them.

In this month also news arrived that Baldwin,
king of the Franks and lord of Jerusalem, had
made a descent with his army on the fortified
port of 'Akkā both by sea and land, having with
him the Genoese vessels which had captured the
port of Jubail, over ninety vessels in all. They
besieged and blockaded the town on every side
and attacked it without intermission, until its
commander and garrison were unable to continue
to battle with them and its inhabitants were too
exhausted to oppose them, so they captured it
forcibly by the sword. The commander of the
town, the amīr Zahr al-Dawla Bannā' Juyūshī,
had previously quitted it, on account of his inability to defend it and hold off the Franks, and
despairing of the arrival of reinforcements or
assistance, sent to them asking for quarter for
himself and for the townspeople. When the city
was captured, he continued his flight until he
reached Damascus. On his entry, which was on
Thursday 28th Sha'ban (26th May), he was

courteously received by Zahīr al-Dīn Atābek, and Shams al-Mulūk Duqāq and Zahīr al-Dīn Atābek gave orders that he should be treated in a manner which revived his spirits and fortified his cheerfulness. He remained at Damascus until the way was smoothed for him to return to Egypt, and thereafter set out on his way back. He arrived there safely and made his apology for the defeat which he had suffered, and his apology was accepted although at first they had blamed him and were violently incensed at his action.

In this year, the king Shams al-Mulūk Duqāq, son of the sultan Tāj al-Dawla Tutush, lord of Damascus, was seized by a prolonged illness, accompanied by digestive disorders, which necessitated his removal to 'Illat al-Daqq, where he remained, growing daily in weakness and exhaustion. When he was on the point of death, and all hope of his recovery was lost, his mother, the Khātūn Safwat al-Mulk,[1] begged him to make his testament and disclose his wishes, and not leave his kingdom and his children without guidance. Thereupon he nominated the amīr Zahīr al-Dīn [Tughtagīn] Atābek to the governorship of Damascus after his death and the tutorship of his young son Tutush b. Duqāq b. Tāj al-Dawla, until he should come of age, and having charged him to give the prince a good upbringing and spoken to him of all that was in his mind, he passed away to the mercy of God on 12th Ramadān of this year (8th June, 1104).

---

[1] She had been given in marriage to Zahīr al-Dīn by Tāj al-Dawla, father of Duqāq.

Now prior to this event Zahīr al-Dīn Atābek had been in the throes of an illness of which he came near to dying, but by the goodness of God his health resisted the malady and he recovered. He set about conciliating the troops and the civil population by a benevolent policy, and showed consideration to the amīrs and officers of state ; he spent freely from the treasury in bestowing robes of honour, dignities, gifts and presents ; he modelled his conduct on the precepts of the Faith [1] ; he inspired fear in the lawless and the evildoers, and was bountiful to excess in rewarding the loyal and well-doing ; all hearts were attached to his cause by his liberality and he won over the waverers by solicitous attention and openhandedness. Thus his control of affairs was securely established and the people were united in obedience to him.

Before his death, al-Malik Shams al-Mulūk had sent his brother al-Malik Irtāsh,[2] son of the sultan Tāj al-Dawla, to the castle of Ba 'albek, to be detained there in confinement under the charge of its commander, Fakhr al-Dawla Gumushtagīn al-Tājī, his father's freedman. Zahīr al-Dīn Atābek regarded it as part of his duty to the sons of Tāj al-Dawla to send instructions to this freedman to release Irtāsh and convey him to Damascus. On his arrival Zahīr al-Dīn went out to meet him, received him with great honour and ceremony and obeisance, and established him in

---

[1] Lit. " he commanded (men) to the good and restrained (them) from the disapproved," a Qur'anic phrase which became stereotyped in this sense.

[2] Usually known as Bektāsh, from the spelling adopted by the later historians.

the place of his brother Shams al-Mulūk. He issued orders to the amīrs, officers, and troops, to render obedience to the prince's commands, and to serve him with all loyalty, and installed him on the throne of the kingdom on Saturday 24th Dhu'l-Hijja of this year 497 (17th September, 1104). Thus affairs were securely established and he enjoyed the confidence of the people.

But in accordance with the predestined decree, against which neither prevention nor guard is of avail, there were found those who plotted to disturb this arrangement and overturn this settled disposition of affairs, by causing the king Muhyī al-Dīn Irtāsh to become estranged from Zahīr al-Dīn Atābek and from the Khātūn Safwat al-Mulk, the mother of Shams al-Mulūk. His mother instilled into his mind fear of these two, and led him to imagine that they would probably intrigue against him and kill him, though in fact the position was exactly contrary to the tales told to him by the mischief-makers. He became afraid of them in consequence and when it was suggested to him that it would be advisable to abandon the city and kingdom of Damascus and return to Ba 'albek, so that his adherents and the soldiery should join him there, he left the city secretly in Safar of the year 498 (began 23rd October, 1104). Āytakīn al-Halabī, lord of Bosra, also fled thither in pursuance of an agreement made between them with a view to this evil strife. They began to lay waste in concert the region of the Hawrān and corresponded with Baldwin, king of the Franks, asking aid of him ; moreover they went to him and stayed with him for a time in the midst of the

Franks, inciting them to march against Damascus and urging them to ravage its districts. But their manœuvres came to no result and they gained no profit by them, and when they despaired of receiving assistance, and their hopes of a favourable answer were disappointed, they set off together towards al-Rahba through the desert. After their departure Zahīr al-Dīn's position was securely established and he assumed sole control of affairs and governed on his own authority. Under his administration and good government, Damascus and its dependencies were prosperous and in flourishing condition. At this time also there befel by the decree of God the death of Tutush, the son of the king Shams al-Mulūk Duqāq mentioned above. It happened also that prices were low and grain was abundant and the people took a pleasure in the cultivation and improvement of their estates within and without Damascus, owing to the benevolence and generous dealings of Zahīr al-Dīn, and to the prevalence of justice amongst them and the prevention of causes of oppression.

In this year a report arrived from Tarābulus that Fakhr al-Mulk Ibn 'Ammār, its lord, had gone out with his 'askar and the town levies and marched to the castle which was built by St. Gilles over against them. They made an assault upon it and the garrison were taken by surprise and killed. Its contents were plundered and it was set on fire and reduced to ruins. Fakhr al-Mulk, having obtained from it a great quantity of weapons, money, rich stuffs and silver, returned to Tarābulus safely and laden with booty on 19th Dhu'l-Hijja (12th September). It was reported also that

Bohemond, lord of Antioch, had taken ship and gone to the Franks, to ask them for assistance and reinforcements against the Muslims in Syria. He stayed in their country for a time, and then set out to return to Antioch.

A.H. 498

(23rd September, 1104, to 12th September, 1105)

In this year Zahīr ad-Dīn Atābek was seized by an illness, which grew worse and could not be shaken off. He feared that it might prove fatal and was filled with anxiety for his family, his children, his men-at-arms, and his subjects, should anything happen to him. Moreover, letters and envoys were constantly arriving from Fakhr al-Mulk ibn 'Ammār at Tarābulus, asking for aid and reinforcement against the Franks who were besieging his city, and urging him to make haste to send to his assistance all the troops who could come to him, in order to relieve him of his distress and allay his anxiety. Now the amīr Sukmān b. Ortuq and the amīr Jikirmish, lord of Mosul, had made a compact to prosecute the Holy War against the polytheists and to aid the Muslims, and when Zahīr ad-Dīn was attacked by his alarming illness, he conceived the idea of sending an invitation to the amīr Sukmān b. Ortuq to come to Damascus with his 'askar, in order that he might nominate him as his successor and that the defence of Damascus might be entrusted to him. At the same time there reached Sukmān letters from Ibn 'Ammār urging him to hasten to respond to his appeal and set out to his assistance, and promising him a large sum of money in return for his aid. Sukmān, on learning the contents of the letters, agreed to the proposals which had been made to him. After hasty preparations, he bent his course towards Damascus and pressing on his journey night and day in the intensity of his zeal and eagerness, crossed the Euphrates for the object to the prosecution of which he had been exhorted and to attack the Franks. When he arrived at al-Qaryatain and news of his movements was brought to the atābek, Zahīr al-Dīn's officers and associates upbraided him for his precipitancy in making this plan without seeking counsel, pointing out the folly of his judgment in summoning Sukmān, and giving him cause to fear the consequences of his action. They said to him : " When the amīr Sukmān b. Ortuq reaches Damascus, and deprives you of control of it, what will become of you and of us ? Were you not acquainted with the fate of Atsiz, and how, when he called in the sultan Tāj al-Dawla, son of Alp-Arslān, and handed over Damascus to him, he at once proceeded to compass his destruction and spared neither him nor his family ? " Thereupon Zahīr al-Dīn awoke to his error and realized the extent of his heedlessness and sorely repented, so that by reason of this to his bodily sickness there was superadded sickness of heart. But while he and his officers were deliberating what action to take with regard to Sukmān, and what treatment to accord him on his arrival,[1] the report arrived from al-Qaryatain that

---

[1] This is apparently the meaning of the phrase *tadbīr bihi hālahu*, but the reading offers difficulties ; I. Athīr has *bi'ayyi hīlatin yaruddūnahu*.

the amīr Sukmān, at the very hour of his arrival and encampment with his 'askar at al-Qaryatain, was attacked with a grievous illness, with which he terminated his predestined span, and passed to the mercy of his Lord. His officers immediately prepared his body for transportation and set off to return with it whence they had come. The atābek was so greatly rejoiced at this turn of affairs, that from that time began his fortune and the restoration of health to his body. Glory be to Him who orders the lives of His creatures by His wisdom and who determines all events by His power. They went to the province of al-Jazīra (Mesopotamia) ; this was early in Safar of this year (end of October).

In this year also arrived the news of the death of St. Gilles, the leader of the Franks who were besieging the fortress of Tarābulus, on 4th First Jumādā (22nd June, 1105), after an armistice had been concluded between him and Fakhr al-Mulk Ibn 'Ammār, lord of Tarābulus. The terms agreed upon were that the suburbs of Tarābulus should belong to St. Gilles with the proviso that he would not cut off supplies from the town, nor prevent travellers from entering it.

On 1st Sha'bān (18th April) Zahīr al-Dīn Atābek set out for Ba 'albek with the 'askar and encamped before it, as he was displeased with the freedman Gumushtagīn al-Tājī, its governor, on account of several matters which had come to his ears about him and of which he disapproved. When Zahīr al-Dīn descended upon him and besieged him, Gumushtagīn, perceiving what was in his mind, sent to him proffering submission and homage, denying the charges brought by his culumniators, clearing himself of what had been attributed to him, and swearing to his innocence of the allegations trumped up against him. Zahīr al-Dīn thereupon dropped the charges made against him, received him back into favour, confirmed his authority, and ordered his courtiers to refrain from their malignity towards him. Thence he continued his advance to the district of Hims, where he marched on Rafanīya and encamped before it. A large contingent joined him from Jabal Bahrā, and together they made an assault on Rafanīya when its people and garrison were off their guard, and killed all those who were in the town and its dependencies and in the castle built above it by the Franks. All that could be burned in the castle and elsewhere was burned, and the castle itself destroyed. The forts of Rafanīya were captured as well and their defenders put to death, and the 'askar returned to Hims.

In Rajab (March–April) the king Fakhr al-Mulūk Rudwān, lord of Aleppo, came out and collected a great host, with the intention of marching to Tarābulus to assist Fakhr al-Mulk Ibn 'Ammār against the Franks who were besieging him. The Armenians who were in the castle of Artāh had surrendered the castle to him, because of the injustice and grievous tyranny which they suffered from the Franks. On learning of this, Tancred left Antioch to march on Artāh and recover it, and having assembled all the Franks who were in his territories he laid siege to the castle and moved with his army against Fakhr al-Mulūk to hold him off from it. Now Fakhr al-Mulūk had collected and levied all the troops that he could from the province of Aleppo, as well as the young men of the city,[1] for the object of waging the Holy War. On approaching each other, the armies engaged in battle ; the Muslim infantry held their ground, but the cavalry were routed, and the footsoldiers were slaughtered. None escaped but those whose salvation God had decreed ; and when the broken remnants reached Aleppo and the losses among both horse and foot were reckoned up, they were found to be about three thousand souls. When the news of this reached the Muslims who were in Artāh, they fled to a man. The Franks then marched on the city of Aleppo ; its population fled from it in panic, and numbers of them were plundered and enslaved. This was on 3rd Sha'bān (20th April), and the people of Syria,[2] after enjoying security and peace, were brought into a state of distress and anxiety.

In this year also there came up from Egypt a vast army, exceeding in number ten thousand horse and foot, under the command of the amīr Sharaf al-Ma'ālī, the son of al-Afdal. Letters were sent to Zahīr al-Dīn Atābek praying for his assistance and support to the waging of the Holy War

---

[1] al-'ahdāth al-halabīyīn. It is difficult to assign a precise meaning to al ahdāth, which may be loosely applied to young men generally, apprentices, or even the town rabble. On the other hand, from certain passages (e.g., p. 175 below), it would appear that they were a definite military organization, and in these instances the term is provisionally translated by " armed bands " or " gens d'armes."

[2] Shām, which is usually applied to Damascus itself, is used by Ibn al-Qalānisī to denote the area extending roughly from Ba 'albek to Aleppo.

against the infidels, but he was unable to accede to the request, on account of certain matters which hindered him from sending aid. He proceeded with the 'askar to Bosra, and encamped before it with the intention of besieging it, because the king Irtāsh b. Tāj al-Dawla and Aytagīn of Aleppo were in the town and were engaged in the negotiations with the Franks of which an account has already been given. Then he changed his mind and, judging that the wisest course would be to join the Egyptian army in order to support them in the Holy War, he set out thither, reached the outskirts of Ascalon and encamped near the Egyptians. The Franks, on hearing of this, collected their forces and marched towards Ascalon. The armies joined battle on 14th Dhu'l-Hijja (27th August) of this year, between Yāfā and Ascalon, and the Franks gained the victory over the Muslims, killing the governor of Ascalon and capturing some of the commanders. The Egyptian 'askar fled to Ascalon and the 'askar of Damascus to Bosra. It is said that the number of Muslims who were killed was about equal to the number of Franks who were killed. Zahīr al-Dīn, on returning with the 'askar to Bosra found that the king Irtāsh and Aytagīn of Aleppo, despairing of support from the Franks, had proceeded to al-Rahba, where they stayed for some time and then separated.

A.H. 499

(13*th September*, 1105, *to* 1*st September*, 1106)

In this year the Franks marched out to the

Sawād of Tiberias,[1] and began the construction of the castle of 'Al'āl between the Sawād and al-Bathanīya.[2] It was one of those castles which are described as impregnable. When Zahīr al-Dīn Atābek learnt of this intention of theirs, he became anxious to prevent its completion, lest, once done, it should prove difficult to undo. Setting out with the 'askar, he marched against them before they [3] became aware of the disaster that threatened them, fell upon them and slew them to the last man. Having obtained possession of the castle, with all the war material, animals, and utensils of the Franks that it contained, he returned to Damascus with their heads, and with the Franks he had captured, and an immense quantity of booty taken from them, on Sunday 14th Second Rabī' (24th December).

In this month also, there appeared in the western sky a comet with a tail resembling a rainbow, extending from the east to the centre of the heavens. It had also been seen near the sun in the daytime before it began to appear at night, and it continued for a number of nights and disappeared.

On 26th First Jumādā (3rd February, 1106), the report was received of the assassination of Khalaf b. Mulā 'ib,[4] lord of Afāmiya, by a party of the Bātinīya, dispatched from Aleppo by the

---

[1] The cultivated land in the region of the Upper Jordan.
[2] The district between the Jordan and the Haurān (modern Ajlūn), with its capital at Adhra'āh (Dar 'ā).
[3] Reading *hum* for *huwa*.
[4] An Arab of the tribe of Kilāb, nominated to the governorship of Afāmiya by the Fatimid Caliph of Egypt in 489/1096.

man known as Abū Tāhir the Persian goldsmith, who had taken amongst the Bātinīya the place of al-Hakīm al-Munajjim the Bātinī, after his death. His emissaries acted in collusion with one of their missionaries known as Abu'l-Fath of Sarmīn, who was living at Afāmiya. This man had arranged it with the townspeople, who made a hole in the city wall to give the assassins access to the governor. When they approached him and he became aware of them, he faced them boldly, but one of them dashed at him and drove a dagger into his belly. He then threw himself into the tower, trying to reach one of the harem apartments, but another of them delivered a second blow, and he died in a few minutes. The assassins raised the battle-cry upon the tower and proclaimed their allegiance to al-Malik Rudwān. The sons and general of the murdered man came in from the wall, but the Bātinīya seized the place from them and killed a number. His son Musbih b. Khalaf b. Mulā 'ib escaped and made his way to Shaizar, where he remained for a time until he was permitted to leave it. After this affair, Tancred arrived at Afāmiya in the hope of seizing it ; with him was a brother of Abu'l-Fath of Sarmīn, the missionary, a prisoner in his hands. He imposed upon the Bātinī a fixed tribute, and having received payment of this sum withdrew.

In this year also Qilij Arslān b. Sulaimān b. Qutulmish arrived with a large army, and moving on al-Ruhā encamped in its vicinity. The officers of Jikirmish who were occupying Harrān sent an invitation to him to take over that city and he marched towards them and took possession of it.

The people were filled with joy at his arrival to take part in the Holy War, but after a short stay he fell ill of a disease which forced him to return to Malatiya, while his officers remained at Harrān.

The report arrived that Musbih b. Mulā 'ib, who escaped from the coup de main at Afāmiya, had taken refuge with Tancred, lord of Antioch, and had urged him to return to Afāmiya and raised his hopes of seizing it, owing to the shortage of provisions in it. Accordingly, Tancred marched thither, encamped before the town and blockaded it, and at length received its surrender by capitulation on 13th Muharram of the year 500 (14th September, 1106). When the Bātinī Abu'l-Fath of Sarmīn fell into his hands, he put him to death by torture, and carried away Abū Tāhir the goldsmith and his companions with him as prisoners, but he did not observe the terms of capitulation which he had granted. The supplies of food at Afāmiya were completely exhausted, and the captives remained in his hands until they ransomed themselves by the payment of a sum of money to him,[1] when he released them and they went to Aleppo.

A.H. 500

(2nd September, 1106, to 21st August, 1107)

In this year the ravages of the Franks in the district of the Sawād, Hawrān, and Jabal 'Awf were greatly increased. When the reports of this

[1] Text : " to them," i.e., to the Franks, if the reading is correct.

arrived and the population of those parts sent petitions to Zahīr al-Dīn Atābek, he assembled the 'askar, with additional forces from the Turkmens, and marching out with them established a camp in the Sawād. The amīr 'Izz al-Mulk, governor of Tyre, had previously set out from that city with his 'askar on an expedition against the castle of Tibnīn in the territories of the Franks, and had attacked its suburb, killed all its inhabitants, and plundered it for booty. When the news of this reached Baldwin, king of the Franks, he marched against him from Tiberias. The atābek marched to a castle in the vicinity of Tiberias, in which was a body of Frankish knights, and having attacked and captured it, he slew all who were in it, and retired to al-Madān.[1] The Franks turned back to deal with him, and when they approached him the 'askar withdrew in haste towards the district of Zurrā.[2] The scouts of both armies encountered one another, and they determined to draw up for a general engagement. The Muslims were in high spirits. On the following day, the 'askar mounted, having prepared for battle in accordance with this purpose, and advanced to the site of their encampment, where they found that the Franks had already moved off and were retreating to Tiberias, whence they withdrew to 'Akkā. Thereupon Zahīr al-Dīn led the 'askar back to Damascus.

In this year also a succession of letters reached the [Saljūqid] sultan Ghiyāth al-Dunyā wal-Dīn Muhammad, son of Malik Shāh, from Zahīr al-Dīn

---

[1] al-Madān is defined by William of Tyre (R.H.C.Occ. I, 583) as the plain east of the junction of the Jordan and the Yarmuq.
[2] In the Hawrān.

Atābek and Fakhr al-Mulk Ibn 'Ammār, lord of Tarābulus, informing him of the widespread disorder which the Franks had wrought in the land, of their seizure of the fortresses and castles in Syria and on the coast, and of their slaughter of the Muslims and blockade of the port of Tarābulus, appealing to him for aid and reinforcement, and urging him to send prompt assistance to the people. The Sultan, on learning of this state of affairs, deputed the amīr Jāwalī Saqāwa, with one of the chief commanders of his 'askar, to set out with a large 'askar of Turks, and assigned al-Rahba and the Euphrates districts to him as a fief. At the same time he wrote to Baghdād and to the amīr Saif al-Dawla Sadaqa b. Mazyad[1] and to Jikirmish, lord of Mosul, instructing them to strengthen him with money and troops for the Holy War, and to do their utmost to assist and reinforce him. His order was received with displeasure by both these lords ; the amīr was repulsed by Ibn Mazyad, and proceeded towards Mosul to request from Jikirmish what the sultan had assigned to him. But Jikirmish hesitated to assist him, so he fell upon the fort of al-Sinn[2] and plundered it, and a great host [of volunteers] joined him. Jikirmish now went out to engage him, but Jāwalī Saqāwa captured him and exterminated his 'askar. His son fled to Mosul and held the city, whereupon Jāwalī Saqāwa followed him up, put his father

---

[1] Sadaqa (reigned 1086–1107) chief of the Arab tribe of Mazyad, and founder of an independent dynasty in Lower 'Iraq, with its capital at al-*H*illa, built in 1101. He and his son Dubais (1107–1134) were constantly engaged in guerilla warfare with the Saljūqid governors of Baghdād, and their plundering raids on Baghdād and its neighbourhood became celebrated exploits.

[2] At the confluence of the Lower Zāb with the Tigris.

Jikirmish to death, and sent his head to Mosul. When his son learned of this he wrote to Qilij Arslān b. Qutulmish, summoning him to his aid from Malatiya and promising to surrender to him the city and all the districts which he held. Now Jikirmish had collected a vast revenue from the Jazīra and Mosul, and was popular amongst his subjects, just in his government, and noted for his uprightness in all his territories. When therefore Qilij Arslān was apprised of the contents of the letter which was written to him by the son of Jikirmish, he agreed to his request, and setting out towards him with his 'askar arrived at Nasībīn. The son of Jikirmish, summoned by him from Mosul, went to join him, and Qilij Arslān entered Nasībīn, since he had with him only a portion of his 'askar, the remainder being in Anatolia, to assist the king of Constantinople against the Franks. When the 'askar of Qilij Arslān drew near to the 'askar of Jāwalī Saqāwa, and the vanguards of both sides engaged in battle, a party of the troops of Qilij Arslān defeated a party of the troops of Jāwalī Saqāwa, killing some and taking others prisoner. Thereupon Jāwalī set out with the main body to attack the army of Qilij, having learnt that he had sent to summon the remainder of his 'askar from Anatolia, and that he had only a small force with him. He made for the district of the Khābūr, and went thence to al-Rahba, encamped before it, and besieged it. At the same time he wrote to Muhammad, who governed the town on behalf of the king Shams al-Mulūk Duqāq, lord of Damascus, and had with him the king Irtāsh b. Tāj ad-Dawla, who had fled from Damascus after the death of his brother the king Duqāq, summoning him to surrender it to him, but he paid no heed to his letter, and gave him to despair of his request. Jāwalī remained there for a time prosecuting his siege of the city. Here he was joined by the amīr Najm al-Dīn Il-Ghāzī b. Ortuq, with a great company of his 'askar of Turkmens, and he sent a request for support in his attack on the town to the king Fakhr al-Mulūk Rudwān, who joined him with his 'askar, having first made a truce with Tancred, lord of Antioch. But when he left Aleppo, and Joscelin, lord of Tell Bāshir, learned of his absence from the city, he made a series of raids upon the districts of Aleppo in all directions. Jāwalī remained in his lines before al-Rahba from the beginning of Rajab (began 26th February, 1107), until 22nd Ramadān (17th April), when the Euphrates rose with its customary flood, and Jāwali's troops embarked in boats and sailed up towards the city walls, with the collusion of some of the townsmen. But they were unable to effect anything with their co-operation, and the troops made instead an assault on the wall, captured the town, and set about plundering it, confiscating the goods of many of the inhabitants, and forcing them to produce their hidden treasures by torture. After a time Jāwali ordered the plundering to cease, promised the people security, and restored them to their dwellings. The citadel surrendered to him five days later, on 28th Ramadān (23rd May). Jāwalī then confirmed the appointment of Muhammad as governor of the town, and swore him to allegiance, but a few days later he arrested him on account of some matter which had come to his ears and roused his displeasure with him, and had him confined in the citadel. The king Irtāsh also became one of the dependants of Saqāwa, and was no longer free to act on his own behalf. Now this Muhammad, the governor, had sent previously to Qilij Arslān b. Sulaimān, appealing for his aid and assistance in defending the city against Jāwalī. Qilij Arslān consequently advanced with his 'askar towards al-Rahba, but when he heard of its capture, he turned back and halted at al-Shamsānīya, having no intention of coming to blows with Jāwalī. Meanwhile, Jāwalī set out and after a halt at Māksīn determined to advance towards the province of Mosul. With him was Fakhr al-Mulūk Rudwān, and it chanced that they marched on the 'askar of Qilij, and the two parties joined combat on Thursday 19th Shawwāl (13th June).

It was then mid-summer, the heat was intense, and the ground scorching, and most of the horses on both sides perished. The 'askar of Qilij Arslān charged on the 'askar of Jāwalī, and Jāwalī sought out Qilij Arslān in the press and struck him several blows with his sword, without producing any effect on him. The 'askar of Qilij Arslān was routed, the lord of Āmid separated from him during the battle, along with the lord of Mayyāfāriqīn, and the remainder fled. The sword did execution on the forces of Qilij Arslān, and Qilij himself in the rout fell into the Khābūr and perished in the water, and was not seen again. Some days later he was found dead. Jāwalī returned to Mosul, and the king Fakhr al-Mulūk Rudwān in fear of him left him and returned to Aleppo. Jāwalī seized Najm al-Dīn Il-Ghāzī b. Ortuq and demanded of him repayment of the money he had spent on the Turkmens, but came to terms with him and agreed to accept instead a sum of money to be paid to him. He took hostages from him pending the payment of this sum, and Il-Ghāzī continued to furnish them to him [1] subsequently.

Now Qilij Arslān had dispatched one of his principal commanders to Anatolia with a great host of Turkmens, to reinforce the king of Constantinople against Bohemond and those Franks who were with him, making their way to Syria. These troops therefore set off to join the king of the Greeks and the armies of Greeks which he had assembled. When the opposing forces had mustered their full strength they set their ranks and engaged in battle. The Greeks were victorious over the Franks and drove them in a shameful rout which destroyed the greater part of them by death or captivity. The remnant of them who escaped broke up into small parties to make their way back to their own country. Qilij Arslān's Turkish troops also separated to their own places, after he had honoured them with ceremonial banquets and robes and distributed bounty amongst them.

When Jāwalī Saqāwa returned from [2] al-Rahba and encamped before Mosul, he sent messages to

---

[1] Text: *aqāma lahu bihā*, perhaps "Jāwalī retained them as a guarantee of his good conduct," or (substituting *qāma* for *aqāma*) "Il-Ghāzī paid him the amount."

[2] Reading *min* for *'ilā*.

its inhabitants and the garrison in the city, who, being unable to defend it against him or keep him at a distance, surrendered it to him, after receiving from him a guarantee of security for all within its walls. The son of Qilij had taken refuge in the city, and Jāwalī seized him and had him conveyed to the [Saljūqid] Sultan Muhammad, with whom he remained until he escaped from the camp at the beginning of the year 503 (began 31st July, 1109), and made his way back to his father's kingdom in Anatolia. It is said that when he arrived there, he formed a plot against his uncle's son and having killed him, firmly established himself in the kingdom in his stead.[1]

In this year the Turkmen amīr al-Ispahbad arrived at Damascus from his own province. Zahīr al-Dīn, having received him with honour and entertained him, assigned to him as an apanage Wādī Mūsā (Petra), Mo'ab, al-Sharāt, al-Jibāl, and the Balqa', and he set out for these districts with his 'askar. Now the Franks had penetrated into those parts and had killed, enslaved, and plundered all that they could lay hands on in them. When the Ispahbad reached them, he found their population in the utmost fear and misery on account of what they had suffered from the Franks. So he established himself there, but the Franks, on hearing of his arrival, marched towards him through the desert, and encamped opposite the place in which he was encamped. They left him

---

[1] This passage apparently refers to Malik-shāh (500–510), whom Qilij left in command of Mosul on his advance against Jāwalī (Ibn al-Athīr X, 297).

unmolested until they found an opportunity against him, then attacked him when he was off his guard, and he fled with most of his 'askar. The remainder perished and the Franks took possession of his baggage-train. He arrived at 'Ain al-Katība in the district of Hawrān, at a time when the 'askar of Damascus was encamped before it. Zahīr al-Dīn received him with expressions of sympathy for what had befallen him and of consolation for what he had lost, indemnified him, and bestowed upon him a gift which retrieved his fortunes.[1]

A.H. 501

(*22nd August*, 1107, *to* 10*th August*, 1108)

In this year Baldwin, king of the Franks, collected his broken faction and God-forsaken army and marched on the port of Tyre. He encamped in face of the town and began the construction of a castle in its outskirts on Tell al-Ma 'shūqa. He remained for a month, after which the governor of the town purchased his withdrawal for seven thousand dinars, and he took them and withdrew.

In this year also the Sultan Ghiyāth al-Dunyā wal-Dīn Muhammad, having [defeated and slain Sadaqa b. Mazyad,[2] and] settled the affairs of al-Hillah, set out to return to Isfahān at the beginning of the month of [Shawwāl].[3] Before

---

[1] Ibn al-Athīr (X, 318) records the return of the Ispahbadh Sabāwū from Damascus to al-'Irāq in the following year (501).

[2] See above p. 76 n.1.

[3] The month is omitted in the text, and has been supplied from Ibn al-Athīr, X, 318.

setting out he laid it as a duty upon the amīr Mawdūd and the 'askar to march on Mosul, reduce it by siege, and take possession of it. Mawdūd and the army therefore proceeded on their way and encamped before Mosul. Now Jāwalī, lord of the city, had driven out most of the people, and his troops had behaved themselves ill in it and committed every kind of excess. So he betook himself to al-Rahba and deputed one of his officers in whom he had confidence to remain in Mosul and defend it. The 'askar of the sultan had remained before it for some time, when seven of the townsmen resolved upon conniving at its capture, and opening one of the city gates delivered over the town to Mawdūd. Upon entering he made a great slaughter of the troops of Jāwalī, but gave quarter to the garrison in the citadel, and dispatched them and all that was with them to the Sultan.

In Sha'bān of this year (began 16th March), the situation of Fakhr al-Mulk Ibn 'Ammār at Tarābulus became critical, owing to the siege of the Franks, and the length of time which it had lasted, the long-drawn-out watch for the coming of reinforcements, and the continued procrastination in sending assistance. In consequence of this, he sent to Damascus, asking that the amīr Ortuq b. 'Abd al-Razzāq, one of the amīrs of Damascus, should visit him, in order that he might discuss with him what was in his mind. The amīr consented to this, and having asked and received permission to go from Zahīr al-Dīn, set out towards him. Meanwhile, Fakhr al-Mulk had left Tarābulus

by land with about five hundred horse and foot,
taking with him a quantity of gifts and precious
objects to be presented to the Sultan when he
went to visit him at Baghdād. When Ortuq
reached him and they met together, it was decided
between them that Fakhr al-Mulk should go to
Damascus in his company. He proceeded to
Damascus accordingly, and was lodged at Marj
Bāb al-Hadīd (the meadow by the Iron Gate)
outside the walls. Zahīr al-Dīn showed him every
possible honour and mark of respect, and the
amīrs and commanders of the troops presented
him with as many horses, mules, camels and other
gifts as each of them found it within his means
to give.

Now Fakhr al-Mulk had left as his lieutenants
in the defence of Tarābulus Abu'l-Manāqib, who
was his uncle's son, and the principal officers of
his troops and his guard,[1] and having bestowed
upon them six months' pay, he bound them by
oaths of allegiance and fidelity. His cousin,
however, revolted against him and declared his
allegiance to al-Afdal, the son of the Amīr al-
Juyūsh, in Egypt. When Fakhr al-Mulk learned
of his action, he wrote to his officers bidding
them arrest him and remove him to the castle of
al-Khawābī. This was done, and Fakhr al-Mulk
proceeded on his way to Baghdād, in the company
of Tāj al-Mulūk Būrī, son of Zahīr al-Dīn Atābek.
For the Atābek had learned that at the Sultan's
court there were envious rivals of his, who were
undermining his position by insidious slanders and
seeking to injure him and to bring him into dis-

---

[1] *Ghilmān*, slaves, i.e., members of the Turkish 'askar or guard.

favour with the Sultan. On this account he dispatched along with his son a quantity of presents and precious objects, such as horses, rich stuffs, and other articles which are suitable for sending as gifts. He appointed as wazīr to him Abu'l-Najm Hibat-Allāh b. Muhammad b. Badī', who had been chief accountant (*mustawfī*) to the martyr-Sultan Tāj al-Dawla. He gave this man full control over the prince, and empowered him to act as envoy between him and those to whom he was sent. The start of the journey was made on 8th Ramadān, 501 (21st April, 1108). When they arrived at Baghdād, Fakhr al-Mulk was received by the Sultan with such marks of honour and esteem as even exceeded his hopes. The Sultan commanded a number of the great amīrs to go with him to give him assistance and reinforcement in repelling those who had invested his city, and to inflict condign punishment upon them, and drive them off. He gave instructions to the 'askar which was detailed to go with him to make a brief halt by the way at Mosul and wrest it from the hands of Jāwalī Saqāwa, and thereafter to proceed to Tarābulus. The result of this was the events which have been related above. Meanwhile, Fakhr al-Mulk was detained [at the Sultan's court] so long that he grew impatient and returned to Damascus in the middle of Muharram 502 (end of August, 1108).

As for Tāj al-Mulūk, son of Zahīr al-Dīn, the affair for which he had been sent proceeded to his utmost satisfaction, and he received from the Sultan gratifying favours both for his father and for himself. Having been honoured by the bestowal of magnificent robes from the Caliph as well as from the Sultan, he returned to Damascus and reached it at the end of Dhu'l-Hijja of this same year (early August, 1108).

Fakhr al-Mulk Ibn 'Ammār, on his return to Damascus, remained there for some days, and set out thence with a troop of cavalry which had been detached from the 'askar of Damascus to accompany him, together with his own cavalry. [He marched to the port of Jabala] [1] and entered it, and the inhabitants gave him their allegiance. The people of Tarābulus sent to al-Afdal in Egypt, begging him to send them a governor by sea, accompanied by vessels with grain and provisions, that he might take over command of the town. In response to their appeal, Sharaf al-Dawla, son of Abū Tayyib, came to them as governor on behalf of al-Afdal, bringing with him supplies of grain. As soon as he arrived and established himself in the town, he arrested all the partisans and officers of Fakhr al-Mulk Ibn 'Ammār, together with his stores, equipage, and furniture, and had them all sent to Egypt by sea.

In this year also Zahīr al-Dīn Atābek marched out by night with the 'askar to Tiberias, and dividing his troops into two detachments, sent one of them into Palestine, and with the other made a raid on Tiberias. The lord of the town, called Gervase,[2] one of the chiefs of the Franks who were noted for knightliness, courage, gallantry, and prowess in combat, a man of the stamp of King Baldwin in his leadership of the Franks, came out against him with his men-at-arms. When they

---

[1] These words are missing in the printed text. [2] *Jarfās.*

engaged in battle, the Turkish cavalry surrounded him and his companions, and most of them were killed. Gervase himself was captured with some others, and they were taken to Damascus. Some of them were sent as a present to the Sultan, and Gervase and those of his companions who were in captivity with him were executed, after they had offered a sum of money for their release, but the atābek refused to accept it.

In this year Baldwin marched with his forsaken army of Franks to the port of Sidon, invested it by land and sea and built a wooden tower for an assault upon it. The Egyptian fleet arrived to defend it, and gained a victory over both the Genoese fleet and the land forces. News also reached the Franks of the approach of the 'askar of Damascus for the defence of Sidon, whereupon they withdrew and returned to their own places.

A.H. 502

(11th August, 1108, to 30th July, 1109)

In this year the lord of 'Arqa sent an envoy to Zahīr al-Dīn Atābek requesting assistance from him to repel the attacks of the Franks, and desiring the despatch of an officer to take over the town. Zahīr al-Dīn accordingly dispatched one of his trusty officers, who took over control and remained as governor of the town, in expectation of the arrival of the 'askar and the fulfilment of Zahīr al-Dīn's promise to bestow a robe of honour and rewards upon him. But there occurred at that time heavy falls of snow and rains that hindered the march of the 'askar to 'Arqa ; the provisions in the town ran short and supplies were cut off from it, and the Franks made haste to besiege it. Thereupon Zahīr al-Dīn set out towards it, but found that the Franks had already invested the place, and that his own strength was insufficient to drive them off. He retired to the castle of al-Akma,[1] and encamping before it, began an attack upon it. When the Franks learned of this, they marched against him with about three hundred knights in order to reinforce the garrison in al-Akma, and joined them under cover of night. Their spirits were so raised by this that the atābek, in view of the increased strength of the garrison, judged it necessary to retire, and withdrew like one defeated. The Franks were emboldened against him, and in their pursuit of the 'askar took an immense booty in horse and other animals. The troops dispersed amongst the woods and mountains and reached Hims in the most wretched and pitiable condition, though there had been no fighting at all. Thereafter the Franks returned to 'Arqa, and its provisions being exhausted, they gained possession of it by capitulation.

In Sha 'bān of this year (6th March to 3rd April, 1109) Raymond,[2] the son of the St. Gilles who had formerly besieged Tarābulus, arrived from the land of the Franks by sea with sixty vessels, loaded up with Franks and Genoese, and encamped before Tarābulus. A dispute arose between him and

---

[1] Perhaps represented by the modern Akun, on the lower slopes of Lebanon, 32 km. S.W. of *H*ims and 9 km. S.E. of Qubai 'at.
[2] *Raimand*, i.e., Bertram son of Raymond.

de Cerdagne,[1] the son of St. Gilles' sister, and Tancred, lord of Antioch, came to him in order to support de Cerdagne. King Baldwin, lord of Jerusalem, also arrived with his army and restored peace between them. De Cerdagne returned to 'Arqa, and finding a certain Frank in the fields there, he desired to strike him, but the Frank struck and killed him. When this news reached Raymond, son of St. Gilles, he sent one of his officers to take over 'Arqa. The Franks now descended with their hosts and levies upon Tarābulus, and set about attacking it and blockading its population from 1st Shawwāl (4th May) to 11th Dhu'l-Hijja of this year (12th July). They set up their towers against the city wall, and when the townsfolk saw with their own eyes the army and fighting men they repented bitterly, and were convinced of their doom. Their spirits were lowered by universal despair at the delay of the Egyptian fleet in bringing provisions and reinforcements by sea, for the stores of the fleet had been exhausted and the direction of the wind remained contrary, through the will of God that that which was decreed should come to pass. The Franks pressed their attack upon the city, and delivered an assault from their towers, and captured it by the sword on Monday 11th Dhu'l-Hijja (12th July) of this year. They plundered all that was in it, took the men captive, and enslaved the women and children ; the quantities of material that fell into their hands from its merchandise and storehouses, and the books in its college and in the libraries of private owners, exceed all computation.

[1] al-Sardānī

The governor of the city and a number of his troops, who had asked for quarter before its capture, were spared ; and after it was occupied, they were set free and arrived at Damascus a few days later. The townsmen were cruelly handled, their money was confiscated and their treasures dug up from their places of concealment and they were reduced to the utmost destitution and bitter distress.

It was agreed between the Franks and the Genoese that a third of the town, with what had been plundered from it, should belong to the Genoese, and two-thirds to Raymond son of St. Gilles, and they set aside for King Baldwin from the choicest of the booty, a portion with which he was content. Meanwhile, Tancred, since he had not gained what he desired from supporting de Cerdagne, had withdrawn, and attacked and captured Bulunyās,[1] giving a promise of security to its population, in Shawwāl (May) of this year. Thereafter he descended upon the port of Jabala,[2] in which Fakhr al-Mulk Ibn 'Ammār was living. The town was but scantily stocked with foodstuffs and he blockaded it and its inhabitants without intermission until Friday 22nd Dhu'l-Hijja (23rd July), when he sent an envoy to them, promising them immunity, and on their acceptance of his terms, took possession of it by capitulation. Fakhr al-Mulk Ibn 'Ammār marched out of it without molestation, though Tancred had promised to show a benevolent regard for him and to grant him the town as a fief.

[1] Text : Banyās. Bulunyās (Balanea) was near the coast, ten miles south of Jabala.
[2] Text : Jubail.

A little later there arrived the Egyptian fleet, such a fleet as had never before been dispatched by the Egyptians in regard to the number of men and vessels and quantity of equipment and provisions, for the purpose of defending Tarābulus and of strengthening it by abundant food stuffs, men and money for the space of a year, and also for the strengthening of the coast towns and population belonging to Egypt. They arrived at Tyre on the eighth day after the capture of Tarābulus, having been forestalled in their purpose, by reason of the calamity preordained for its people. The fleet remained on the coast for a time, and distributed the provisions in the various districts. The people of Tyre, Sidon, and Bairūt sought to retain it, and made representations of their lamentable condition and their incapacity to fight against the Franks, but the fleet could not stay and weighed anchor to return to Egypt when the wind became favourable.

In Shawwāl (May) of this year reports were received that the amīr Sukmān al-Qutbī,[1] having besieged the city of Mayyāfāriqīn and blockaded its people for a number of months, had captured it by capitulation, after its provisions had given out and its inhabitants were reduced to starvation.

In the same year, Bohemond, lord of Antioch, arrived from the land of the Franks on his way back to his kingdom with a great host. He halted in

---

[1] He was a Turkish general of the Saljūqids, who had seized Akhlāṭ, one of the principal cities of Armenia, at the western end of Lake Van, from its former Kurdish rulers in 1100. Mayyāfariqīn (Martyropolis) at this time was in the possession of an independent atābek, Khumartāsh.

the vicinity of Constantinople, and its king went out against him, accompanied by a great host of Turkmens from the districts bordering on his territories. They fought against one another for some days, and the king sought to disunite them by every means, until they broke up, and became dispersed throughout the land. Bohemond made his peace with the king, and being admitted to his presence he and those with him paid homage to him.[1] Thus God, to Him be praise, delivered us from them and diverted their fury from Islam.

In this year a succession of envoys from King Baldwin came to Zahīr al-Dīn with proposals for an armistice and the establishment of amicable relations. An agreement was reached between them that the Sawād and Jabal 'Awf should be divided into thirds, the Turks to have one-third, and the Franks and peasantry two-thirds. The compact was concluded on this proposition, and the terms written down on this basis.

When the Franks captured Jabala, Fakhr al-Mulk Ibn 'Ammār had left the town and gone to Shaizar, the lord of which, Sultān b. 'Alī b. al-Muqallad b. Munqidh al-Kinānī, received him and his followers with honour, and proposed that he should remain with him. He refused the invitation and set out for Damascus to rejoin Zahīr al-Dīn Atābek, who welcomed him, assigned him a residence, and bestowed on him the town and districts of al-Zabdānī as a fief in Muharram of the year 503 (August, 1109).

[1] Literally : " trod his carpet."

A.H. 503

(31st July, 1109, *to* 19*th July,* 1110)

When the Franks finished with Tarābulus, after capturing it and putting the affairs of the city and its districts into order, they marched to Rafanīya. Zahir al-Dīn also, learning that they entertained this purpose, marched towards Rafanīya with the 'askar to protect it, and pitched his camp at Hims over against them. The Franks were unable to besiege or to invest the town, and there passed between them and Zahīr al-Dīn some correspondence and negotiations, which led to both parties agreeing to make an amicable settlement regarding their respective territories and to establish peaceful relations. A treaty was concluded on the terms that the Franks should receive one-third of the produce of the Biqā' (Coele-Syria) and that the castles of al-Munaitira and Ibn 'Akkār[1] should be delivered up to them, that they should abstain from their plundering and ravaging in the provinces and outlying districts, that the castles of Masyāf,[2] Hisn al-Tūfān and Hisn al-Akrād should be included in the terms of the treaty, and that their inhabitants should pay a stipulated sum annually to the Franks as protection-money. The Franks observed these conditions for a short time, but they did not long continue within the terms of the agreement and returned to their customary ravaging and destroying.

In First Jumādā of this year (began 26th

---

[1] Ibn 'Akkār is apparently *Hi*sn 'Akkār north of *T*arābulus.
[2] Text : Ma*s*yāth.

November) news was received from al-'Irāq of the
arrival at Baghdād of the Sultan Ghiyāth al-
Dunyā wal-Dīn [1] Muhammad son of Malik-Shāh,
and of his despatch of letters to all his territories,
announcing his firm resolve to proceed to the Holy
War. It was reported also that he had issued a
command to Zahīr al-Dīn Atābek to make no
advance until such time as the troops should arrive
in Syria, when he should join with them and take
control of their operations, because he had dispatched a constant succession of letters with
appeals for assistance and reinforcements against
the infidel opponents. But certain obstacles arose
in the way of that design, and various hindrances
which diverted him from his object. When the
time of waiting lengthened out, and the boldness
of the infidels was increased by the dilatoriness of
the Sultan's armies, Zahīr al-Dīn's zeal for the
cause of Islām and his Turkish resolution led
him to prepare to journey in person to Baghdād,
to pay homage at the high court of the Successor
of the Prophet, the Caliph al-Mustazhir, and the
stations of the Sultanic majesty of Ghiyāth al-
Dunyā wal-Dīn, and to appear before them and
make complaint of what had befallen the Muslims
within their realms, of the seizure of cities, the
slaying of men and enslavement of women and
children, and of their covetous ambition to reach
out to the conquest of the provinces of al-Jazīra
and al-'Irāq. Having made preparations for the
journey, he took with him Fakhr al-Mulk Ibn
'Ammār, lord of Tarābulus, and his personal
officers, and all that he could dispose of in the

---

[1] The printed text has by error Rukn al-Dunyā wal-Dīn.

way of swift Arab horses, rare Egyptian stuffs and precious objects and gifts of every costly kind, such as were suitable for presentation to those high quarters, and set out through the desert by way of al-Samāwa. As his lieutenant in Damascus he appointed his son Tāj al-Malūk Būrī, and counselled him in regard to his duty of remaining on the alert in defence and protection [of his dominions], of benevolent conduct towards his subjects, of dissimulating to the Franks, and maintaining the amicable relations which had been established with them until his return. After he had set out, however, and had reached the valley in the desert called Wādi'l-Miyāh (Valley of Waters), he received the report of a statement circulated by the alarmists in Baghdād, that the Sultan had invested with the governorship of Syria certain amīrs who were singled out by name, and indicated in this connection. This report caused him such disquietude as made it necessary for him to abandon his journey and he commissioned Fakhr al-Mulk Ibn 'Ammār, with certain of his officers in whom he had confidence, to go on to Baghdād together with the gifts and treasures which he had brought with him, and to represent him in putting an end to the state of affairs which had caused him to abandon his journey. Fakhr al-Mulk reached Baghdād with the gifts which he had brought, and was received with pleasure at his coming and regret at the return of the atābek, that he had not prosecuted his journey and seen in person the fulfilment of his desires beyond his utmost hopes, and the demonstration of the falsity of those alarmist reports as baseless calumnies. A succession of letters arrived [from Baghdād] about these matters, conveying messages of a gratifying and reassuring nature, and apologising for the spread of this calumny and these false reports.

As Zahīr al-Dīn Atābek was returning from Wādi'l-Mīyāh he had received information that the freedman Gumushtagīn al-Tājī, the governor of Ba 'albek, had communicated with the Franks, seeking a friendly accommodation with them and inciting them to raid the frontier districts, and had sent his brother the freedman Bāitagīn al-Tājī to the Sultan, that by slanderous intrigue he might find a way to rouse discord and dissension.[1] When Zahīr al-Dīn heard of this report and of the despatch of Bāitagīn, he summoned a troop of his 'askar and gave them instructions to proceed to the roads and highways by which he must necessarily pass on his journey, and to fetch him to him, but he failed to obtain any news of Bāitagīn. Zahīr al-Dīn himself with the 'askar turned aside from his road [to proceed to Ba 'albek] and at the same time wrote to his son Tāj al-Mulūk, ordering him to set out with the 'askar to Ba 'albek, and to encamp before it. Tāj al-Mulūk hastened to carry out his command, and setting out thither, encamped before it when the townsmen were off their guard and not expecting him. Thereupon he addressed a letter to the freedman, summoning him to return to his allegiance and surrender the place to him, warning him of the consequences of persisting in his disobedience and rebellion, and threatening him if he maintained an attitude which must lead to the

[1] i.e., to set the Sultan against Zahīr al-Dīn.

shedding of blood. Notwithstanding that he couched this warning and ultimatum in the strongest terms, Gumushtagīn rejected his demands, and persisted in his opposition and insubordination. Shortly afterwards, Zahīr al-Dīn came up with his ʿaskar and the forces of footsoldiers which he had collected, and disposed his troops in battle positions opposite Baʿalbek. He set up catapults against it, and began the construction of an engine of war and breaching, in order to find the weak spots in its defences, and to take advantage of the opportunity offered by them. A number of troops from the town bands and the garrison made their submission to him, and he showed them favour and bestowed robes upon them. He then made an assault upon the wall, and killed a number of its defenders. When the townsfolk saw the energy with which he fought and his persistence in maintaining the siege, they inclined towards making submission to him. The freedman sought the remission of his fault and promised to surrender the town and citadel upon a definite stipulation and the assignment to him of a specified fief. He asked that one of the commanders might come to him to discuss matters with him and bring them to a successful conclusion for himself. So he sent the amīr Baltāsh to him, on account of his standing with the government. A settlement having been reached on the conditions he had proposed, he surrendered to Zāhīr al-Dīn both town and citadel, which was exceedingly formidable and inaccessible, one of the most celebrated of fortresses and a marvel of construction, and went out to him. The atābek followed his generous custom of pardoning those who had done evil to him and raised rebellion against him, giving him in exchange for Ba 'albek the castle of Sarkhad, which is likewise celebrated for its strength and inaccessibility, and restoring to him the property and estates of which he had deprived him, and . . .[1] to Damascus. Zāhīr al-Dīn Atābek made over the governorship of Ba 'albek to his son Tāj al-Mulūk Būrī, and established a garrison in it under trustworthy officers in whom he had confidence, and settled its affairs. The space of time spent in besieging the city was thirty-five days, and it was surrendered on 22nd Ramadān 503 (14th April, 1110). Zāhīr al-Dīn gave orders to relieve the inhabitants of Ba 'albek from oppressive imposts and to remit a portion of their land tax, and he restored to them properties which had been wrongfully seized from them in former times, whereupon the people showered blessings upon him and expressions of gratitude reached him from all sides. He set out thereafter to return to Damascus, where he received news of the Sultan's return from Baghdād to Isfahān in Shawwāl of this year (beg. 23rd April).

News arrived of the death of the amīr Ibrāhīm [son of] Yanāl (Inal), lord of Āmid ; he was a man of evil conduct, and spoken of as a tyrant to its people, so that a number of its inhabitants had left the city because of his persistent oppression of them and his injustice towards them. Thus there was general relief at his loss, and hope of

[1] A word or words missing in the text, perhaps "sent him."

better conditions after his death. He was succeeded by his son,[1] who was a man of more upright character and more humane nature than his father. In this year also Tancred marched out from Antioch with his host and his God-forsaken rabble to the Syrian frontiers,[2] and having captured Tarsūs and the adjacent territories and expelled the representative of the king of the Greeks from them, returned to Antioch. Next he marched out to Shaizar, and after ravaging its territory, imposed upon it a tribute of ten thousand dinars, to be paid to him at once. He then besieged Hisn al-Akrād, which was surrendered to him by its inhabitants, and proceeded to 'Arqa. King Baldwin and the son of St. Gilles had in the meantime invested the port of Bairūt both by land and sea. Tancred returned to Antioch, and Joscelin,[3] lord of Tell Bāshir, journeyed to the port of Bairūt, in order to assist the Franks who were investing it, and ask their support against the 'askar of the amīr Mawdūd,[4] which was investing al-Ruhā. The Franks set about constructing a tower and planting it against the wall of Bairūt, but when it was completed and they moved it up it was broken by stones from the catapults and rendered useless. Thereupon they set to work upon another, and the son of St. Gilles constructed a third tower. During this time nineteen war vessels of the Egyptian fleet arrived by sea, and having overcome the

[1] Sa 'd al-Dawla Āikaldī (Āigildī) or Il-Aldī.
[2] Cilicia and the districts bordering on Anatolia.
[3] Jūsalīn.
[4] Mawdūd, son of Altūntāsh and nephew of Karbūqā, the former Turkish governor of Mosul (see above p. 83). He was not the brother of Sultan Muḥammad (Ghīyāth al-Dunyā wal-Dīn).

vessels of the Franks and captured some of them, they entered Bairūt with supplies. The spirits of the population were raised by this success. King Baldwin sent to al-Suwaidīya, asking aid of the Genoese who were there with their ships, and forty of their vessels came to Bairūt in response, laden with fighting men. The Franks now attacked both by land and sea with their entire forces, on Friday 21st Shawwāl (13th May). They set up two towers against the wall and fought with the utmost vigour. The commander of the Egyptian fleet was killed, together with a great host of the Muslims, and never before nor after did the Franks see a more hard-fought battle than this. The people in the town lost heart and became assured of their destruction. At the close of this day the Franks made an assault on the town and captured it mightily by the sword ; the governor who was in it fled with a party of his troops, but he was brought to the Franks, and put to death with all his companions, and they plundered all the treasure he had taken with him. The city was sacked, its inhabitants enslaved or made prisoner, and their goods and treasures confiscated. Shortly afterwards there arrived from Egypt three hundred horsemen as a reinforcement for Bairūt but when they reached the Jordan province [1] a small detachment of Franks came out against them, and the Egyptians fled before them to the hills and many of them perished. When the affairs of Bairūt had been set in order, King Baldwin departed with the Franks and encamping before

[1] The province of Urdunn included most of Samaria and Galilee in addition to the valley of the Jordan.

the port of Sidon, sent an envoy to its inhabitants summoning them to surrender the town. They asked of him a respite for a space of time which they specified, and he granted them a respite after exacting from them a sum of six thousand dinars to be paid to him as annual tribute, their former tribute having been two thousand dinars. Thereafter he departed for Jerusalem to perform the pilgrimage.

On 8th Dhu'l-Qad'da of this year (29th May) there appeared in the sky a comet from the East with a tail extending southwards. It continued until the end of Dhu'l-Hijja (mid-July) and then disappeared.

In this year also the Sultan Ghiyāth al-Dunyā wal-Dīn wrote to the amīr Sukmān al-Qutbī, lord of Armenia and Mayyāfāriqīn, and to the amīr Sharaf al-Dīn Mawdūd, lord of Mosul, commanding them to set out with their troops to the Holy War against the Franks and the defence of the territories of Mosul. Having collected their troops and recruited their levies, they set out and halted at Jazīrah Banī Numair, until the governors of all the outlying districts had joined them, together with a great host of volunteers. They were joined also by the amīr Najm al-Dīn Il-Ghāzī son of Ortuq, with a great host of Turkmens, and the Muslim armies assembled in such force as all the Franks would not suffice to withstand. They agreed unanimously to open the Holy War by making for al-Ruhā and blockading it until God should facilitate its capture, in view of its strength and impregnability. Setting out therefore with all their forces, they encamped before it, between the 10th and 20th of Shawwāl (3rd to 12th May), and surrounded it on all sides like a girdle, preventing all ingress and egress. The city was short of provisions, and the inhabitants reached the verge of destruction. The price of foodstuffs rose to a height and the siege and blockade was maintained over a long space of time. When the Franks learned of this condition of affairs, they set about gathering their forces and levies and preparing their armaments and taking measures for its defence. In face of these circumstances unanimity was restored between them ; Tancred, lord of Antioch, the son of St. Gilles, lord of Tarābulus, and King Baldwin, the chiefs of the governors of the provinces among the Franks, met together and made a solemn agreement with one another to remain steadfast in battle and to meet adversity with resolution. When a clear understanding was established between them, they set out with all their host towards al-Ruhā. The news also reached Zahīr al-Dīn Atābek, together with information of the agreement reached between the Franks, and setting out with the 'askar from Damascus he encamped at Salamīya. Here he learned that the Franks had attacked Rafanīya on their way, and that when they encamped before the town its governor, the amīr Shams al-Khawāss, made a sortie with his cavalry and killed a number of them. On Zahīr al-Dīn's arrival at the camp of Salamīya, he was joined by a great host [of volunteers] who assembled together from all parts of Syria. News was brought that the Franks had reached the Euphrates and were preparing to cross it in the direction of [1] al-Ruhā. The atābek at once set out and made towards the district of al-Raqqa and Qal 'at Ja 'bar. Having crossed the Euphrates, he delayed there until he heard news of the Franks and learned that they had resolved not to cross over, owing to the distribution of squadrons and scouting parties of the armies of Islām throughout all these parts and on all the roads leading to the river.

When the Muslims learned that the Franks were in their neighbourhood, they agreed amongst themselves to give them a clear passage so that they might be able to attack them in the open ground east of the Euphrates. They withdrew therefore from al-Ruhā, at the end of Dhu'l-Hijja (ended 19th July), and encamped in the land of Harrān with the intention of deceiving the enemy and leading them into a trap. Harrān had previously come into the possession of the amīr Mawdūd, and he had given it to Najm al-Dīn Il-Ghāzī son of Ortuq. The Muslims refrained from attacking the Franks until they should be close upon them and the 'askar of Damascus should join them. The Franks, perceiving the object of this manœuvre and that the Muslims had acted thus by agreement amongst themselves, became alarmed, and with premonitions of disaster and defeat turned back in panic upon their tracks to the banks of the Euphrates. On the receipt of information of their movements, the Muslims advanced in their wake, and the foremost of the cavalry overtook them when some of their leaders had just crossed the

---

[1] " In the direction of " is a conjectural restoration by the editor of the text.

river. Their transport and baggage train fell as booty to the Muslims, who annihilated an immense number of their followers by slaughter, capture and drowning in the Euphrates. The hands of the Muslims were filled with spoils, plunder, captives, and animals, but they were unable to cross the river to overtake the remainder by reason of their occupation with the siege of al-Ruhā and their return thither. The Franks had evacuated all the helpless civilians from the city, leaving a garrison of Armenians to defend it, and had provisioned it with the stores which accompanied the relieving army, in order to strengthen it. Its lord, Baldwin the Little,[1] also left the city and set out in company with the retreating Franks. The army of Islām remained on the Euphrates for some days, encamped opposite them, and then withdrew to prosecute the siege of al-Ruhā. Zahīr al-Dīn Atābek, on learning of their retirement in this manner, withdrew to return to his own government in order to protect it from the Franks, after dispatching a numerous contingent from his camp to assist the besiegers of al-Ruhā. He arrived at Damascus, and those of his 'askar whom he had sent to al-Ruhā remained there until the besieging army evacuated the country, when they were given permission to return to their own places, after the bestowal of honours and bounties upon them.

The frequent exchange of envoys between the atābek Zahīr al-Dīn and the amīr Sharaf al-Dīn Mawdūd led to the consolidation of the friendship

[1] *Baghdawīn al-ru'aiyis*, literally " the chieflet."

and the establishment of unity of purpose between them, and strengthened the bonds of comradeship. When the stay of the army of Islām at al-Ruhā was prolonged by reason of its strength and power of resistance, and the supply of provisions to the camp began to fail and their stores to give out, necessity compelled them to retire from it, and they dispersed, after first organizing a detachment to remain behind and harass al-Ruhā from a base at Harrān. Najm al-Dīn Il-Ghāzī conceived an aversion to Sukmān al-Qutbī, on account of an old quarrel which broke out afresh between them, and fled from 'Harrān to Mārdīn ; Sukmān then seized the son of his brother Balak, and carried him with him in chains to his own town. After the dispersal of the Muslim armies from ar-Ruhā, its lord, Baldwin the Little, returned and entered the city, though raids were continually being made on its borders.

The king Fakhr al-Mulūk Rudwān, lord of Aleppo, on learning of the defeat of the Franks, had gone out into the districts of Aleppo, and had recovered such of them as the Franks had captured, and raided the province of Antioch, taking a quantity of booty until, on hearing the report of their return, he returned to Aleppo. Shortly afterwards the Franks arrived and ravaged part of the province of Aleppo, killing and taking captive a great number of persons. Tancred on his return descended on al-Athārib, and captured it after a long siege and blockade in Latter Jumādā of this year.[1] He spared its garrison, and those

---

[1] An obvious error for " of the following year," i.e., Latter Jumādā 504 (15th December, 1110 to 12th January, 1111).

who desired to go out went out, and those remained who preferred to remain. Thereafter a treaty of friendship was agreed upon between the king Fakhr al-Mulūk Rudwān and Tancred, on the conditions that the king should pay him annually a tribute of twenty thousand dinars from the revenues of Aleppo, with ten head of horses, and the release of the prisoners, and peace was restored upon this basis.

In this year also King Baldwin, lord of Jerusalem, arrived in the district of Ba 'albek with the object of plundering and creating devastation in the district of the Biqā'. A correspondence ensued between him and Zahīr al-Dīn Atābek in regard to this, until it was agreed to establish amicable relations between them on the condition that one-third of the produce of the Biqā' should belong to the Franks, and two-thirds to the Muslims and the peasantry. A protocol was drawn up between them on these terms in Safar of this year,[1] and he set off to return to his own province, retaining possession of the plunder from Ba 'albek and the Biqā' which was in his hands and the hands of his troops.

Reports were received in this year of the arrival of one of the kings of the Franks by sea, with more than sixty vessels laden with men-at-arms, for the purpose of making the pilgrimage and raiding the lands of Islām. He went up towards Jerusalem, and when Baldwin came out to meet him, it was agreed between them to attack the Islamic

[1] Began 30th August, 1109, but probably again for Safar 504 (beginning 19th August, 1110).

territories. On their return from Jerusalem, they encamped before the fortified port of Sidon on 3rd Second Rabī' of the year 504 (19th October, 1110) and blockaded it by land and sea. The Egyptian fleet was then stationed at the port of Tyre, but it was unable to bring support to Sidon. The Franks made a tower and moved it forwards towards the town, having draped it with branches of vines, mats and damp ox-hides, as a protection against missiles and greek fire. When they had completed its construction in this skilful fashion, they moved it up at intervals of several days on pulley-wheels inserted beneath it. On the day of the attack, when it had been brought close up to the wall they moved it forward, having placed in it supplies of water and vinegar to put out fires, and fighting machines. When those in Sidon saw what was afoot, their hearts sank, and they feared a repetition of a disaster like that at Bairūt. The qādī and a number of the principal men of the town were sent out to the Franks, and they asked Baldwin for a guarantee of safety. He agreed to their request and promised also security to the troops who were with them in respect of their lives and property, and to allow those who wished to leave the town to proceed to Damascus. When they had sworn him to these terms, the governor and controller of the administration, together with all the troops and guards and a great number of the townsmen, went out and proceeded to Damascus on 20th [First] Jumādā 504 (4th December, 1110), the siege having lasted forty-seven days. After establishing a garrison in the town and regulating its affairs, Baldwin returned to Jerusalem, but a short time later he returned to Sidon, and exacted from those who had remained in it a tribute exceeding twenty thousand dinars, whereby he reduced them to poverty and stripped them of their possessions, and confiscated the property of all of them who were known to have any residue.

A.H. 504

(20th July, 1110, to 9th July, 1111)

In this year news arrived that a company of travelling merchants, chafing at their prolonged inaction, lost patience and set out from Tinnīs, Damietta and Misr [1] with a great quantity of merchandise and moneys. The Egyptian fleet was unable to go to sea, but they took upon themselves the risk and set sail. They fell in with some Frankish vessels and were captured, and merchandise and moneys to the value of more than a hundred thousand dinars were seized by their captors, who held them as prisoners and tormented them, until they ransomed themselves by all that remained of their deposits at Damascus and elsewhere.

On returning from Sidon, Baldwin marched to Ascalon, and made an attack upon it. Its governor Shams al-Khilāfa opened negotiations with him, and a settlement was reached between them, the terms of which were that on receipt of a sum of

---

[1] Misr, the name usually applied to Fustāt, now Old Cairo ; the modern Cairo, founded in 969, being at this time restricted to the royal suburb.

money from the governor, Baldwin would retire
and refrain from molesting Ascalon. Now Shams
al-Khilāfa was more desirous of trading than of
fighting, and inclined to peaceful and friendly
relations and the securing of the safety of travellers,
and he levied from the people of Tyre seven thousand dinars, to be paid to him in the space of a year
and three months. When the news of this reached
al-Afdal, the ruler of Egypt, in Shawwāl (12th
April to 10th May), he disapproved of his action
and bore him a secret grudge on that account, but
concealed it from all his associates, and equipped a
strong 'askar to proceed to Ascalon under a
governor to replace Shams al-Khilāfa. When it
approached Ascalon, and Shams al-Khilāfa
learned its purpose, he rebelled against al-Afdal
and raising the standard of revolt drove out all
the regular troops who were under his command.
His reasons for this action were a fear that they
might turn against him at the instigation of al-
Afdal (since he was well aware of several actions
on account of which al-Afdal was dissatisfied with
him and bore him a strong ill-will) and also because
he had entered into correspondence with Baldwin,
desiring his friendship and assistance with men
and provisions, and promising that if he should be
overtaken by any calamity, he would deliver up
the city to Baldwin, and ask Baldwin to compen-
sate him for it. Al-Afdal, on learning of this, was
afraid lest this arrangement should be carried out,
and wrote to him to allay his suspicions, dissimulating with him, and assigning Ascalon to him as
a fief. He further confirmed him in possession
of his fief in Egypt, and put a stop to all interfer-

ence with his property in horses, merchandise, and household possessions in Egypt. Shams al-Khilāfa, in fear of the townspeople, called in a company of Armenians and established them in the town, and this state of affairs lasted until the close of the year 504. The townsmen were indignant at his action, and a party of Kutāma [1] set upon him as he was riding, and wounded him. He fled to his house, but they pursued him, dispatched him and plundered his house and property, as well as the houses of several of the respectable citizens [2] and the common people. The report of this was brought to the postmaster,[3] who hastened to the town. The inhabitants submitted to his authority, and sent the head of Shams al-Khilāfa to al-Afdal in Egypt, together with a full account of his actions. Al-Afdal was gratified by the news, and rewarded those who brought the good tidings, but ordered the prosecution and incarceration of the assassins for what they had plundered from his house and seized of his property and the property of the townsfolk. The postmaster arrested a number of the townsfolk and conveyed them to Egypt, where they were incarcerated on their arrival.

In First Jumādā of this year (15th November to 14th December) the Sultan Ghiyāth al-Dunyā wal-Dīn Muhammad, son of Malik-Shāh, arrived at Baghdād from Hamadhān. Here he received letters and envoys from Syria, acquainting him

---

[1] The Kūtama were the Berber troops of the Fāṭimid Caliphs of Egypt.

[2] lit. " the witnesses," see p. 49, n. 1.

[3] Sāhib al-Sayyārah.

with the state of affairs and the activities of the Franks after their return from the Euphrates, and the disaster at Sidon and al-Athārib and in the districts of Aleppo. On the first Friday of Sha 'bān (17th February, 1111) a certain Hāshimite sharīf [1] from Aleppo and a company of Sūfīs, merchants and theologians presented themselves at the Sultan's mosque, and appealed for assistance. They drove the preacher from the pulpit and broke it in pieces, clamouring and weeping for the misfortunes that had befallen Islām at the hands of the Franks, the slaughter of men, and enslavement of women and children. They prevented the people from carrying out the service, while the attendants and leaders, to quieten them, promised them on behalf of the Sultan to dispatch armies and to vindicate Islām against the Franks and the infidels. On the following Friday they assembled again, went to the Caliph's mosque, and repeated their performance with much weeping and clamour and appealing for help, and lamenting. Shortly afterwards the princess, the Sultan's daughter and wife of the Caliph, arrived at Baghdād from Isfahān, in such magnificence and with such quantities of jewellery, moneys, utensils, carriages and riding beasts of all kinds, furniture, varieties of gorgeous raiment, attendants, guards, slave-girls, and followers, as exceeds all reckoning. Her arrival coincided with these appeals for assistance, and the tranquillity of the city and joy at her coming were marred and disturbed. The Caliph, al-Mustazhir

----

[1] *Sharīf* (pl. *ashrāf*), a lineal descendant of Muḥammad through his daughter Fāṭima, the wife of 'Alī ; or more generally a descendant of Muḥammad's clan, the Banū Hāshim.

B'illāh, Commander of the Faithful, was indignant at what had happened, and determined to seek out him who had been its instigator and cause, in order to mete out to him condign punishment. The Sultan prevented him from doing so, and excused the action of those people, and directed the amīrs and commanders to return to their governments and make preparations for setting out to the Holy War against the infidels, the enemies of God.

In Latter Jumādā of this year (15th December to 12th January), the envoy of the tyrant [1] of the Greeks arrived with gifts, precious objects, and letters, the purport of which was an exhortation to attack the Franks and inflict summary chastisement upon them, to unite to drive them out of these territories, and abandon all remissness in regard to them, and to put forth the utmost exertions to exterminate them before they were too firmly established in their menacing position and their malice became uncontrollable. He stated that he had prevented them from traversing his dominions to the lands of the Muslims and had gone to war with them, but if their ambitious designs upon the land of Islām led to a constant succession of their armies and reinforcements proceeding thereto, he would be impelled by imperious necessities to come to terms with them and to give them free passage and assistance in their aims and objects, and concluded with

---

[1] The Arabic text has here, as in some other passages, not the word *malik* (king), but *mutamallik*, lit. " would-be king," or " self-proclaimed king." The reason for the distinction is obscure.

exhortations and incitements in the strongest of terms to take concerted action to fight them and root them out of these lands.

In this year also King Baldwin, lord of Jerusalem, violated the truce agreed upon between the atābek and himself, and wrote to the son of St. Gilles, lord of Tarābulus, summoning him to bring his army and join him at Tiberias. Having collected his forces, he set out in the direction of Jerusalem, to dispose of a matter which he had in mind, but was seized on the way by an illness which detained him for some days, and after his recovery from it he became convinced that no further action calling for his attention was likely on their part. On learning of his intention Zahīr al-Dīn Atābek set out with his 'askar and encamped at the station called Ra's al Mā', whence he marched to the Lejāh. The Franks followed him up to al-Sanamain and the atābek, by breaking up his forces so that detachments should operate against them from various directions, and posting cavalry patrols on the crossings and roads to prevent supplies from reaching them, put them in such straits that they were compelled to revert to the the rule of peace and amicable relations. Negotiations were carried on to this end until it was agreed that Baldwin should have half the yield of Jabal 'Awf and the Sawād and al-Jabanīya, in addition to what he possessed, as well as of those neighbouring districts which were in the hands of the Bedouins of the Āl al-Jarrāh. This stipulation was set out in writing between them, and each of them returned to his own government at the end of Dhu'l-Hijja of this year (early July, 1111).

After the appeal for assistance at Baghdād which has already been described, it had been agreed by the Sultan Ghiyāth al-Dunyā wal-Dīn that he should dispatch his troops and command his amīrs to prepare for setting out to the Holy War. They made preparations accordingly, and the first of them to set out for the provinces of the Franks was the amīr the isfahsallār [1] Sharaf al-Dīn Mawdūd, lord of Mosul. He marched with his 'askar to Sanjatān, and captured Tell Murād and a number of castles thereabouts by the sword and by capitulation. He was joined by the amīr Ahmadīl with a powerful 'askar, who was followed in turn by the amīr Sukmān al-Qutbī from Armenia and Diyār Bekr. They joined forces in the land of Harrān, where a letter reached them from Sultān b. 'Alī b. Munqidh, lord of Shaizar, informing them that Tancred, lord of Antioch, had descended upon the land of Shaizar and had begun to build Tell ibn Ma 'shar opposite it and [was preventing] [2] the transport of grain to it. He therefore appealed to them for assistance and urged them to come to him. On learning of this they set out for Syria, and crossed the Euphrates in the middle of Muharram of the year 505. They encamped before Tell Bāshir on 19th Muharram (28th July, 1111) and remained there awaiting the arrival of the amīr Bursuq b. Bursuq, lord of Hamadhān, who had been ordered by the Sultan to proceed to join them. He arrived with part only of his 'askar, and was himself suffering from gout;

[1] A military title frequently conferred at this period, from Persian *sipah-sālār*, commander-in-chief.

[2] The word *man 'ahu*, which is not in the text, seems to be required by the sense.

Sukmān al-Qutbī also was ill, and the two disagreed with each other's plans. Meanwhile the volunteers and common soldiers attacked this fortress and made a breach in it. Thereupon Joscelin, lord of Tell Bāshir, sent to the Kurdish amīr Ahmadīl, bribing him with money and gifts and promising to be with him and to take his part. Now the greater number of the regular troops were with Ahmadīl, and when Joscelin begged him to withdraw from the castle and humbled himself to him, he consented to his request in spite of the disapproval of the other amīrs. The illness of Sukmān al-Qutbī grew worse, and Ahmadīl determined upon withdrawal, in his eagerness to receive the grant of Sukmān's lands from the Sultan, since some connection and marriage relations had been established between them. The armies therefore withdrew from Tell Bāshir to Aleppo, where they encamped before the city, ravaged its territories, and created worse devastation than the Franks had done. They had expected that either the king Fakhr al-Mulūk Rudwān, lord of Aleppo, would himself come out to join them, or else his officers would join them by his command. But he paid no heed to any of them, and shut the gates of Aleppo, took hostages from the townsmen into the citadel, and organized his troops, with the armed bands [1] of the Bātinīs and the loyal citizens, for garrison duty to guard the city wall and prevent the citizens fron ascending it. Besides this he gave a free hand to the brigands [2] to seize whomsoever they could from the fringes of the army.

[1] *ahdāth*, see above p. 70 n. 1.
[2] *al-harāmīya*, apparently in the sense of " irregulars " ; cf. Usāma 86.2.

At the time when these amīrs assembled and crossed the Euphrates, they had corresponded with Zahīr al-Dīn Atābek asking him to join them and committing to him the direction of their enterprise. As a letter of similar import had reached him from the Sultan, the position of affairs as well as his own good judgment demanded that he should set out towards them with the 'askar to lend his aid in the Holy War and strengthen their resolution to protect these lands against the people of polytheism and false doctrine. Having collected what men he could from Hims, Hamāh, Rafanīya, and all the other Syrian strongholds, he marched up to them and joined them outside Aleppo. They received him with honour and marks of high respect, and their spirits were raised and their loins strengthened by his arrival; but in spite of the outward joy they displayed at his coming amongst them, he did not find in them any true determination to wage the Holy War nor to protect the country.

As for Sukmān al-Qutbī, his illness became aggravated, and being on the point of death, he separated from them and returned to his own town, and the report arrived of his death on the way, before he reached the Euphrates. As for Bursuq b. Bursuq, he was carried about on a litter, and could neither act nor speak, while Ahmadīl was firmly set on returning because of Sukmān's lands and his eagerness to receive them as a fief from the Sultan. Zahīr al-Dīn Atābek persuaded them to advance into Syria, and setting out at the end of Safar (beginning of September, 1111), they encamped at Ma 'arrat al-Nu 'mān, where they acted as they had done formerly [at Aleppo]. The troops seized what provisions they required from the district and were unable to carry with them any supplies of food or forage. The ill-will displayed by the generals towards Zahīr al-Dīn at length alienated him from them and inspired him with aversion to a longer stay amongst them ; it was told him, moreover, that the king Fakhr al-Mulūk Rudwān had negotiated with one of the amīrs to form a plot against him and assassinate him. He came to an agreement, therefore, with the amīr Sharaf al-Dīn Mawdūd, by which their friendship and alliance was securely established, and presented to the remainder of the amīrs the gifts which he had brought with him for them together with precious objects, swift Arab horses, and rare Egyptian stuffs. They were accepted from him with profuse expressions of thanks and appreciation and acknowledgment of indebtedness. Mawdūd faithfully carried out his promises to Zahīr al-Dīn, and remained steadfast in friendship to him. The atābek now urged the amīrs to march on Tarābulus, promising to supply them with all the provisions which they should require from Damascus and its government, and, if they should be overtaken by the winter, to provide quarters for them in his cities, but they refused to carry out his suggestion and dispersed like the tribes of Saba.[1] Bursuq b. Bursuq and Ahmadīl withdrew and followed up the 'askar of Sukmān al-Qutbī. The amīr Mawdūd alone remained behind with the atābek, and they set out together from al-Ma 'arra and encamped on the 'Āsī (Orontes).

[1] A proverbial phrase, referring to the legendary dispersal of the ancient South Arabian tribes after the rupture of the dam of Marib.

When the Franks heard of the withdrawal and dispersal of the armies, they assembled and encamped at Afāmiya in full force. On this occasion Tancred, Baldwin, and the son of St. Gilles, notwithstanding their hostility to one another, and their mutual aversion and disagreement, joined forces and formed a united front against Islām and its people. On their advance, Sultān b. Munqidh came out of Shaizar in person with his followers, and at a meeting with the atābek and Mawdūd urged them to engage in the Holy War and belittled the strength of the Franks to them. They set out therefore, and crossing the 'Āsī encamped in the southern part of Shaizar. The troops set up their bazaar in the bazaar of Shaizar, and Mawdūd's 'askar encamped near the town. Ibn Munqidh and his followers showed the greatest zeal in serving them and maintaining a supply of provisions ; he lodged the atābek and Mawdūd and their personal attendants in the castle of Shaizar, and himself, along with his family, attended to them. The Franks encamped to the north of Tell Ibn Ma 'shar. The dispositions of the 'askar were planned with the utmost skill ; the cavalry was posted on all sides of the Franks, patrolling round them, harassing them and preventing all approach to them, and they put them in sore straits. Moreover they cut them off from water and prevented them from approaching the 'Āsī owing to the multitude of archers posted on its banks and on the south side of the river, so that no Frank could come near it without being killed. The Turks became emboldened against them, and made light of them. The cavalry of the Muslims was equal in number to the cavalry of the Franks, but their footsoldiers were more numerous. The Turks advanced against them in battle order, and when the Franks descended to engage them from a hill on which they were camped, they charged upon them from their western flank and plundered a portion of their camp, capturing a number of their tents and some of their baggage, and wheeled round about them. The Franks then withdrew and returned to their former position. This occurred in the month of First Rabī' (7th September to 6th October, 1111). The fear of the Franks for the Turks increased, and they remained for three days, not one of them daring to show himself nor any person to approach them. When the Muslims retired for the Friday prayer in the mosque of Shaizar, the Franks marched off to Afāmiya, but passed by it without halting there. On learning of their withdrawal, the Muslims pursued them and seized their stragglers and all whom they found marching in their wake. They returned to Shaizar and thence marched to Hamāh, and all the people were rejoiced at the discomfiture of the Franks in this wise.

A.H. 505

(10th July, 1111, to 27th June, 1112)

The friendship between Zahīr al-Dīn Atābek and the amīr Mawdūd took firm root.

In this year king Baldwin assembled all whom he could of the Franks and marched to the port of Tyre. The governor 'Izz al-Mulk and the citizens wrote in haste to Zahīr al-Dīn Atābek at Damascus, asking him for help and reinforcement and promising to surrender the city to him. They besought him to make haste to send a large number of Turks and urged that they should come to them speedily to assist and strengthen them, for should there be any delay in sending them assistance necessity would compel them to surrender the city to the Franks, as they despaired of help from al-Afdal, the ruler of Egypt. The atābek dispatched with all speed a large contingent of Turks, consisting of over two hundred horsemen, archers of proved worth, with full equipment. In addition to this contingent, the citizens were reinforced by numbers of footsoldiers from Tyre and Jabal 'Āmilah who embraced their cause, together with footsoldiers from Damascus. The atābek also prepared to dispatch another detachment. When Baldwin learned of the arrangement between the atābek and the people of Tyre, he made haste to invest it with the forces which he had assembled, on 25th First Jumādā 505 (29th November). He ordered the fruit trees and palms to be cut down and constructed permanent dwellings before the city, and delivered regular assaults upon it on several occasions, only to retire discomfited and frustrated in his object. It is said that in one attack the people of Tyre discharged twenty thousand arrows in a single day.

Zahīr al-Dīn on learning that the Franks had invested Tyre marched out and made his camp at Bānyās, whence he dispatched his squadrons together with bands of brigands into the territories of the Franks with a free hand to plunder, kill,

rob, destroy and burn, with the object of causing
them vexation and forcing them to abandon the
siege. The second contingent which he sent to
Tyre attempted to enter the town but was unable
to gain entrance. Zahīr al-Dīn himself marched to
al-Habīs, a strong and forbidding castle in the
Sawād, and after a vigorous attack captured it by
the sword and put the entire garrison to death.
The Franks set about constructing two wooden
towers with which to make the assault on the wall
of Tyre, and Zahīr al-Dīn deployed his forces
against them several times in order to distract
them so that the troops in Tyre might make a
sortie and burn the towers. The Franks became
aware of his object in these manœuvres, and
having dug a trench around them on all sides,
posted armed men along it to defend both it and
the towers, paying no heed either to what he might
do or to the raids which were made upon their
territories and the slaughter of their inhabitants.
When the winter storms commenced, they did no
harm to the Franks since they were encamped on
hard, sandy soil, while the Turks on the contrary
suffered great hardships and bitter distress in
their position, yet they did not cease from raiding
and making booty, and cutting off supplies and
provisions from the Franks, and seizing all that
was conveyed to them.

The Turks also cut the mole by which access
was gained to Sidon, in order to cut off supplies
from it as well, whereupon they changed their
tactics and sent out requests to all parts for supplies
to be sent to them by sea. Zahīr al-Dīn, realising
this, set out with a detachment of his 'askar to the

district of Sidon and raided its suburbs, killing a number of the seamen and burning about twenty vessels on the shore. And withal he did not neglect to send letters to the men of Tyre, encouraging them and urging them to perseverance in face of the Franks and zeal in fighting against them. The construction of the two towers and the battering-rams to be placed within them was completed in about seventy-five days, and on 10th Sha'bān (11th February) they began to be moved forward and employed in the attack. They were brought up close to the city wall and fierce fighting went on round about them. The height of the smaller tower exceeded forty cubits and that of the greater exceeded fifty cubits.[1] On 1st Ramadān (2nd March) the men of Tyre made a sortie from the bastions with greek fire, firewood, pitch, and incendiary equipment, and being unable to penetrate to either of the towers, threw the fire close to the smaller one where the Franks could not protect it from the flames. The wind blew the fire on to the smaller tower, which was completely burned after severe fighting around it and a hand-to-hand struggle in its defence. Many coats of mail, long shields, and other objects were recovered from it as booty. The fire also gained the large tower. The news spread to the Muslims that the Franks had desisted from the attack on the town owing to their preoccupation with the fire in the tower, whereupon they began to withdraw from the fighting round the bastions. The Franks then made a vigorous attack upon them,

[1] The cubit (*dhirā'*) employed in these measurements was probably slightly over 20 inches.

drove them clear of the tower, and put out the
fire that had caught hold of it. Thereafter they
set a strong guard of their picked men to protect
the tower and the catapults on all sides.

They continued their assault upon the city without intermission until the end of Ramadān, and
brought the tower close up to one of the bastions
of the wall, having filled in the three trenches
which were in front of it. The townsmen had
recourse to the underpinning [1] of the wall of that
bastion which was opposite the tower of the Franks
and cast fire at it. The underpinning caught fire
and the face of the wall fell in front of the tower
and prevented it from being moved close up to
the wall. The place which they had intended to
attack was now defended only by a low wall, but
as it was commanded by the city bastions, the
tower could not be brought up to that point. The
Franks cleared away the debris, and dragged the
tower towards another of the bastions of the city
where, having pushed it up until it was close to
the wall, they battered the wall with the rams
which were within it and shook it, so that some of
the stones were dislodged from it and the townsfolk were on the point of destruction. Thereupon
a certain man of Tarābulus, one of the leaders of
the seamen, who was acquainted with forging, and
possessed some understanding and experience of
warfare, set to work to construct grappling irons,
with which to seize the ram, as it was butting the
wall, by the head and the sides by means of ropes,
which were then pulled by the townsmen until the
wooden tower almost rocked with the vigour of

[1] *ta 'līq.*

their pulling on them. Sometimes the Franks themselves would then break the ram, fearing for the safety of the tower, sometimes it would be bent aside or rendered useless, and sometimes it was broken by means of two stones tied together and thrown down upon it from the city wall. The Franks made a number of rams, but they were broken in this fashion one after the other. Each of them was sixty cubits in length, and was slung in the wooden tower with ropes and at the head of each was a piece of iron weighing more than twenty pounds.

When the replacing of the battering-rams had gone on for a long time and the Franks brought the tower close up to the wall, this same seaman took a baulk, long, tough and strong, and erected it on the city bastion which was opposite the tower of the Franks. At the top of this was another baulk of wood, set crosswise and forty cubits in length, which turned on pulley wheels [by tackles] led to a windlass [1] in whatever direction was desired by the man in charge of it, on the same principle as the [yards on the] masts of sailing-ships. At one end of this rotating crosspiece was an arrow of iron, and at the other end were ropes arranged round about it as the man in charge desired. He used to hoist on this contrivance jars of filth and impurities, in order to distract them from the rams by upsetting the contents over them on the tower. This was very disagreeable to the assailants and distracted them from their tasks and operations. The same sailor also took baskets of vine leaves and rushes, and having filled them with oil,

---

[1] Literally, " a screw " (*lawlab*).

pitch, kindling wood, resin, and peelings of canes, put fire in them, and when the fire caught he fixed them on the contrivance we have described, so that they hung over the tower of the Franks and the fire dropped down on top of it. They would make haste to extinguish it with vinegar and water and he would quickly hoist another, at the same time also throwing boiling oil on the tower in small pots. This caused a great conflagration, and when the fire extended and by spreading from one part to another increased in violence, it overcame the two men who were in charge of the top of the tower, one of whom was killed and the other fled below. The fire now gained control of the top storey, and being fed by the wooden structure overcame all who were in the storeys round about, so that they were unable to extinguish it and fled, together with all the Franks who were near it. The men of Tyre then went out to it, and plundered its contents, gaining an indescribable quantity of weapons, arms and equipment as booty.

Thereupon the Franks despaired of capturing the city and prepared to retire. They burned the houses which they had built in their camp to dwell in, as well as many of the vessels belonging to them on the shore, since they had removed their masts, rudders, and equipment for their towers. The number of these vessels was about two hundred, large and small, about thirty of them being war vessels, and they used some of them for the transport of their light baggage. They departed on 10th Shawwāl of this year (10th April), having prosecuted the siege of Tyre for the space of four and a half months, and proceeding to 'Akkā dispersed to their own provinces. The men of Tyre came out and seized as booty everything belonging to them that they could find, and the Turks who had been sent to assist them returned to Damascus. The number of men whom they had lost in the fighting was about twenty, and they received their pay and allowances there every month. No other tower of the Franks either before or after met such a fate as befel this tower, by being burned from top to bottom, and the cause that contributed to this was that the two towers [that of the Franks and the bastion of the city] were equal in height ; had one of them dominated the other, the lower would have been destroyed. The number of the men of Tyre who were lost was four hundred souls, and the losses of the Franks in this engagement, according to a reliable statement, about two thousand souls. The Tyrians, however, did not carry out their promise to surrender the city to Zahīr al-Dīn Atābek, and he did not openly demand it of them, but said, " What I have done I have done only for the sake of God and the Muslims, not out of desire for wealth or kingdom." Blessings and thanks were showered upon him for his noble action, and he promised them that when a similar danger should threaten them, he would hasten to the city and do his utmost to assist it. He then returned to Damascus, having suffered great hardship in warring against the Franks until God delivered the men of Tyre from their distress. The Tyrians set about repairing the damage done by the Franks to the wall, restoring the trenches to their former state and digging them out afresh, and fortifying the city, and the footsoldiers who were in the city dispersed.

On 2nd Sha'bān (3rd February) news was received of the death of Bertram [1] son of St. Gilles, lord of Tarābulus, as the result of an illness which had seized him. He appointed his son to succeed him, but as he was yet a young child, his officers, acting as his guardians, made a settlement on his behalf with Tancred, lord of Antioch. The boy was enrolled amongst Tancred's knights, and received from him the fiefs of Antartūs, Sāfīthā, Maraqīya,[2] and Hisn al-Akrād.

In this year there broke out in Egypt the violent pest whereof a great number, said to be about sixty thousand souls, perished. In the same year the report came from al-'Irāq that the Sultan Ghiyāth al-Dunyā wal-Dīn Muhammad arrived in Baghdād in First Jumādā (5th November to 12th December) and remained there for a time, during which his presence weighed heavily upon the people and prices rose, until he withdrew, when conditions became normal and prices fell. In this year also reports were received of the coming of the amīr Sharaf al-Dīn Mawdūd, lord of Moṣul, with his 'askar, and of his encampment before al-Ruhā and consumption of its green crops for forage in Dhu'l-Qa'da (April). He remained there until Muharram 506 (began 28th June), and afterwards marched to Sarūj, where he sent out his horses to pasture on the crops in an

[1] *Badrān.*
[2] On the coast, opposite the island of Arwād (Aradus).

unguarded moment, without taking precautions against marauding enemy or suspect Muslim. Suddenly, as the horses were dispersed over their pasture-ground, Joscelin, lord of Tell Bāshir, with his Frankish knights swept down upon them from the district of Sarūj, caught Mawdūd and his companions unprepared, killed a number of them, including some of their leaders, and drove off most of their beasts. Those of the Muslims who were off their guard woke up and prepared to engage him, but he returned to the castle of Sarūj.

In this year also arrived the report of the death of Qarāja, the governor of Hims, after a long illness, which proved fatal. He was an oppressive ruler, and a confederate of brigands and outlaws. His place was taken by his son Khīr-Khān b. Qarāja, who followed his example of tyranny and his pattern of injustice and misrule.

A.H. 506

(28th June, 1112, to 17th June, 1113)

In this year, the men of Tyre, in great fear lest the Franks should return to besiege them, concerted with 'Izz al-Mulk Anūshtagīn al-Afdalī, who was governor of the town, to surrender it to Zahīr al-Dīn Atābek, in virtue of the assistance which he had rendered them in their hour of extreme danger. They therefore dispatched an envoy in whom they had complete confidence to discuss the matter with Zahīr al-Dīn Atābek.

The envoy, on reaching Bānyās, spoke with its governor, the amīr Saif al-Dawla Mas 'ūd, who set out with him to Damascus, that the matter might be decided in his presence. Their arrival at Damascus happened at a time when Zahīr al-Dīn Atābek had gone to Hamāh to settle matters between himself and Fakhr al-Mulūk Rudwān, lord of Aleppo. The amīr Mas 'ūd, fearing that if action was delayed until the return of Zahīr al-Dīn from Hamāh, Baldwin would anticipate them by investing Tyre, and the object desired by the citizens be frustrated, arranged with Tāj al-Mulūk Būrī, who was the atābek's representative in Damascus, that he should accompany him to Bānyās and seize the opportunity by nominating Mas 'ūd to take over Tyre. Būrī agreed to this and went with him to Bānyās, and Mas 'ūd, taking with him a body of the 'askar on whom he could rely, went on to Tyre without waiting for the atābek, and took up his residence there. When news of what had happened reached the atābek, he dispatched a strong detachment of Turks to Tyre to strengthen its defences, and they too reached the town and took up their quarters in it. The Turks were thus firmly established in control of the city ; the cost of their maintenance was sent to them from Damascus, and the apprehensions of the townsfolk were dissipated. The government of the town was conducted exactly as before ; they continued to profess allegiance to the ruler of Egypt, and to strike coins in his name, and no outward change was made in their practice.

Zahīr al-Dīn Atābek wrote to al-Afdal in Egypt informing him that Baldwin had collected his forces to invest Tyre, and that its inhabitants having asked him for reinforcements and requested him to protect them from him, he had made haste to send thither those in whose bravery he had confidence, to defend the city and to hold him at a distance from it, and that they were now established there; further that, when there should arrive from Egypt a governor to take control of the affairs of the city and to defend it, he would hand it over to him and withdraw his representatives, and adding " And I for my part hope that the affairs of Tyre will not be neglected, but that a fleet will be dispatched to provision and strengthen it."

When Baldwin received news of this, he set out immediately from Jerusalem for 'Akkā, only to find that the opportunity was lost, and that the Turks were already in Tyre. He remained at 'Akkā, until a man of the Arabs of Ruzaiq came to him from the town of Ascalon with a message that the Damascus caravan had left Bosra on its way to Egypt with a rich convoy, and offering to guide him to it on condition that he liberated the prisoners of his tribe. Baldwin at once set out from 'Akkā in pursuit of the caravan. Now it happened that a part of the Banū Hawbar had seized part of the caravan, but they had escaped from them and reached the settlement of the Banū Rabī 'a,[1] who detained them for some days but afterwards let them proceed. When they emerged from the pass of 'Āzib, which is two days' journey from Jerusalem for a horseman, and entered the

[1] They were the ruling family of the Tayy Arabs in Transjordan and the Syrian desert.

wādī, the Franks appeared above them. All who were with the caravan fled, and those who climbed the hill escaped with their lives, but lost their property. The Arabs captured most of the men, and the Franks seized all the goods and merchandise in the caravan, while the Arabs pursued those who fled and took them prisoner. Baldwin obtained more than fifty thousand dinars and three hundred captives from it, and returned to 'Akkā. There was not a town [in Syria] but had some merchants among the victims in this caravan.

In this year the son of the king Takash, son of the Sultan Alp Arslān and brother of the Sultan Malik-Shāh the Just, arrived at Hims fleeing from his cousin, the Sultan Ghiyāth al-Dunyā wal-Dīn Muhammad. Being unable to remain at Hims or at Hamāh, he went on to Aleppo, but as the son of Fakhr al-Mulūk Rudwān, lord of Aleppo, was a member of the Sultan's household, he feared to stay there and made his way to Tancred, lord of Antioch, and besought his protection. Tancred promised him protection, and treated him with honour and generosity, so he remained with him and a company of Turks who were in Tancred's service attached themselves to him. On 1st Latter Jumādā (24th November) Tancred left Antioch for the province of Kogh Basil,[1] the leader of the Armenians, who had just died, being consumed with desire to seize his lands, but he was seized on the way by an illness which necessitated his return to Antioch, and his illness becoming acute,

[1] *Kur Basil*. Kogh Basil was the ruler of a small principality in the Eastern Taurus, 1082–1112.

he died on Wednesday 18th [1] Latter Jumādā (11th December).

He was succeeded by the son of his brother, the Sire Roger,[2] who took possession of Antioch and its provinces, and became securely established in them, after a dispute which arose between the Franks in regard to him had been composed by the priests. He demanded from the king Rudwān the stipulated tribute from Aleppo, namely twenty thousand dinars and a certain number of horses, and it was paid by Rudwān at his demand ; he demanded also the tribute from Shaizar, amounting to ten thousand dinars, and its lord too consented to his demand.

Baldwin continued to make incessant raids on the district of al-Bathanīya, one of the provinces of Damascus, as a result of which the road was intercepted, its supplies of food were depleted, and the prices there rose. A succession of letters was sent by Zahīr al-Dīn Atābek to the amīr Sharaf al-Dīn Mawdūd, lord of Mosul, containing an account of these events in these provinces and urging him to join him, that they might take common action to drive back the impious enemies and to gain the merit of the Holy War. Now Mawdūd had been calumniated to the Sultan Ghiyāth al-Dunyā wal-Dīn with various vile accusations trumped up by jealous enemies, which inspired the Sultan with a certain suspicion of him and aversion from him. It was said, for instance, that he was making up his mind to revolt and that he and the atābek were hand and glove with one another, holding like views and animated

---

[1] The text has 8th.   [2] *Sir Rajāl.*

by like ambitions. On learning of this, Mawdūd sent his son and his wife to the court of the Sultan at Isfahān to clear him of these suspicions and justify his conduct, to prove the falsity of the accusations and calumnies which had been trumped up against him and of the intentions which had been attributed to him, and to assert his innocence of them, to regain the Sultan's favour, and make known that his actions were inspired by the same loyal obedience, submissiveness, and faithful service and zeal for the Holy War which the Sultan had ever found in him. Thereafter he assembled his 'askar of Turks and Kurds, and all whom he could muster, and setting out for Syria, crossed the Euphrates in Dhu'l Qa' da of this year (19th April to 18th May).

When the news of this reached King Baldwin, he was disturbed and filled with anxiety. Now Joscelin, lord of Tell Bāshir, had quarrelled with his maternal uncle Baldwin the Little, lord of al-Ruhā, and had joined Baldwin lord of Jerusalem, who gave him Tiberias as a fief. It was agreed between these two that Joscelin should write to Zahīr al-Dīn Atābek, promising friendship, and moving him to desire the establishment of amicable and peaceful relations, also that Joscelin should surrender to him the castle of Thamānīn, in the neighbourhood of the castle of . . .[1] and Jabal 'Āmila, and receive in exchange the castle of Habīs in the Sawād together with half of the Sawād, and should promise on behalf of Baldwin the loyal observance of these conditions and maintenance of friendship and cessation of attacks

---

[1] Perhaps Tibnīn, near Bānyās. The text has a blank.

on any of the provinces of Damascus, provided that the atābek on his part did not attack any of the provinces of the Franks. Zahīr al-Dīn rejected these proposals and set out from Damascus with the 'askar to meet the amīr Mawdūd and join him in the Holy War. They united at Marj Salamīya [1] and, having agreed to attack Baldwin, set out together. The atābek was accompanied by the entire 'askar, together with troops from Hims, Hamāh, and Rafanīya. On the Feast of Sacrifice (10th Dhu'l-Hijja, 28th May) they encamped at Qadas,[2] and marched thence by 'Ain al-Jar in the Biqā' and Wādi'l-Taim to Bānyās, whence a portion of the army proceeded to the district of Thamānīn, but failing to achieve its design there returned.

At this point Baldwin came up with them. On learning that nothing was to be expected of his overtures of peace to the atābek, he had prosecuted his raids and ravages in Syria until the Sultan's army entered his own territory. The atābek showed the utmost honour and respect to the amīr Mawdūd and made large presents of clothing, food, and horses to him and to the commanders of his 'askar and the members of his suite. Thereafter they resumed their march, having given instructions to encamp at al-Quhwāna.[3] Baldwin was joined by Sire Roger, lord of Antioch, and the lord of Tarābulus, and they agreed together to encamp to westward of the bridge of al-Sannabra [4] and thence they would cross to al-Quhwāna to

---

[1] S.E. of Hamāh.

[2] Near Hims; to be distinguished from the better known Qadas (Kadesh Naphthali), by Lake Huleh.

[3] Or al-Uqhuwāna, on the shores of the Lake of Tiberias.

[4] 3 miles from Tiberias, on the Damascus road.

engage the Muslims. They had already unloaded[1] their baggage on the other side of the bridge, unknown to the Muslims, who were also unaware that the Franks had marched on a parallel course with them to this camping ground. The Turks were the first [of the Muslim units] to encamp at al-Quhwāna and some of [2] the Turkish troopers crossed the bridge in search of fodder and corn. They found that the Franks had already pitched their tents, for Baldwin had marched ahead in order to be first at this camping ground, and the lords of Antioch and Tarābulus had encamped behind him, following him up.

Battle was then joined between the foraging party and the Franks. The shout was raised, and the troops sprang to arms and crossed the bridge, thinking that it was Joscelin, since he was lord of Tiberias. The atābek took up his stand on the bridge and a great host of the troops made haste to cross it, amongst those who crossed being the amīr Tamīrāk b. Arslāntāsh with a strong detachment of the 'askar. Battle was joined on both sides without any preparations for an engagement, pitching of tents, settling down in camps, or preliminary skirmishing. Both sides engaged in a hand-to-hand fight, and God the Bountiful, to Him be praise, gave victory to the Muslims after three charges. Of the Franks there were killed in this battle about two thousand men of rank and warriors of note, and the Muslims captured all the tents which they had pitched, together with

---

[1] Reading *ihtattu* instead of *ihtātu 'alā* (" they had surrounded ") of the printed text.
[2] Reading *ba'd* for *ba'd*.

the famous church. Baldwin escaped only after being captured and having his weapons seized. The animals and effects of the footsoldiers were captured, and a great number of them were drowned in the lake. The water was so mixed with blood that the troops abstained from drinking of it for some days, until it was purified from it and became clear again. Those of the Franks who escaped fled for refuge to Tiberias, most of them with wounds. This battle took place on Saturday 11th Muharram 507 (28th June, 1113).

When it was all over, the rest of the Franks, the troops of Tancred and the son of St. Gilles, came up, and having blamed Baldwin for his precipitancy and criticised his plan, they pitched those of their tents that were saved before Tiberias. On the day after the battle a body of the Turkish troopers marched towards Tiberias, and coming out above the Franks in the neighbourhood of Tiberias, proposed to charge down upon them and exterminate them. The Franks were in fear of them and convinced of their own doom, but the Turks, after remaining on the hill all day long, retired to their camp. Thereupon the Franks climbed the hill and fortified themselves on it, owing to the difficulty of its ascent. It lay to the west of Tiberias, and no water was accessible to those on it. The Muslims determined to ascend it and attack them, and the atābek summoned the Arabs of Tayy, Kilāb, and Khafāja, who arrived in great numbers with large and small waterskins and camels for carrying water. The scouts, on ascending the hill from the north, found that it was impossible to fight on it, owing to its impracticability for both horsemen and infantry. The Muslims therefore, knowing that the signs and evidences of their victory were manifest, the enemy humbled, broken, defeated and dispirited, and that the squadrons of Islām had penetrated to the environs of Jerusalem and Yāfā, wrought havoc and destruction in their territories, driven off their livestock and cattle, and plundered all that they found in them, abandoned the project of making the ascent, and matters remained in this state until the end of Safar (middle of August).

After this engagement there arrived from Aleppo a hundred troopers from the ʻaskar of the king Fakhr al-Mulūk Rudwān by way of support, in flagrant violation of his undertaking and his promises. Zahīr al-Dīn Atābek and Sharaf al-Dīn Mawdūd, in disgust that he should have done no more than this, revoked their previous decision to support him and acknowledge him as their over-lord.[1] This happened on 1st First Rabīʻ 507 (16th August, 1113). They dispatched an envoy to the Sultan Ghiyāth al-Dunyā wal-Dīn at Isfahān with the good tidings of this victory, and sent with him a company of Frankish prisoners, with heads, horses, shields, tents and weapons of various kinds.

Thereafter the ʻaskar moved from its encampment to Wādi'l-Maqtūl, whereupon the Franks descended from the hill to their camp and took up a defensive position on a hill in the camp, where provisions, rations, and reinforcements were

[1] lit. " insert his name in the Khuṭba," the allocution at the Friday service in which blessings are invoked on the sovereign by name.

sent to them from all parts of their territories. The Turkish troopers of the 'askar, numbering between ten and a score of regiments, came back from their camp without baggage to engage them, and kept this up for some days, hoping that they would come out to fight with them, but they would not leave their defences, and remained huddled up, horse and foot together, in one place, and not a man of them showed himself. The Turks then set about attacking them, shooting down those of them whom they could approach, and preventing their supplies and forage from reaching them, for they had surrounded them like a girdle or the halo of the full moon at its setting. Their position became critical, and they withdrew from their camp, retiring about three miles in three days. When night fell they made for the hill which they had previously occupied, in order to take refuge on it and defend themselves there. The Muslims were assiduous in pursuing them and eager to capture the troops and spoils which were slipping out of their hands by their continued retirement, but the officers of the 'askar restrained them from precipitate action against the Franks and from attacking them in their camp, and promised them that an opportunity of engaging them would present itself. When the period of waiting grew prolonged, the troops of Mawdūd became impatient owing to their distance from their homes and the delay in their return and the failure to gain their objects. The greater number of them dispersed and returned to their own lands, while others asked for and were granted permission to return. Mawdūd himself determined to remain in Syria in the vicinity of the enemy, awaiting the commands of the Sultan, and the reply to his letter informing the Sultan of what had happened and explaining the situation, in order to act in accordance with his instructions. There was not a Muslim left in the land of the Franks who did not send to the atābek begging that he should guarantee him security and confirm him in the possession of his property[1] and a part of the revenue of Nāblus was brought to him. Baisān was plundered, and not a single cultivated estate was left between 'Akkā and Jerusalem while the Franks remained blockaded on the hill. It was then judged necessary that the atābek and Mawdūd should withdraw, and they returned together to Damascus on 21st First Rabī' 507 (5th September, 1113). Mawdūd took up his residence in the apartments on the Green Maidān, and the atābek showed him the utmost honour and reverence, and manifested his regard for him in every way that he could, and the friendship and affection between them was strengthened and confirmed.

A.H. 507

(18th June, 1113, to 6th June, 1114)

We have already followed the sequence of events of the year 506 into the beginning of the year 507, from a desire to present the narrative as a connected whole without interruption.

On the last Friday of Second Rabī' of the year

[1] taqrīr hālihi.

507 (2nd October) the amīr Mawdūd came as was his custom from his encampment at the meadow outside the Iron Gate to the Cathedral Mosque, in company with the atābek. When the prayers were completed and Mawdūd had performed some supplementary prostrations, they went out together, the atābek walking in front by way of showing respect for him. Surrounding them both were Daylamites, Turks, Khurāsānīs, gens d'armes[1] and armour-bearers, with weapons of all kinds, fine-tempered blades and keen thrusting-swords, rapiers of various sorts and unsheathed poniards, so that they were walking as if in the midst of a tangled thicket of intertwined spikes, while the people stood round about them to witness their pomp and the magnificence of their state. When they entered the court of the mosque, a man leapt out from among the crowd, without exciting the attention of anyone, and approaching the amīr Mawdūd as though to call down a blessing upon him and beg an alms of him, seized the belt of his riding cloak with a swift motion, and smote him twice with his poniard below the navel. One of the blows penetrated to his flank and the other to his thigh. As the assassin struck his second blow swords fell upon him from every side and he was struck with every kind of weapon. His head was cut off that it might be known who he was, but he could not be recognised, so a fire was kindled for him and he was thrown upon it. The atābek had moved on some paces during the occurrence and was surrounded by his own officers, while Mawdūd, controlling himself, walked

---

[1] al-aḥdāth.

on till he was close to the north gate of the mosque. There he collapsed, and was carried to the residence of the atābek, who walked alongside him. The people were at first cast into great commotion and confusion, but afterwards calmed down on seeing the amīr walking on, and thought that he had escaped with his life. The surgeon was sent for and sewed up part of the wounds, but he died, may God have mercy upon him, a few hours later on the same day. The atābek was distressed at his death in this wise, and manifested his intense sorrow, grief, and disquiet ; so also did all the troops and the citizens, grieving at his loss, and there was general mourning for him. He was enshrouded and buried at the hour of afternoon prayer on that day in a tomb inside the Gardens Gate of Damascus, while every eye that witnessed it wept and tears poured down every cheek. His followers began to make preparations for their return to their own places at Mosul and elsewhere, and the atābek gave orders to issue to them all that they requested for their journey. They also took back with them his baggage, jewels, and treasure.

His conduct in government was at first tyrannical [1] and his treatment of the citizens of Mosul unpraiseworthy, so that a great multitude fled from his province because of his tyranny. But when he heard of the Sultan's change of attitude towards him, he renounced that conduct ; his actions became upright, his justness and fairness was manifested, and he made a fresh start along lines which were the very antithesis of his former

---

[1] Reading *jā'irah* ; the text has *hā'irah* (" irresolute ").

reputation. He became assiduous in religious exercises and almsgiving, and in practising and enforcing the precepts of the Faith, so that his doings were noised abroad with praise and his actions with approbation. Thereafter he died the death of a blessed martyr, and he remained buried in his tomb, his grave attended by servitors and Qur'ān-reciters, until the end of Ramadān in this year (early March, 1114), when a party, sent by his son and his wife, arrived to carry his coffin back to them.

The attack on Tyre and the transference of its government to Zahīr al-Dīn Atābek, with his delegation of Mas'ūd to defend and protect it and to organise its garrison, and his despatch of an envoy to al-Afdal to explain the situation in the town, have already been described above. The envoy who was sent to Egypt remained there until Dhu'l-Hijja 506 (ended 17th January, 1113). Al-Afdal, on learning the state of affairs in Tyre and realizing the facts of the situation, sent back the envoy with a favourable answer, to the effect that this arrangement was most satisfactory to him, and admitting the wisdom of Zahīr al-Dīn's judgment in the plan which he had adopted, and praising his design. He gave orders to equip a fleet for Tyre with corn, provisions, money for the pay of the levies and regular troops, and with grain stuffs to be sold to the townsmen. In pursuance of this command the fleet, commanded by Sharaf al-Dawla Badr b. Abu'l-Tayyib al-Dimashqī, who was formerly governor of Tarābulus at the time when the Franks captured it, arrived at Tyre, at the end of Safar 507 (first half of August, 1113) with all that was required, so that prices in the town were lowered and its conditions improved, its situation was firmly re-established and the desire of the Franks to possess it was quenched. With the cargoes of the vessels were magnificent robes of honour of rare Egyptian stuffs, destined for Zahīr al-Dīn, his son Tāj al-Mulūk Būrī, and his suite, and also for Mas 'ūd, the governor appointed as his lieutenant in Tyre. The fleet remained off Tyre until the wind became favourable for its return, when it weighed anchor and left during the last ten days of First Rabī' of this year (5th to 14th September, 1113). King Baldwin sent an envoy to the amīr Mas 'ūd, the governor of the city, desiring of him a truce and the establishment of amicable and peaceful relations, so that no cause of annoyance might remain on either side. Mas 'ūd agreed to his request and matters were arranged between them to their mutual satisfaction. The highways became safe for travellers, merchants, and dealers coming from all parts. Mas 'ūd died (God's mercy upon him) on 10th Shawwāl 507 (20th March, 1114).[1]

Now when the lord of Antioch had separated with his army from King Baldwin to return to Antioch, the son of the king Takash, son of the Sultan Alp Arslān, left him and went to Tyre, whence he sent to Zahīr al-Dīn Atābek asking his permission to come to Damascus. The atābek replied refusing his request in the most delicate manner, with polite excuses and acceptable argu-

---

[1] There is some error here, as Mas 'ūd is referred to in 516 (see below p. 165) as still governor of Tyre.

ments, and when he despaired of finding a refuge with him, he set out for Egypt, where al-Afdal received him with the marks of honour and deep respect in which he delighted, and assigned him revenues sufficient to ensure him a comfortable existence and the realization of his hopes.

In Latter Jumādā news arrived from Aleppo that the king Fakhr al-Mulūk Rudwān, lord of the city, had been seized by an illness, which clung to him and became acute, and that he had died, may God have mercy upon him, on the 28th of that month (10th December, 1113). There was general perturbation in Aleppo at his death, and his officers were grieved at his loss. It is said that he left in his treasury about six hundred thousand dinars in specie, movable property, weapons and vessels. His position was secured after him by his son Alp-Arslān, who was sixteen years of age and had an impediment and stammer in his speech ; his mother was the daughter of the amīr Yāghī Siyān, [the former] lord of Antioch. He arrested a number of his father's courtiers, some of whom he put to death, and seized the property of others. The control of affairs was shared with him by his father's freedman Lu'lu', and both of them governed badly. He also arrested his two brothers, his full brother Malik-Shāh and half-brother Mubārak, son of his father and a slave girl, and put them both to death. His father, al-Malik Rudwān, had at the outset of his reign acted in the same manner, by putting to death his two brothers Tāj al-Dawla Abū Tālib and Bahrām-Shāh, both of whom were exceedingly beautiful.

So the fate of his sons when he died was a recompense for what he had deliberately done to his brothers.

The Bātinīya had by now become strong in Aleppo and their power there was formidable. Ibn Badī', the chief of the gens d'armes in Aleppo, and the principal men of the town were afraid of them because of their numbers, the strength of their corporate organization, and the protection which they assured by their numbers to those of their sect who sought their help. Al-Hakīm al-Munajjim and Abū Tāhir the goldsmith [1] were the first who openly professed this detestable doctrine in Syria, in the days of the king Rudwān. They sought to gain his sympathy by deceitful devices and intrigues, and were supported by a great host of the Ismā'īlīs of Sarmīn, the Jawr, Jabal al-Summāq, and Banū 'Ulaim. Ibn Badī', the prefect of Aleppo, set himself to speak with the king Alp-Arslān son of Rudwān about their movement, and reached a decision with him to use rigorous measures against them and root them out. In pursuance of this design, he arrested Abū Tāhir the goldsmith and all the adherents of his sect, about two hundred souls. Abū Tāhir the goldsmith was immediately put to death, along with the missionary Ismā'īl, and the brother of al-Hakīm al-Munajjim, and the other leaders in their movement who have been referred to. The remainder were imprisoned and their properties were confiscated. Some of these were interceded for, some were set free, some were thrown from the top of the citadel, and some were executed. A number escaped, fled

[1] See above p. 58.

to the Franks, and dispersed throughout the country.

The king Alp-Arslān now found it necessary to look to someone to assume control over his affairs and supply his deficiencies, and his choice fell upon Zahīr al-Dīn Atābek, lord of Damascus. He therefore wrote to him to this effect, placed himself under his guidance, and relied upon him to bring order into his affairs. At first he begged him to come to Aleppo and supervise its administration, but the course of events made it necessary for him to proceed in person with his suite to visit the atābek in Damascus, in order to meet him and have matters put on a sound footing between them. He arrived in the middle of Ramadān of this year and the atābek received him with the honours due to the arrival of one of his rank, invited him into the citadel of Damascus, and seated him on the throne of his uncle Shams al-Mulūk Duqāq, son of Tāj al-Dawla, while he and his courtiers stood in homage to him. He also brought and presented to him all the gifts and precious objects suitable to his rank which he was able to offer, and made presents likewise to all who had come in his company. Alp-Arslān remained thus for some days, and set out to return to Aleppo on 1st Shawwāl (11th March), along with Zahīr al-Dīn Atābek, who accompanied him to Aleppo and stayed there for some days with the greater part of his 'askar. Some of Alp-Arslān's associates advised him to arrest a number of his principal military officers and also his wazīr Abu'l-Fadl b. al-Mawsūl, who was upright in administration and noted for his beneficent activities and avoidance of evil. He carried out this advice, but Zahīr al-Dīn Atābek took into his own service from amongst them the amīr Gumushtegīn al-Ba 'labakkī, the commander of his 'askar. Alp-Arslān rejected the sage counsel and laudable direction of the atābek, and when the latter saw for himself the iniquity and folly of Alp-Arslān's conduct, and realized the viciousness of his government and that matters were falling out contrary to his expectations [1] he decided that the best thing that he could do was to return to Damascus. On his return he was accompanied by the mother of the king Rudwān, at her own desire and choice. When he reached Damascus, a correspondence was carried on between him and Baldwin, king of the Franks, with a view to the conclusion of an armistice and establishment of amicable and peaceful relations between them, in order that the provinces might be restored to cultivation after their devastation and the roads be secured from the malice of evil-doers and robbers. An agreement was reached between them to this effect, and each of them took an oath to the other to observe faithfully and loyally the terms of the treaty and live in friendship and peace. Thus the roads and provinces were made safe, conditions became normal, and produce was abundant.

In this year also news was received from Shaizar that on the Easter day of the Christians a company of the Bātinīya composed of a hundred footsoldiers from Afāmiya, Sarmīn, Ma 'arrat al-Nu 'mān and Ma 'arrat Masrīn made an assault on the castle of Shaizar when its garrison were off their

---

[1] Or perhaps " the opposition of his destiny " (*ikhtilāf at-taqdīr*).

guard, and having seized it and driven out many of its defenders they closed the gate of the fortress, mounted to the citadel and captured it together with its towers. The Banū Munqidh, lords of Shaizar, had gone out to witness the festival of the Christians. This attack had been organized a long time before, and the Banū Munqidh had shown every kindness to these men when they came on their errand of mischief. The men of Shaizar, before they entered, hastened to the outer tower [1] and pulled up the women from the windows [of the citadel] by ropes so that they remained safely under their care.[2] Here they were joined by the Banū Munqidh, lords of the castle, who climbed up to them, and shouting *Allāhu Akbar* engaged the Bāṭinīs until they forced them back into the citadel. The Bāṭinīs became disheartened and subdued, and the men of Shaizar attacked them in increasing numbers, put them to the sword, and killed them to the last man. All those who were of their views in the town were put to death, and a strict watch was kept against a repetition of this attempt.

A.H. 508

(7th June, 1114, to 26th May, 1115)

In this year news arrived from Aleppo that Bābā,[3] known as Lu'lu', the freedman [4] atābek

---

[1] *al-bāshūra,* i.e., the barbican.
[2] Text : *sāru ma 'ahum,* but the masc. plural of the verb is frequently found (*e.g.,* in Usāma) replacing the feminine.
[3] A term applied by Turkish rulers to their tutors or guardians.
[4] Or eunuch.

of the king Tāj al-Dawla Alp-Arslān, son of the king Rudwān, lord of Aleppo, had plotted against him and conspired with a number of his associates to attack and murder him on a suitable opportunity presenting itself against him. When the opportunity occurred, they leapt upon him and killed him in his palace in the citadel of Aleppo. After his death there was general confusion, for his administration both of his own affairs, and of his army and his subjects was vicious and disordered to a degree which left no hope of good or betterment, so he went his way unlamented and without sorrow at his loss.

In this year also a great earthquake occurred in Syria. The earth shook with it, and the people were anxious, but as the tremors ceased, their souls were restored from palpitation and distress to tranquillity, and their hearts were comforted after disquiet and fear.

In this year also the amīr Najm al-Dīn Il-Ghāzī b. Ortuq encamped before Hims, the governor of which was Khīr-Khān b. Qarāja. Now when Najm al-Dīn drank wine and it got the better of him, he habitually remained for several days in a state of intoxication, without recovering his senses sufficiently to take control or to be consulted on any matter or decision. Khīr-Khān, who knew of this disgraceful habit and unexampled heedlessness in him, on learning that he was in this state, made a sortie from the citadel of Hims with his men-at-arms and surprising him in his camp, took advantage of the opportunity against him, seized him, and carried him into Hims. This happened in Sha 'bān of this year (January, 1115). When the news of this reached Zahīr āl-Dīn Atabek he was annoyed and wrote to Khīr-Khān, upbraiding him and showing his displeasure at what had been done to Il-Ghāzī. Khīr-Khān therefore changed his attitude towards him, and after keeping Il-Ghāzī in detention for some days, released him and let him go his way.[1]

A.H. 509

(27th May, 1115, to 15th May, 1116)

In this year the might of the Franks in Rafanīya was increased, and having fortified it to the utmost and placed a strong garrison in it, they set about laying waste and ravaging with the utmost ferocity. Zahīr al-Dīn therefore turned his attention to acquiring information on their conditions and to investigation of their activities within their provinces, and to watch for an opportunity to attack them when he should learn that they were off their guard. He gave orders to the principal officers and commanders of his 'askar to make preparations and hold themselves in readiness to set out in a certain direction to acquire the mèrit of the Holy War and to deal with a matter of importance. Thereafter he made a rapid night march towards Rafanīya and came upon the garrison as they were lying unguarded in their quarters, unconscious of danger until disaster surrounded them on every side. The Turks made

---

[1] In the text a brief account of the death of Baldwin is erroneously inserted after this passage, and repeated in its correct place below (p. 157).

an assault upon them and battered their way into the town and captured it. All its inhabitants fell into captivity and suffered the yoke of humiliation and violence, some being killed and others taken prisoner. The amount of booty which the Muslims gained from their baggage train, beasts, and belongings filled their hands and rejoiced their hearts, and was such as to exhilarate their spirits. This happened on Thursday 2nd Latter Jumādā of this year (22nd October, 1115). The Muslims returned to Damascus, victorious, rejoicing, and booty-laden, without having lost a single man. With them were the prisoners and the heads of the slain, and they were led in procession through the town so that the rejoicing was redoubled by the spectacle of them, and the loins of the army were strengthened in the cause of the Holy War and the raiding [of the infidels].

When the report was noised abroad in the districts of 'Irāq and the Court of the Sultan of the vigour and boldness with which God had endowed Zahīr al-Dīn Atābek in fighting against the abominable Franks, and what He had granted him of victory over them and slaughter among them, in the defence of the people of Syria and warding off the Franks from them, and of his upright government over them, so that men blessed his name in the assemblies of the citizens and merchants and spoke of him with gratitude in the companies of traders from all parts, a number of high officers at the court of the Sultan Ghiyāth al-Dunyā wal-Dīn became jealous of him and sought to disparage and calumniate him, desiring to do him an injury, and with the design of thwarting his hopes and undermining his position with the Sultan. The Sultan's confidence in him was disturbed, and the fact became known and spread abroad in every direction. Zahīr al-Dīn, being informed of this by letters from his friends, who sought his welfare and were anxious on his behalf, was filled with disquietude. For this reason he set about making preparations to proceed on a visit to the court of the Caliph al-Mustazhir and the court of the Sultan Ghiyāth al-Dunyā wal-Dīn at Baghdād, the City of Peace, in order to make formal acknowledgment of their patronage,[1] and to pay homage to them and gain their goodwill by hastening to them, to lay before them a true account of his situation and to remove by visiting them the impression which had been created in men's minds. . . .[2] He was advised to abandon this project and warned against it, and efforts were made to make him overlook the matter, but he paid no heed to this advice and answered no questions. He prepared for his journey with the utmost energy and thoroughness, and made ready various acceptable gifts to take with him, such as crystal vessels, jewellery, Egyptian stuffs of various sorts, and swift Arab horses, suitable for conciliating these high dignitaries.

He set out with his domestic officers and a body of his guards on whose loyalty he could depend, on Sunday 24th Dhu'l-Qa 'da of this year (9th April, 1116). When he approached Baghdād and the news of his arrival was announced, he was met by

---

[1] Reading *littawallī ma 'ahum.*
[2] Text *ka'annahu;* read perhaps *limakānihi* " owing to his position."

a number of the domestic officers from the high prophetic household of the Caliph and from the court of the Sultan, together with the officers of state and the notables of the population, who showed him the utmost honour and respect. The warmth of this reception increased the joy of his friends,[1] and broke the power of his detractors and enemies. He made plain the objects for which he had come, and heard nothing but expressions of apology, of praise of his action and of eulogy of his activities, which set him at ease and removed his disquietude. When he proposed to return to Damascus, and received permission to depart, he was honoured by rich robes and magnificent gifts, and received from the Sultan a diploma investing him with the military and financial government of Syria, and giving him a free hand in disposing of its revenues at his own discretion and choice.[2] So he set out to return to Damascus with all his affairs in excellent order, safe and sound both himself and all his company, and increased in power and honour, and entered it on Tuesday 12th First Rabī' (25th July, 1116).

A.H. 510

(16th May, 1116, to 4th May, 1117)

In this year news arrived that Bertram [3] son of St. Gilles, lord of Tarābulus, having assembled his

---

[1] The text is obscure ; the rendering given above is based on the reading *mā* for *wamā*.

[2] The full text of this diploma is quoted here by the author.

[3] By error for Pons son of Bertram.

forces and used his utmost endeavours, had marched towards the Biqā' to lay it waste by devastation and ravaging. The Isfahsallār Saif al-Dīn al-Bursuqī, lord of Mosul,[1] had at this time arrived at Damascus with part of his 'askar in order to assist Zahīr al-Dīn Atābek against the Franks and to join in the expeditions against them, and the atābek received him with the utmost honour and the respect due to his rank. It happened at this moment that news was brought of the approach of the Franks to the Biqā', and they agreed to move out against them together. By means of forced marches night and day they succeeded in making an attack on the Franks when they were off their guard and lying unsuspectingly in their camp. The 'askar advanced upon them before they were able to mount their horses or seize their arms, and God granted the Muslims the victory over them. They plied the sword amongst them, slaying, taking captive, and plundering; the foot-soldiers, who were a great multitude collected by the Franks from their provinces, they completely annihilated, and having made captive their principal knights and commanders and their outstanding warriors, they put the remainder to death. None of them escaped save their leader Bertram son of St. Gilles and the commander called the Constable [2] and a small party along with them, who were saved by the swiftness of their horses and the protection of their destiny. The Turks obtained possession of vast quantities of equipment, horses,

---

[1] Āq-Sunqur al-Bursuqī, governor of Baghdād from 498–1105. Mosul was added to his command in 507–1113, on the death of Mawdūd.
[2] *Kund Istabl.*

transport animals, and baggage. Expert eye-witnesses have stated that the losses in slain in this engagement of the Frankish cavalry, serjeantry [1] and footmen and the Christian cavalry and footmen [2] amounted to more than three thousand souls. Zahīr al-Dīn Atābek and Saif al-Dīn Āq-Sunqur al-Bursuqī returned with their 'askar to Damascus, rejoicing in the glorious victory and the rich booty and the abundant blessings, not a man of either of the 'askars having been lost nor any misfortune or injury having befallen them. When they reached the city with their prisoners and the heads of the slain, the population came out from the city to see them and rejoiced at the spectacle, mingling their joy with praises to God, the Lord of victory and Giver of power, and gratitude to Him for the manifest succour which He had afforded them in this signal victory. Āq-Sunqur al-Bursuqī remained at Damascus for some days thereafter, and set out to return to his own town, after a firm friendship and affection had been established between him and Zahīr al-Dīn, and an agreement had been made between them to support one another in the Holy War, whensoever any occasion should arise or danger befall.

In this year also reports were received from Aleppo that Lu'lu', the freedman who had seized the authority in it and had brought about the assassination of his master's son the king Alp-Arslān b. Rudwān, was killed in Dhu'l-Hijja (April)

---

[1] Arabic *sarjundīya*, which looks like a Perso-Arabic formation (" head-troops ") ; cf. Usāma (ed. Hitti, 67, 6-7).

[2] i.e., Eastern Christian (Armenian, etc.), in contradistinction to the Franks.

as a result of a plot formed against him by the officers of the late king.

A.H. 511

(5th May, 1117, to 23rd April, 1118)

In this year reports were received from 'Irāq of the death of the Sultan Ghiyāth al-Dunyā wal-Dīn Muhammad, son of Malik-Shāh (may God have mercy upon him) at Isfahān, as the result of an illness which attacked him and lingered with him until he died on 11th Dhu'l-Hijja of this year (5th April, 1118). He was succeeded in the Sultanate by his son Mahmūd, and his authority was duly established and recognized.

In this year also news arrived from Aleppo that the Isfahsallār Yāruqtāsh, the freedman who held the chief military command in Aleppo, had made a truce and established peaceful relations with the Franks, and had surrendered to them the castle of al-Qubba. It was said also that the amīr Āq-Sunqur al-Bursuqī had left al-Rahba with his 'askar and had marched to Aleppo and invested it, in the desire to take possession of it. But his hopes were not realized, and he broke off the siege and returned to Mosul. News arrived also that the above-mentioned Isfahsallār Yāruqtāsh had been driven out of the citadel of Aleppo and that the chief military command and supervision of finances had been remitted to the amīr Abu'l-Ma 'ālī al-Muhassin b. al-Malhamī, the army inspector from Damascus, who took over control of its affairs and governed its territories.

In the middle of Muharram of this year (about 20th May) the Franks made an assault on the suburbs of Hamāh on the night of an eclipse of the moon, and killed about a hundred and twenty of its inhabitants.

News was brought of the death of the Duke of Antioch.

In Muharram of this year the amīr Najm al-Dīn Il-Ghāzī son of Ortuq arrived with his 'askar at Aleppo, and took over control of its affairs for the period of Safar (4th June to 2nd July). His plans having miscarried, he left the town, but his son Husām al-Dīn Timurtāsh remained behind him.

In this year reports arrived from Constantinople of the death of Alexios, king of the Greeks [1] ; he was succeeded in the kingship by his son John, whose authority was established and who followed in the footsteps of his father.

In this year news arrived also of the perishing of Baldwin, King of the Franks and lord of Jerusalem, by reason of an illness which lingered with him and was the cause of his death in Dhu'l-Hijja (26th March to 23rd April, 1118). He was succeeded in his rule by the King Count. . . .[2]

A.H. 512

(24th April, 1118, to 13th April, 1119)

In this year various reports and rumours from the land of the Franks gained wide currency, concerning their desire to possess themselves of

---

[1] *Mutamallik al-Rum Alikzāikas*, see above p. 112 n.
[2] *Kundahrī* or *Kundahū*.

fortresses and cities and their decision to proceed against them with destruction and devastation, owing to the neglect of Islām to make raids upon them and to prosecute the Holy War. It was said that they were engaged in preparations to this end, and Zahīr al-Dīn Atābek sent out letters to the commanders of districts and high officials, urging them to co-operate in repelling the malice of the accursed ones by assisting one another and persevering in the common cause. News arrived that the amīr Najm al-Dīn Il-Ghāzī had set out with his 'askar for Damascus, in order to join Zahīr al-Dīn Atābek and deliberate on the action to be taken and measures to be adopted. Before he set out he sent envoys to the Turkmen tribes inviting them to carry out the obligation of Holy War and urging them to instigate one another [1] to enrol for that purpose and to assemble their forces. The amīr arrived at Damascus from Aleppo with some of his suite and household officers, and had a meeting with the Atābek, at which they covenanted with one another to devote their entire means and energies to warfare with the infidel enemy and to drive them back, before they could make mischief in these fortresses and cities. It was agreed between them that the amīr Najm al-Dīn Il-Ghāzī b. Ortuq, for the better executing of his undertaking, should proceed to Mārdīn [2] in order to assemble the Turkmens from his provinces, and urge them to destroy the factions [3] of infidelity

---

[1] Reading *at-tabā 'uth*.

[2] This reading is based on a conjectural emendation of the text (which can hardly be correct as it stands) reading *'an yasīra* after *'alā* and *'ilā* in place of *wālī*.

[3] Reading *ahzāb* for *ikhrāb*.

and error. It was considered desirable that the amīr Zahīr al-Dīn should go with him to reinforce their purpose and facilitate the realization of their hopes. They set out together during the first ten days of Ramadān 512 (16th to 25th December) and Zahīr al-Dīn left him and returned in Safar of the year 513 (14th May to 11th June, 1119), after they had exacted a promise from the Turkmen tribes to set their affairs in order and to make preparations for moving into Syria with their numerous hosts and invincible determination, that they might unite for the succour of the Faith and the rooting out of the stiff-necked misbelievers. Zahīr al-Dīn remained at Damascus until the appointed time of meeting drew near, and set out for the district of Aleppo on 1st First Rabī' 513 (12th June, 1119).

A.H. 513

(14th April, 1119, to 1st April, 1120)

When Zahīr al-Dīn Atābek arrived at Aleppo to join forces with Najm al-Dīn, according to the plan arranged between them, at the expiration of the period specified in their deliberations, he found the Turkmens already assembled thither from every quarter [1] and every direction, in vast numbers and manifest strength, as lions seeking their prey and gerfalcons hovering over their victims. News reached them that Roger,[2] lord of Antioch, had marched out of his city with an army

[1] lit. "ravine." [2] *Rujīr.*

which he had assembled, composed of parties of Franks and Armenian footsoldiers from all their provinces and districts, so that their number exceeded twenty thousand horse and foot beside camp followers—an immense army indeed—completely equipped and perfectly armed, and that they had encamped at the place known as Sharmadā,[1] or some say Dānīth al-Baqal, between Antioch and Aleppo. When the Muslims learned this, they flew towards them with the wings of hawks flying to the protection of their nests, and no sooner was eye matched with eye and each side approaching the other than the Muslims charged down upon them and encompassed them on all sides with blows of swords and hails of arrows. God Most High, to whom be the praise, granted victory to the party of Islām against the impious mob, and not one hour of the day of Saturday seven[teen]th First Rabī' 513 (28th June, 1119) had passed ere the Franks were on the ground, one prostrate mass, horsemen and footmen alike, with their horses and their weapons, so that not one man of them escaped to tell the tale, and their leader Roger was found stretched out among the dead. A number of the eyewitnesses of this battle have related that they made a circuit of the scene of this combat in order to see the glorious sign wrought by God Most High, and that they saw some of the horses stretched out on the ground like hedgehogs because of the quantity of arrows sticking into them. This victory was one of the finest of victories, and such plenitude of divine aid was

[1] 24 miles W. of Aleppo. See on the site of this battle Dussaud, *Topographie . . . de la Syrie*, 220-221.

never granted to Islām in all its past ages. Antioch was left defenceless and bereft of its protectors and trusty men-at-arms, a prey to the attacker, and an opportunity to the seeker.

But the opportunity of attacking it was neglected owing to the absence of Zahīr al-Dīn Atābek from this battle, since the Turkmens had hurried ahead to engage the Franks without making preparations for the battle, in accordance with the predestined decree, and owing to the preoccupation of the troops in taking possession of the spoils, wherewith their hands were filled and their spirits fortified, and with whose beauty their hearts were rejoiced. " These are their dwellings wasted," and " Praise be to God, Lord of the Worlds." [1] Zahīr al-Dīn Atābek returned to Damascus after this victory and entered it on Saturday, the penultimate day of First Jumādā 573 (6th September, 1119).

In this year also some who came from Jerusalem told of the discovery of the tombs of the prophets al-Khalīl (Abraham) and his two sons Isaac and Jacob, may blessing from God be upon them and peace. They related that they were all together in a cave in the land of Jerusalem, and that they were as if alive, no part of their bodies having decayed, and no bones rotted, and that suspended over them in the cave were lamps of gold and silver. The graves were then restored to their former condition. This is the story precisely as it was told, but God is more knowing of the truth than any other.

[1] Qur'ān 27, 53 and 1, 1.

A.H. 514

(2nd April, 1120, to 21st March, 1121)

In this year the report arrived from Aleppo that the amīr Najm al-Dīn Il-Ghāzī son of Ortuq had abolished the tolls levied on the people of Aleppo, together with the duties on natural products and other contributions, and had rescinded the oppressive innovations and objectionable imposts introduced by the evildoers. This action of his was received with gratitude, praise, appreciation and blessings. It was related that a great storm of hail had fallen at Mārdīn, in unaccustomed violence and unprecedented amount, which killed the cattle and destroyed most of the vegetation and trees. In this year also Najm al-Dīn dismantled Zaradnā, and the amīr Balak son of Ortuq defeated Gavrās [1] the Greek near the castle of Sirmān in the land of Arzinjān, killing about five thousand of the Greeks and capturing their commander Gavrās.

In this year also news was received of the arrival of the Count, king of the Franks, with a number of ships. He took possession of most of the fortresses.

In this year a truce was made between Najm al-Dīn Il-Ghāzī son of Ortuq, lord of Aleppo, and the Franks, and it was agreed to establish amicable and peaceful relations and that each of the two parties should refrain from doing injury to the other.

[1] 'Afrās or Ghafrās, i.e., Theodore Gavras, duke of Trebizond, who had been asked for assistance against the Ortuqids by the ruling prince of Arzinjān (of the house of Mangūchak).

It was reported that Joscelin had made a raid upon the Arabs and Turkmens dwelling in Siffīn and had seized some of them and a quantity of their livestock on the bank of the Euphrates, and on his return had destroyed the fort of Buzā 'a.[1]

A.H. 515

(22nd March, 1121, *to* 11*th March,* 1122)

In this year news arrived of the assassination of al-Afdal, son of the Amīr al-Juyūsh, the holder of authority in Egypt (God's mercy upon him) on the second day of the Festival of the Fast-breaking (13th or 14th December), as the result of a plot which was organized against him for a time when an opportunity should present itself. . . . It was asserted that the Bātinīs were responsible for his assassination, but this statement is not true. On the contrary it is an empty pretence and an insubstantial calumny. The real cause, upon which all accurate and indisputable narratives concerning this affair are agreed, was an estrangement between him and his lord, the [Fātimid] Caliph al-Āmir bi-ahkāmi'llāh, arising out of al-Afdal's constraint upon him and restraining him from following out his inclinations, and the aversion which he had shown to him on several occasions. . . . When he was killed al-Āmir manifested unconcealed joy before all the courtiers and men of rank in Misr and Cairo. It is said also that the place of his assassination was in Misr on the middle of the

[1] Between *H*amāh and Aleppo.

bridge at the head of al-Suwaiqatān [1] on Sunday, the last day of Ramadān 515 (11th December, 1121). He was fifty-seven years of age at this time, having been born at 'Akkā in the year 458 (1066). He was a firm believer in the doctrines of the Sunna, upright in conduct, a lover of justice towards both troops and civil population, judicious in counsel and plan, ambitious and resolute, of penetrating knowledge and exquisite tact, of generous nature, accurate in his intuitions, and possessing a sense of justice which preserved him from wrongdoing and led him to shun all tyrannical methods. All eyes wept and all hearts sorrowed for him ; time did not produce his like after him, and after his loss the government fell into disrepute.

In this year also reports were received of the appearance of the Georgians from the Durūb [2] and their descent on the territories of the king Tughrul. The latter asked for assistance from the amīr Najm al-Dīn Il-Ghāzī son of Ortuq, lord of Aleppo, and also from the Turkmens and from the amīr Dubais b. Sadaqa b. Mazyad. They consented to his urgent request, and set out to join him with a great host. The army of the Georgians fled in terror, and the Muslims pressed upon them and besieged them in the Durūb ; but the Georgians turned upon the Muslims, and having put them to flight, killed large numbers of them. Thereafter they advanced on the city of Tiflīs and captured it by the sword, and put its inhabitants to death.

---

[1] Literally " the two small markets."
[2] i.e., the Pyles, the passes west of Darband. Tughrul b. Muhammad, later Saljuqid Sultan of al-'Irāq, was governor of Qazwīn, Gīlān, and the N.W. frontiers (cf. Bundarī, p. 134).

A.H. 516

(12th March, 1122, to 28th February, 1123)

It was said that the amīr Najm al-Dīn b. Ortuq marched out of Aleppo with his 'askar and having crossed the Euphrates encountered the Franks, but they did not engage him in battle, and after destroying whatsoever he could lay hands on in their territories, he returned to al-Funaidiq, in the environs of Aleppo.

In this year also the Egyptian fleet arrived at Tyre carrying marines and a section of the troops. The commander privily intended to dupe the amīr Saif al-Dawla Mas'ūd, who was governor in Tyre on behalf of the amīr Zahīr al-Dīn Atābek, and when Mas'ūd went out to greet the commander of the fleet, they invited him on board and arrested him as soon as he set foot on the commander's vessel. Thus the plot was successfully carried out and the town fell into their hands. When the fleet set sail and reached Egypt, bearing the amīr Mas'ūd, he was received with honour, lodged in a house and supplied with all that he required.

The reason of this stratagem was that a succession of complaints had been sent by the men of Tyre to al-Āmir and al-Afdal, relating the injuries which Mas'ūd was inflicting upon the civil population, his disregard of their customs, and opposition to them.[1] It was considered necessary in consequence to take measures against him and to terminate the governorship which he held, but the result of his leaving the town and of the bad

---

[1] Reading *al-muwāqafati* for *al-muwāfaqati* (" agreement with ").

management of its affairs was that it was lost to the Franks.

In this year also the report arrived that the amīr Nūr al-Dawla Balak son of Ortuq had set out with his 'askar during Rajab (5th September to 4th October), and having marched against the Franks at al-Ruhā, had fallen upon them and defeated them at Sarūj, taking prisoner their commander Joscelin together with Galeran,[1] the son of his maternal aunt, and a number of their leaders.

News arrived also of the death of the amīr Najm al-Dīn Il-Ghāzī son of Ortuq from an illness which befel him, while stopping in a village called al-Fuhūl in Diyār Bakr, in the government of Mayyāfāriqīn, on 6th Ramadān (8th November) of this year. His place was taken after his death by his son Shams al-Dawla Sulaimān and the latter's brother Timurtāsh, who took possession of Mārdīn. They remained in concord for some time, but a quarrel afterwards broke out between them, on which both of them were unyielding.

A.H. 517

(1st March, 1123 to 18th February, 1124)

News was brought from Aleppo that an armistice had been concluded between the amīr Badr al-Dawla son of 'Abd al-Jabbār b. Ortuq, lord of Aleppo, and the Franks, on the condition of the surrender of the castle of Athārib to the Franks. It was surrendered to them accordingly and they

---

[1] *Kalyān.*

entered into possession of it. Friendly relations were maintained on this footing, the provinces prospered on both sides, and the roads became safe for travellers between the districts of the two parties. This was in Safar (April) of this year.

In this year also news was brought of the advance of Baldwin, King of the Franks, with his army on 9th Safar (8th April) towards the province of Aleppo in order to attack the amīr Balak b. Ortuq, who was besieging the castle of Karkar.[1] Balak advanced towards him and the two armies met in the vicinity of Manzara. Baldwin was defeated and captured and became a prisoner in Balak's hands along with a number of his principal knights. Balak confined him in a dungeon in the castle of Khartbart (Kharput) together with Joscelin and the leaders of the Franks.

At the end of Safar (end of April) Zahīr al-Dīn Atābek led out the 'askar and delivered an assault on the suburb of Hims, which he plundered and set on fire, together with some of the houses of the city. But since Tughān Arslān son of Husām al-Dawla had come to Hims to assist its lord Khīr-Khān, Zahīr al-Dīn withdrew from it and returned to Damascus.

News arrived from Aleppo that the amīr Balak b. Ortuq had descended upon it in First Rabī' of this year (May), and having burned its crops and blockaded the city, at length obtained possession of it by capitulation on Tuesday 1st First Jumādā (26th June) from Badr al-Dawla, son of his uncle

[1] ? Qarqar, on the right bank of the Orontes, a little to the north of the site of Afāmiya (Dussaud, *Topographie*, 242).

'Abd al-Jabbār b. Ortuq.[1] He had already obtained possession of the city of Harrān in the month of First Rabī'.

In this year also news was brought of the arrival in Egypt of a numerous force of the army of the Luwāta [Berbers] from the region of the west. They ravaged its provinces, and al-Ma'mūn Abū 'Abdallāh, son of al-Batā'ihī, the successor of the martyred al-Afdal, son of the Amīr al-Juyūsh, went out towards them with the Egyptian army by the command of the Imām al-Āmir son of al-Musta'lī. He met them and inflicted a severe defeat upon them, killing and capturing a great multitude, and imposed upon them a fixed tribute to be paid by them each year. Thereupon they returned to their own places and al-Ma'mūn returned to Misr, booty-laden and victorious, and rejoiced at his good success. The report also arrived that the Egyptian fleet had met the Venetian fleet at sea, and that a battle was fought in which the Venetian fleet gained the upper hand over the Egyptian fleet and captured from it a number of galleys.

In the first ten days of First Rabī' of this year (between 28th April and 8th May) the amīr Balak

[1] The following genealogical table will make clear the relationships of the Ortuqids :—

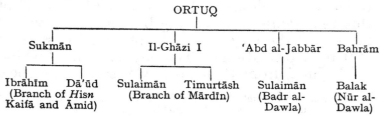

	ORTUQ		
Sukmān	Il-Ghāzi I	'Abd al-Jabbār	Bahrām
Ibrāhīm Dā'ūd (Branch of *Hisn* Kaifā and Āmid)	Sulaimān Timurtāsh (Branch of Mārdīn)	Sulaimān (Badr al-Dawla)	Balak (Nūr al-Dawla)

b. Ortuq captured the castle of al-Bāra and took its bishop prisoner.

In this year also the report arrived from Khartbart that King Baldwin the Little and Joscelin, the leaders of the Franks, together with others of the captives of the amīr Balak who were imprisoned in the fortress of Khartbart, had devised a stratagem amongst themselves and had seized the castle and fled. . . .[1] King Baldwin and he escaped, and they could not recapture him. On the same day also the Bishop of al-Bāra escaped from his confinement. In the same month the amīr Nūr al-Dawla Balak marched with his 'askar to Khartbart and besieged its citadel until he recovered it from the Franks who had taken it by surprise. He established a garrison in it to protect it and be on their guard in its defence.

In this year also the news was received that Mahmūd b. Qarāja, governor of Hamāh, had marched out with his men-at-arms and made towards Afāmiya, the suburb of which he attacked. An arrow from the castle struck him in the hand, and when it was extracted his hand festered, and growing worse, caused his death. He was debauched, tyrannical, and unscrupulous, and had put a number of the leading citizens of Hamāh to death unjustly and illegally on the ground of slanderous accusations brought by them against one another. When Zahīr al-Dīn learned of this, he dispatched one of his trusty officers to Hamāh to take over the town and govern it.

In this year also befel the disaster to the 'askars of Zahīr al-Dīn Atābek of Damascus and Saif

[1] lacuna in MS.

al-Dīn Āq-Sunqur al-Bursuqī, when they joined forces and made an attack on 'Azāz, in the province of Aleppo. They pressed on its siege by breaches and battles until its capture had become an easy matter, but the Franks assembled together from every quarter and sought to drive the 'askar away from it. The two armies met, and the army of the Muslims was broken and dispersed, with severe losses in killed and captives. Zahīr al-Dīn returned to Damascus in First Jumādā of this year (27th June to 26th July). In the month of Ramadān (23rd October to 21st November) of this same year the chamberlain 'Alī b. Hāmid proceeded to Egypt as an envoy from Zahīr al-Dīn Atābek [1].

A.H. 518

(19*th February*, 1124, *to* 6*th February*, 1125)

In this year the Franks gained possession of the port of Tyre by capitulation. An account has already been given of the causes which compelled the removal from Tyre of its governor, the amīr Saif al-Dawla Mas 'ūd, and his being taken on the fleet to Egypt, so that it is not necessary to repeat this. When the governor who had been dispatched from Egypt after Mas 'ūd arrived in the town, he gained the goodwill of the townsmen and wrote to Zahīr al-Dīn explaining the situation. The latter replied that the responsibility in this matter rested with those who had conceived it, and that the governor must look for assistance to their measures and dispositions. It befel that when the Franks

[1] This paragraph appears to be misplaced from A.H. 519.

learned of this state of affairs, and that Mas'ūd had been removed from the governorship of Tyre, their desire for it was stirred up and they persuaded themselves that the opportunity for capturing it was now come ; whereupon they set about gathering their forces and making preparations to besiege and invest it. When the governor was informed of what was afoot, he, realizing that he could not resist the Franks nor hold out against their siege on account of the shortage of troops and provisions in the town, wrote to apprise al-Āmir, lord of Egypt, of this. Thereupon it was judged necessary to restore the government of Tyre to Zahīr al-Dīn Atābek, in order that he should take measures for its defence and protection and for the warding off [of the Franks] from it, as he had been wont to do. The diploma of investiture was written in his name, and he deputed as its governors a body of men who had neither ability, capacity, nor bravery. In consequence of this its affairs fell into disorder, and the desire of the Franks was directed towards it. They set about forming a camp and making preparations for the blockade, and having encamped outside the city in First Rabī' of this year (18th April to 17th May), they blockaded it by fighting and siege until the supplies of food in the city ran short and its provisions were exhausted. Zahīr al-Dīn marched with the 'askar to Bānyās for the defence of Tyre. Letters were dispatched to Egypt with appeals for assistance to be sent to the city, but when day after day passed their hearts sank and the citizens came to the brink of destruction. Zahīr al-Dīn, being made aware of the true state of affairs and the impossibility of remedying the critical situation of the town, and despairing of assistance being sent to it, opened negotiations with the Franks, and finessed, cajoled, threatened, and incited, until an agreement was reached to surrender the city to them, on the conditions that all who were in it should be given a guarantee of security, and that those of the troops and citizens who desired to depart should do so with as much of their property as they could remove, and those who desired to stay should stay. The atābek then took up a position with his 'askar facing the Franks and the gate of the city was opened, and permission given to the people to depart. Each of them carried with him all light property that he was able to carry and left all heavy property behind. They filed out thus between two ranks, without a single Frank molesting any one of them, until the entire body of troops and citizens had left, and none remained behind but those who were too weak to leave. They were dispersed throughout the country and some of them came to Damascus. The date of the surrender of the city was 23rd First Jumādā 518 (7th or 8th July, 1124).

In the same year news was received that the Franks had assembled from their provinces, descended upon Aleppo, and set about fighting with its inhabitants and besieging the city. The siege was prolonged until the supplies of food in the town became deficient and its people were on the brink of destruction. When they were reduced to extremity and their endurance was exhausted, they wrote to the amīr Saif al-Dīn Āq-Sunqur al-Bursuqī, lord of Mosul, complaining of their situation and describing what had befallen them, and begging him to send them support against the Franks and deliver them from the hands of the infidels. He was much distressed thereat and his happiness was dissipated, and he made preparations at once to set out to their assistance and turned his attention to repelling their enemies. When he reached them in Dhu'l-Hijja of this year (January, 1125) and the Franks received news of him and of his approach towards them, and of the exceeding might of his army, they fled in panic and withdrew in defeat. The vanguard of the cavalry pursued them, picking up all upon whom they could lay hands from among their companies,[1] and not one fugitive amongst them turned aside to any halting place until they were safely within Antioch. In their camp they had erected houses and huts to protect them from heat and cold, and they were determined to remain there to prosecute their siege, but God Most High—to Him be the praise!—showed mercy upon the people of Aleppo and delivered them from disaster and snatched them from the coils of destruction. By this noble action Āq-Sunqur al-Bursuqī acquired great merit and renown, and having entered Aleppo, he governed it with uprightness and protected the interests of its people, and made every effort to defend the city and keep the enemy at a distance from it. Thus its affairs were set in order, its districts restored to prosperity, its roads made safe, and caravans frequented it with their merchandise and objects of trade.

---

[1] This appears to be the meaning of the reading *fī a 'nāqihim* in the text, but perhaps read *fī a 'qābihim* " from amongst their rearmost men."

In the winter of this year no rain fell in the land of Syria during December, January, and the greater part of February ; the crops perished and prices rose, and famine became general in most of the Syrian districts. Thereafter God overtook His servants with His mercy and the sending down of rain after they had despaired of it, restoring the earth thereby to life after its death,[1] and recovering the seed crops after their loss, and all hearts were gladdened and care and distress were removed from them. Prices became high in this year in Aleppo, Damascus, and all its territories as far as al-Rahba, al-Qal 'a, and Mosul. This state of affairs lasted into the year 19 and many poor people perished of starvation.

A.H. 519

(7th February, 1125, to 26th January, 1126)

In this year news arrived from the quarter of Baldwin, king of the Franks, lord of Jerusalem, of his assembling of troops and making preparations to invade the region of Hawrān in the government of Damascus, in order to ravage and devastate it. He began to dispatch raiding parties to the districts near Damascus, placing them in sore straits, and laying ambushes on the roads for those who journeyed to them. On receiving confirmation of this news, Zahīr al-Dīn Atābek set about making preparations to encounter him and assembling his allies to wage the Holy War against him. He sent

[1] A Qur'ānic reminiscence.

letters to the amīrs, leaders and principal men of the Turkmens, informing them of the state of affairs, asking for their help against the Franks, and promising them generous treatment and reward. Meanwhile, having received news that the Franks were near Tiberias and intending to advance on the immediate neighbourhood of Damascus by way of Marj al-Suffar and Sharkhūb, he led out his ʿaskar and camped at Marj al-Suffar, whence he wrote to the governors of the provinces to send him reinforcements of foot-soldiers. At this moment the Turkmens arrived, to the number of two thousand horsemen, men of great valour, filled with desire for the Holy War and eager to be first in the fight, and a great host assembled to assist him. The Franks, on learning that the Atābek and the ʿaskar were encamped at Marj al-Suffar, marched towards him and set up their tents over against him, so that both armies were face to face and the outposts of the two forces engaged in skirmishes.

On Monday 27th Dhu'l-Hijja of this year (25th January, 1126), there were assembled, in accordance with the predestined decree of God and His ineluctable wisdom, a great host from the armed bands and untried youths of Damascus, the men of the Ghūta, the Marj, and the outlying districts, and the armed bands of the Bātinīya, noted for courage and gallantry, from Hims and elsewhere, and from al-ʿAqaba, Qasr al-Hajjāj, and al-Shāghūr,[1] both footmen and horsemen,

---

[1] All three were suburban districts to the south of Damascus, if by al ʿAqaba is meant the " Pass of Shuhūra," between the city and the village of al-Kiswa (see below).

fully armed, together with others accompanying those who had volunteered out of religious zeal. They set out to join the ranks before the battle was begun, when the news had spread of the strength and multitude of the army of Islām and of its superiority over the party of the Franks and its exceeding might, and no one doubted but that the Franks were doomed to destruction on that day and would fall an easy prey to the Muslims. It fell out that a strong party of the Turkmen troops made an attack on the fringes of the Franks and gained the advantage over them, whereupon the Franks, moved by fear, and knowing that they could do nothing against such a multitude, but certain only of their own destruction, withdrew in a body from the camp which they had occupied, to return to their own districts, in the utmost fear and panic and humiliation. A body of the Turkmens became engaged with a detachment of them as they were on the march, and captured a rich booty in their baggage train and animals, in addition to seizing the famous church which they had in their camp. Thereupon the army became emboldened against them and charged upon them, while the Franks, on their part, fled without venturing to turn against their pursuers, or to wait for stragglers, so panic-stricken were they. The Muslims pressed upon them and harassed them so mercilessly that at length they were forced to throw themselves upon their pursuers, be the issue for them or against them. Rallying their ranks, they turned to face the Muslim cavalry and charged upon them with their famous onset, broke them and drove them in flight, killing all those of the rearmost who were deflected by fear or betrayed by destiny. The flight of the 'askar became a headlong rout, and the Franks turned against all the footmen, who were an immense number and a vast host, and put them to the sword until they made an end of them. They pursued and slaughtered the fugitives until they reached the pass of Shuhūrā,[1] and approached the city [of Damascus] from Sharkhūb, notwithstanding the greatness of this distance and the powers of endurance of their horses. Zahīr al-Dīn Atābek and the 'askar reached Damascus at the close of the same day, and arranged between themselves to attack the Franks early the following morning in order to inflict a decisive defeat upon them, but they found that they had already set off to return to their own district, for fear of the determination of the Muslims to attack and pursue them. God disposes as He wills.

A.H. 520

(27th January, 1126, to 16th January, 1127)

In this year the report was received from Mosul of the martyrdom of the amīr isfahsallār Saif al-Dīn Āq-Sunqur al-Bursuqī, lord of the city, in the cathedral mosque there at the hands of the Bātinīs in Dhu'l-Qa'dà of this year (beg. 18th November).[2] This amīr (God's mercy upon him) was upright in conduct and action, of laudable character, a lover of justice and fair dealing,

---

[1] The important pass giving access to the plain of Damascus, about ten miles south of the city (Dussaud, 318).
[2] Details of the assassination omitted.

frequent in his religious observances, praiseworthy in his aims, fond of welldoing and welldoers, and generous to men of learning and religion. The people grieved for him and mourned his loss in this tragic fashion, and when Zahīr al-Dīn Atābek learned of it, he was troubled and distressed at the news.

Al-Bursuqī was succeeded by his son, the amīr Mas 'ūd, who was noted for the nobility and purity of his character, and famous for his gallantry and capacity.[1] The domestic officers, wazīr, and secretaries of his father all continued in his service, and he maintained the laudable conduct and aims of his father ; his power was thus firmly established and his affairs rightly and excellently ordered.

In this year Zahīr al-Dīn Atābek marched towards Tadmur (Palmyra) and remained on campaign until he recovered the town from the hands of those who governed it, and who had assassinated its former governor, the son of Zahīr al-Dīn's brother. The town was captured on Thursday 12th Second Rabī' (6th May), and it was decided that it should be given as an apanage to the amīr Shihāb al-Dīn Mahmūd son of Tāj al-Mulūk Būrī son of Zahīr al-Dīn Atābek. It was delivered up to him accordingly and he went out to it, accompanied by some of [Zahīr al-Dīn's] trusty officers, to whom the guardianship both of him and of the town had been assigned.

In this year also, when Zahīr al-Dīn returned from Aleppo, the first signs of illness were showing in him. He entered Damascus in Sha 'bān (beg.

---

[1] Reading *ghanā'* for *'anā'*.

August 22nd) and in the same month Amīn al-Dawla Gumushtagīn, governor of Bosra, came to him from Egypt bringing the reply to the letter with which he had been sent. In his company there came the amīr al-Muntadī b. Musāfir al-Ghanawī, the ambassador of al-Āmir, ruler of Egypt, bringing magnificent robes of honour and costly Egyptian presents.

In this year also the position of Bahrām, the propagandist of the Bātinīya, grew so formidable that he became a factor to be reckoned with in Aleppo and Syria. He lived in extreme concealment and secrecy, and continually disguised himself, so that he moved from city to city and castle to castle without anyone being aware of his identity, until he appeared in Damascus in pursuance of an agreement which Najm al-Dīn Il-Ghāzī son of Ortuq had made with the amīr Zahīr al-Dīn Atābek, and with a letter containing strong recommendations on his behalf. He was received with honour as a measure of precaution against his malice and that of his organization, and every consideration was shown him, and protection was assured him after suffering many vicissitudes of fortune. He moved about from place to place and gained a following among the ignorant and witless mob, and foolish peasantry, men lacking both intelligence and religion, who sought in him and his party a means of protecting themselves and injuring others. He found an ally in the Wazīr Abū 'Alī Tāhir b. Sa'd al-Mazdaqānī, who, even though he was not of his way of thinking, assisted him to spread his malicious devices and to manifest his secret objects. When his organization came into the open and extended far and wide, and this wazīr of Zahīr al-Dīn consented to become an accomplice in his activities and to strengthen his hands in his operations, he requested of Zahīr al-Dīn Atābek a castle in which to take refuge and a fortress in which to defend himself. Zahīr al-Dīn accordingly delivered up to him the frontier fort of Bānyās in Dhu'l-Qa'da 520 (November to December, 1126), and when he had established himself in it, he was joined there by his rabble of varlets, half-wits, peasants, low fellows and vile scum, whom he had seduced by his lying and his false pretensions, and had won over to his side by his intrigues and deceits. This public establishment of their cause [1] created a grievous calamity and a public terror ; men of learning, piety, and religious authority, the people of the Sunna and the Tradition of the Fathers, and true Believers of honourable and peaceful life were sore distressed, and none of them dared say a word about these people or complain about any man of them, in order to ward off their malice and guard against their vengeance upon him. For they set about killing all those who opposed them, and supporting all who gave them assistance in their impious ways, so that neither Sultan nor Wazīr would condemn them, nor could any general or amīr break the edge of their malice.

In this year also the Franks marched on Rafanīya and regained possession of it from the Muslims after a siege.

[1] Reading *sababihim*.

A.H. 521

(17th January, 1127, to 5th January, 1128)

An account has been given above of the martyr-dom of amīr Saif al-Dīn Āq-Sunqur al-Bursuqī, lord of Mosul, in the mosque of the city at the hands of the Bātinīs, and of the succession of his son, the amīr Mas'ūd, in his place. When his authority was firmly established and his might became formidable, he grew arrogant and being puffed up by his youthful impetuousness he conceived the idea of taking the field against the cities of Syria, trying to seize the Muslim fortresses, and throwing himself into the Holy War against the Frankish bands with adversaries of resolution and upright-ness, vigour and bravery in acquiring the merit of the Raid and the Holy War. The news of his activities was brought to Zahīr al-Dīn Atābek, accompanied by tales illustrating the prince's jealousy of him, on account of the respect and fair reputation which he had won, and by reports that he was determined to arm and gather his forces in order to set out for the provinces of Syria and to sow in them disorder and devastation. Zahīr al-Dīn Atābek, on learning of these proposals, the like of which would not be put forward by any man of sense, nor be contemplated by any prudent and intelligent person, determined to make prepara-tions for marching against him with his 'askar and quench his desire by the massacre of his own party. But it was not more than a few days later that the pitcher of his youth was broken and the decree of his predestination descended upon him in the outskirts of al-Rahba through the assault of a severe illness which carried him off to that predestined end from which there is no refuge and against which there is no protector. Thus his sword was shattered, and his counsellors and his army forsook him, his defenders abandoned him to fate, and his intimates and trusted officers separated from him. At the same time perished his wazīr, his partner and adviser in his folly, by reason of a severe illness which came suddenly upon him and led him into the snares of death. A number of the principal Turkish slaves of his father fled with the standards which he had caused to be made for his purpose, and which had been fashioned with the utmost skill in accordance with his specifications and choice, and brought them to Zahīr al-Dīn Atābek, in order to present them to him and by this means to gain his goodwill. He received them graciously and showed them exceeding honour and favour, took them into his own service and included them in the number of his trusted officers and private associates, and rewarded them for their adhesion to him by bountiful deed and high pay.

In Sha'bān of this year (12th August to 9th September, 1127) Baldwin, king of the Franks, lord of Jerusalem, marched with his army to Wādī Mūsā (Petra), and having plundered and enslaved its inhabitants and scattered them, he withdrew and left them. In Latter Jumādā (15th May to 13th June) of the same year the report was received that the amīr Khutlugh Abah al-Sultānī had been appointed governor of the city of Aleppo, and had occupied its citadel by means of a party of secret agents which had been selected for the purpose. He had been but a short time in possession when his affairs fell into disorder and an enmity sprang up between him and the town bands of Aleppo, who besieged him in the citadel until the 'askar of the amīr 'Imād al-Dīn [Zankī] Atābek arrived at Aleppo. Khutlugh Abah was then surrendered to 'Imād al-Dīn from the citadel and imprisoned, until at the request [of his enemies] he gave permission to blind him, and this was done.

A.H. 522

(6th January to 24th December, 1128)

[1] In this year the illness of Zahīr al-Dīn Atābek increased in violence and persisted with him until it sapped his strength and weakened his bodily frame, and brought him to the brink of that event which no device can ward off nor any force prohibit. Thereupon he summoned his son the amīr Tāj al-Mulūk, together with the amīrs of his kingdom, his household officers, his trusted advisers and the leaders of the troops, and informed them that he felt in himself the approaching end of his span. "Naught remains (he continued) but my injunctions concerning the action to be taken and the conduct of government after my death and its carrying on in future. This my son Tāj al-Mulūk Būrī is my eldest son, who has been trained up to occupy my place after me and who is looked to in order to fill the gap of my loss. I have no doubt as to the uprightness of his conduct, his desire to

---

[1] This passage is slightly abridged.

do that which is best, and his love [of justice], nor that he will follow in my footsteps in preserving the hearts of the amīrs and troops and act according to my example in dealing equitably with the notables and subjects. If he accepts this my testament, and walks in the way of approval in extending justice and fair dealing to all, and removes from them by his good government all causes of anxiety and fear, that is what is expected of such an one as he and hoped for from his uprightness and good action. If he turns aside from this conduct to follow any other way, and inclines from the uprightness which is sought of him in secret and in open, he will now himself call you to witness against himself in such a case, and declare sentence against himself in such a turn of events." Thereupon Būrī, saying "Nay, but I shall faithfully carry out [your testament] as you would desire, and I shall not transgress the path of rectitude" confirmed his pledge to him to this effect with an emphasis which conveyed his sincerity to Zahīr al-Dīn and satisfied him. Thereafter he was called to the mercy of God on the forenoon of Saturday 8th Safar of this year (11th February), and all hearts and eyes mourned his loss, and no voice was heard but was afflicted with sorrow, mindful of his generous actions and giving thanks for his reign. His son Tāj al-Mulūk Būrī assumed control after him, and dealt beneficently with his personal followers, his subjects and his army.

This blessed amīr (Zahīr al-Dīn) had gone to the utmost lengths in enforcing justice and restraining from oppression. He restored to a number of the

subjects a quantity of neglected properties in the
outskirts of the city, which had been seized from
them by violence in the time of insolent and
tyrannical governors, or had been subjected to the
payment of tribute in kind or ruined by ravishing
hostile hands, and assessed them at their old-
established rate of land-tax and duties, removing
from them all causes of oppression and injury, and
relieving their owners from all disputation regarding their title at all places and times. By this
measure he gained the gratitude and fervent
prayers of the people.

Following this he had addressed a petition to the
Commander of the Faithful, the Caliph al-Mustarshid billāh, at the time of his journey to Baghdād,
and visit to the courts of the Imām al-Mustarshid
and the Sultan Ghiyāth al-Dīn. In this petition,
having exposed the condition of neglected areas in
the government of Damascus and of cultivated
estates and land fallen out of cultivation which
had no owner, that there was nothing to be gained
from leaving them uncultivated, and that neither
courtier nor citizen received any benefit from them
owing to their ruinous state and the disappearance
of their workshops and [consequently] of the
duties [formerly levied on them],[1] he asked the
Caliph for permission to sell them to whosoever
desired them and sought to bring them under
cultivation, in order that the benefit of their crops
and produce might be gained, and to apply the
revenues accruing from their sale to the purpose of
the troops enrolled for the Holy War. The Caliph

---

[1] *ma 'āmilihā wa rusumihā*, but perhaps read *ma 'ālimihā* " boundary
marks and lines of division."

accorded him full and emphatic permission to carry out this proposal, declaring it lawful to him, and assuring legal possession to those who acquired an estate by purchase from him, and endorsed the petition to that effect, by granting execution and invalidating legal disputation in regard thereto, and forbidding the revocation of any part of his decision or the revision of his decree ; moreover he confirmed his acceptance of the atābek's proposals by the noble sign-manual of the Imām al-Mustarshid, and brought in to witness thereto witnesses of known probity. The atābek then carried out the sale of these properties to those who desired them, and a number of estates which had been desolate wastes, lying in ruins and of no value or use to anyone, were put into cultivation, their springs of water made to flow, and restored to the most flourishing of their former states. . . .

THE REIGN OF TAJ AL-MULUK BURI B. ATABEK

Now when the preordained decree was executed upon Zahīr al-Dīn Atābek (God's mercy upon him) and his son, the amīr Tāj al-Mulūk, reigned in his place, he confirmed his father's wazīr Abū 'Alī Tāhir b. Sa 'd al-Mazdaqānī in his wazirate and maintained him in his position as his personal representative, and did not remove any governor of his of proved loyalty from his post or source of income, but on the contrary increased their emoluments and bestowed upon them robes of honour and rich bounty. He also confirmed the fiefholders in their fiefs and all recipients of state salaries in their stipends, so that he was greatly praised and blessed by all. To his wazīr al-Mazdaqānī he showed great liberality, and assigned to him the tenth part of his revenue together with the fees payable on presentation of petitions regarding fiefs,[1] salaries and grants for mainten-ance. When the power of the Bātinīs increased and their malevolence redoubled in consequence of his father's policy of giving them protection and humouring them in order to ward off their malice, he had privily formed a decision concerning their organization which he did not communicate to any of his intimates or more trusted courtiers. When, therefore, God empowered him over them, he began to take action by devising a means to punish them and by exterminating them, and took those steps which will be related in their proper place.

An account of what befel in Damascus and its districts by reason of the Bātinīya and the destruc-tion and obliteration of landmarks resulting from their activities during the remainder of the year 522.

A sufficient account has already been given of Bahrām, the missioner of the Bātinīya, and the cause which necessitated the deliverance to him of the frontier castle of Bānyās. When he had established himself in Bānyās he set about fortify-ing it and rebuilding what of it was in ruins or out of repair. In all directions he dispatched his missionaries, who enticed a great multitude of the ignorant folk of the provinces and foolish peasantry from the villages and the rabble and scum, persons

---

[1] huqūqu'l 'ardi 'ani'l-'iqtā 'āti.

without intelligence to restrain them from mischief or fear of God to prevent them from wrong-doing. Their evil power was thereby increased and the true nature of their false doctrine made manifest ; their hands and tongues were lengthened with slander and abuse against the men of repute amongst the subjects, and with greed and spoliation against lonely travellers on the highways, whom they seized with violence and used despitefully, and with the slaying of men outrageously and unjustly. They were assisted to these depths of misdoing by the wazīr Abū 'Alī Tāhir b. Sa 'd al-Mazdaqānī, who carried his partisanship to extreme lengths. But he suffered the dire consequences and bitter penalty of his action when an agreement was established between him and Bahrām the missioner to furnish [one another with] aid and support—an agreement made in flat disregard of and disobedience to God, and inspired by the desire to take joint action against those who sought to injure them and pursue a common aim against those who had evil designs upon them. Tāj al-Mulūk was by no means pleased at this nor did he consent to it ; but sound statesmanship, a strong spirit of forbearance, and penetrating knowledge moved him to close his eyes, with whatever pain, to their activities and to bear patiently their rankling injury. Meanwhile he secretly meditated taking steps against them, without disclosing his design until such time as he should find an opportunity which facilitated his object and a clear predominance over the enemies of God, whereupon the opportunity would be seized and the quarry hunted down.

Now it chanced that Bahrām the missioner, since it was the will of God that he should perish, conceived the idea of slaying Baraq b. Jandal, one of the chiefs in Wādī'l-Taim, not for any cause which impelled him to do so, or for any crime which required him to take action against him, but in sheer disregard of the fate of tyrants who shed inviolate human blood and in culpable ignorance of the warning of God to those who seek to do so and venture upon it in His words " And whoso slayeth a Believer of set purpose, his recompense shall be Hell, to dwell therein to eternity ; God shall be wrath with him and shall curse him, and shall make ready for him a mighty chastisement."[1] So Bahrām used deceit with Baraq until he came into his hands, when he put him in fetters and killed him in cold blood. There was general lamentation at the murder in this way of such a man notwithstanding his youth, his gallantry, and personal beauty, and imprecations and reproofs were openly uttered against his murderer in all gatherings and assemblies, and by all, both far and near. His brother Dahhāk b. Jandal, with his clan and family, impelled by the ardour of their Muslim pride and their passion for the honour of the family to seek revenge for his blood, assembled and made a compact together and swore to one another to remain steadfast in meeting their enemies, to devote themselves to the pursuit of their vendetta and to spend their life-blood and their souls in attaining their revenge. They set about making preparations to this end with steadfastness and watchfulness for an opportunity, until

---

[1] Qur'ān, Sūra IV, v. 95.

their predestined doom laid Bahrām and his band by the heels, and God decreed their uprooting and extirpation. With forces gathered together from all quarters, and swelled by adherents who came in from every side, Bahrām marched out from Bānyās in the year 522 and made in the direction of Wādī'l-Taim in order to crush these persons of whom we have spoken, but they were prepared to meet him and watching for an opportunity to engage him in battle. When they were made aware of his approach to them, they rose to meet him in a body like lions rising from their lairs to defend their cubs, and flew at them as mountain-hawks at partridges. On approaching his broken faction and Godforsaken host they charged upon them when they were in their camp and off their guard. Shouting the battlecry, they took them unawares, and ere the horseman could mount his steed or the footsoldier could seize his weapons death overtook the greater part of the Bātinīs, by smiting with the sword, abrading with the poniards of fate, sprinkling with the arrows of destruction, and stoning with the rocks of predestination.

Bahrām meanwhile was in his tent, surrounded by a company of his partners in his folly and error, ignorant of what had encompassed him and his sectaries. On hearing the uproar and shouting they had leapt up to seize their weapons, but the men of Wādī'l-Taim rushed upon them with their keen swords and death-dealing poniards and killed the whole company. Bahrām's head and hand was cut off, after he had been dissected by swords and knives, and one of the slayers who took these, along with his ring, to Egypt, carrying the joyful tidings of his death and destruction, was vested with a robe of honour and rewarded. The news of this event spread far and wide, and all the people were united in joy and congratulation at their destruction, and derived the fullest share of pleasure from this victory.

In consequence of this, the numbers of the Bāṭinīs were diminished and their power of offence was weakened. The place of Bahrām was taken by his friend Ismā'īl the Persian, his comrade in error and violence, and his accomplice in intrigue and rebellion, who set about enticing the witless, exactly as Bahrām had done, and even surpassed him in folly to an extent which made plain the weakness of his intelligence and his malignity. Round him gathered the remnants of the abominable sect from all provinces and districts, and all those of them who were scattered throughout the country. The wazīr Abū 'Alī Ṭāhir b. Sa'd al-Mazdaqānī maintained towards Ismā'īl the same policy as he had observed towards Bahrām, by assisting him to achieve his purposes, in order to guard himself against their malice and out of desire for his own safety, not knowing that the end of such actions is bitter repentance and wide digression from the path of security. As it has been said, "Many an one who gives himself up is saved by his surrender, and many an one who guards against evil finds therein his bane." The complaints of the people, men of rank and commons alike, continued to multiply, and their losses at the hands of the deluded fanatics to succeed one another, until Tāj al-Mulūk, son of Zahīr al-Dīn Atābek, set about their extirpation and whetted the blade of his determination to purify the provinces of them. He considered that the most advisable step necessitated by his plans for attaining this object was to make away in the first instance with the wazīr Abū 'Alī, since he was the most certain mark at which to aim and the first to be sought. He therefore laid upon one of his household officers in whom he had confidence the duty of killing him, and arranged with him that he should strike his head with a sword when he himself gave him the signal. On Wednesday 17th Ramadān 523 (4th September, 1129), the wazīr presented himself as usual with all the amīrs and commanders in the Rose Pavilion at the Palace of the Citadel at Damascus, and various matters were transacted and discussed in the council with Tāj al-Mulūk and those present, until the hour of their withdrawal and return to their houses. The wazīr rose to withdraw after them, according to his custom, and at that moment Tāj al-Mulūk gave the signal to his antagonist, who struck his head several blows with his sword and killed him. His head was then cut off, carried with his dead body to the ashheap at the Iron Gate, and thrown upon it, that all the people might see the act of God upon one who plotted and sought other helpers than Him. His body was burned with fire some days later, and reduced to ashes strewn by the winds. "This is the reward for that which his hands wrought, and God is not unjust towards His creatures." [1]

The report of this spread immediately, and the

[1] Reminiscence of Qur'ān 22, 10.

town bands at Damascus, assisted by the mob and the refuse of the city, rose with swords and naked poniards and put to death all the Bātinīs and their adherents [1] upon whom they could lay hands, and every person connected with them or related to them. They pursued them into their dwellings, fetched them out of their places, and dispatched them all either by dismemberment with swords or by slaughter with poniards, and they were thrown out upon the dungheaps like abandoned carrion. A large number of individuals among them who had taken refuge with various high quarters in order to protect themselves, and who hoped for safety through their intercession, were forcibly seized and their blood was shed without fear of consequences. By the next morning the quarters and streets of the city were cleared of the Bātinīs and the dogs were yelping and quarrelling over their limbs and corpses. " Verily in this is a sign to men of intelligence." [2]

Amongst those who were captured was the man known as Shādhī the freedman, the pupil of Abū Tāhir the Bātinī goldsmith who was formerly at Aleppo. This accursed freedman was the root of all the trouble and evil, and was repaid with the severest punishment, at which the hearts of many of the Believers were comforted. He was crucified, along with a few others of the sect, on the battlements of the wall of Damascus, in order that it might be seen how God had dealt with the oppressors and brought signal chastisement upon the infidels. The chamberlain Yūsuf b. Fīrūz, military

---

[1] Text *asbābihim*, perhaps for *ashyā 'ihim*.
[2] Another Qur'anic reminiscence.

governor of the town, and its worthy mayor, Thiqat al-Mulk Abū'l-Dhuwād Mufarrij b. al-Hasan ibn al-Sūfī, had displayed the utmost zeal in urging on the destruction of the abominable sectaries. They adopted in consequence elaborate precautions against the sudden onslaught of emissaries who might be sent against them from the Bātinīya of Alamūt, the centre of the Bātinīya,[1] by wearing iron and surrounding themselves with large numbers of guards carrying quantities of weapons ready for action. So disaster came upon the evildoers and rejectors of God, and felicity to the upright and heedful of admonition.

As for Ismā 'īl the missioner, who was living at Bānyās, and those who were with him, when they heard the report of this disaster, they were filled with despair and humiliation and began to lay the blame upon one another, while their supporters dispersed throughout the country. Ismā 'īl himself, knowing that disaster threatened him if he remained at Bānyās and being unable to put up an obstinate resistance, sent to the Franks, promising to deliver up Bānyās to them, in order to seek safety with them. He surrendered it to them accordingly, and he with a number of others came into their hands and slunk away from Bānyās into the Frankish territories in the utmost abasement and wretchedness. Ismā 'īl was smitten by the disease of diarrhœa, and dying of it was buried in Bānyās at the beginning of the year 524. So

---

[1] The castle of Alamūt (" Eagle's Nest ") in the mountain region, N.E. of Qazwīn (Kasvin), in North-Western Persia, which was seized by the founder of the Batini sect, Hasan-i Sabbāh, in 1090, and remained the mother-convent of the order until its destruction by the Mongols. (See the *Geographical Journal* for January, 1931.)

this district was rid of them and purified from their uncleanness.

A.H. 523

(25th December, 1128, *to* 14*th December,* 1129)

An account of the defeat of the Bātinīs and of matters relating to other persons during the years 22 and 23 has already been given, as required by the sequence of the narrative.   When the Franks heard the news of the disaster among the Bātinīs and the transference of Bānyās from them into their own hands, it stirred up in them a covetous desire for Damascus and its provinces.   After much talk about marching on it, they sent out their envoys to the districts to gather the men-at-arms and call up their levies, and all who were in their territories of al-Ruhā, Antioch, Tarābulus, and the coast-lands assembled to join them.   They were reinforced also from sea by the king Count,[1] he who took the place of Baldwin amongst the Franks when he died, having with him a vast host.   Having joined forces they halted at Bānyās, where they established a camp and set out to collect supplies and provisions for their stay.   Reports of their movements were brought by a number of persons who had seen them, and their numbers were reckoned to exceed sixty thousand horse and foot, the majority being footsoldiers.

When Tāj al-Mulūk learned of their resolution, he made preparations to deal with it and turned his attention to laying in large stocks of equipment,

---

[1] Fulk, Count of Anjou, and the new force of Knights of the Temple.

arms, war stores and appliances which were required in order to overcome all difficulties. He
sent letters to the amīrs of the Turkmens by the
hands of envoys who were specially deputed to
ask them for reinforcement and aid, and he
promised such an amount of money and grain as
moved them to hasten to answer his summons.
He was joined by all the men of valour and might
in battle from their various tribes, eager to perform the obligation of Holy War and hastening
to raid the infidel antagonists, and he hastened to
deliver to them what they required for their food
and fodder for their horses.

The accursed ones set out from Bānyās, advancing slowly and in battle order towards Damascus.
On the ————¹ of Dhu'l-Qa 'da 523 (16th
October to 14th November), they halted at
the Wooden Bridge ² and the famous plain
adjacent thereto, and encamped there. The 'askar
had that morning moved out of Damascus, and
had been joined by the Turkmens from their
encampments around the city and by the amīr
Murra b. Rabī 'a with his Arab auxiliaries. They
broke up into squadrons [which surrounded the
Franks] on all sides and took up positions facing
them, in the hope that a detachment of the
Franks might come out [against them] when they
would hasten to advance upon them and meet
them in battle. But not a knight of them came
out, nor did a single footsoldier appear ; on the
contrary they drew in their flanks and remained
fast in their camp. The Muslims stayed in this

¹ Blank in the text.
² Near Darayya, about six miles S.W. of Damascus.

position for several days, expecting them to advance towards the city, but nothing was to be seen of them save their assembling, their perambulation round their camp, and the glitter of their helmets and weapons. Enquiries were made as to what they were doing and what it was that delayed their advance and caused them to remain stationary. It was said that they had dispatched the bravest of their cavalry and stoutest of their footsoldiers to Hawrān with mules to collect such provisions and corn as were required for a long stay and a siege, and that they could not move nor had they any strength until the return of these persons.

On hearing of this state of affairs Tāj al-Mulūk made haste to detail a detachment consisting of the doughtiest of the Turks of Damascus, with his Turkmen allies and the Arabs who had come with the amīr Murra, to whom he added the amīr Saif al-Dawla Sawār with the 'askar of Hamāh, and instructed them to set out at the close of the same day, to march with all speed through the night and reach in the morning the district of Burāq,[1] for it was estimated that the accursed ones would then have reached that place on their way back from Hawrān. They hastened to carry out his instructions, and by daybreak were at their destination in overwhelming force, for they had with them the entire train of their 'askar, consisting of an innumerable body. The Muslims at once opened an attack upon the Franks, many of whom were killed by arrows before they could complete their mounting. Thereupon they formed battle-ranks

---

[1] At the northern edge of the Lejā, about 25 miles S. of Damascus.

and stood in a solid phalanx. The Muslims charged upon them, but they held their ground, until, when the army of Islām had repeatedly returned to the attack and made great slaughter amongst them, they became discouraged and lost heart and were convinced of their doom. Their leader and hero Guillaume [1] turned and fled with a party of knights, whereupon the Turks and Arabs made a mighty assault and surrounded the remainder with blows of swords and thrusts of lances and showers of arrows, and ere more than a part of the day had gone they were prostrate upon the ground and befouled with dust beneath the horses' feet. The victors took from them a spoil with which their hands were filled, consisting of horses, arms, prisoners, men-at-arms, and mules of all sorts, in quantity beyond reckoning. None of them escaped to their camp except the few knights whose fleet and well-conditioned horses carried them to safety. The Turks and Arabs returned to Damascus at the close of the same day victorious, booty-laden and rejoicing.

The people were overjoyed at this felicitous day and noble victory and their spirits were raised and their breasts dilated. The 'askar determined to deliver an assault upon their camp early upon the following morning as soon as all the units arrived. A strong body of horsemen went forward to open the attack upon them, thinking as they saw the multitude of fires and the smoke rising in the air, that they were still occupying the camp. But when they approached it, they found that the Franks had retired at the close of that night, when the

---

[1] *Kilyām Dabūr* (i.e., the Constable Guillaume de Bures).

news [of the disaster at Burāq] reached them.
They had burned their baggage, their train, their
equipment and their weapons, since they had no
animals left on which to load them, when they
realized that the position was now such that they
could not possibly hold on, knowing as they did
that the Turkish troops far outnumbered them and
that they were too weak to withstand their attack,
so they had no choice but to retire, neither turning
aside for isolated units nor stopping for stragglers.
The troops went out to their camp and gained an
immense quantity of their furnishings and provisions as booty. They found also a number of the
wounded in the battle, who were dead when they
entered and were buried in their places, while their
horses were prostrate with numerous wounds.
The rearguard of the fugitives was overtaken by
the 'askar, who killed a number of persons separated from the main body. The Franks pressed on
their retreat with the utmost speed for fear lest
the Muslims should overtake them. Then the
people felt secure and went out [of Damascus] to
their farms, and dispersed to their own abodes and
places of work, freed from sorrow and anxiety,
and visited by unlooked-for and undreamt-of
mercy and goodness from God—to Him be praise
and thanks for this abounding favour and perfect
gift, such as will make the flow of His benefits
perennial and call forth an increase of His bestow-
als and appointments.

The Turkmens returned to their abodes with
copious spoils and rich robes of honour, while the
host of the infidels dispersed to their castles in the
most abject state of abasement and loss of horses,

of baggage, and of stout-hearted warriors. So
the hearts of the Muslims were relieved from terror,
and restored to security after fear, and all men felt
assured that after this disaster it were scarcely
possible for the infidels to assemble in full force,
so many of their knights had perished, such
numbers of their men were destroyed, and so much
of their baggage lost.

A.H. 524

(15th December, 1129, to 3rd December, 1130)

In this year, news was received of the arrival at
Aleppo of the amīr 'Imād al-Dīn Atābek Zangī
son of Āq-Sunqur, lord of Mosul, together with
his 'askar, with the determination to prosecute
the Holy War. He wrote to Tāj al-Mulūk Būrī
son of Zahīr al-Dīn Atābek, requesting his assistance and aid in the conflict with his Frankish
adversaries, and messengers went to and fro
between them in regard to this matter, until Tāj
al-Mulūk agreed to his request, and dispatched an
officer to him to swear him to loyalty and friendship and bind him by oaths to observe his engagement and have confidence in the good faith [of
Tāj al-Mulūk]. Having obtained the amīr Zangī's
confirmation of this promise with binding guaran-
tees in which he could trust with tranquillity of
mind, he at once detached the principal officers
of his 'askar with a body of five hundred horsemen,
and wrote to his son Bahā al-Dīn Sawinj at Hamāh,
instructing him to set out with his 'askar, and join
the 'askar of Damascus, which was commanded by

the amīr Shams al-Umarā al-Khawāss with a number of amīrs and officers. Sawinj, in accordance with his instructions, quitted Hamāh with his men-at-arms and full war equipment, and the joint forces proceeded together to the camp of 'Imād al-Dīn Atābek. He received them with honour, and treated them with the utmost liberality, but after neglecting them for some days he perfidiously plotted against them, arrested Sawinj b. Tāj al-Mulūk and a number of the officers, and plundered their tents, baggage, and animals. Some of them escaped by flight, and the Atābek placed the remainder in confinement, had them carried to Aleppo, and ordered them to be detained there.

On the same day he marched to Hamāh, which was stripped of its garrison, and took possession of it and all that was in it. Thence he marched to Hims, the lord of which, Khīr-khān b. Qarāja, was accompanying him with his 'askar, devoted to his service, and obedient to his commands. It was he indeed who had supported him and instigated him in his treachery towards and seizure of Sawinj ————¹ [and 'Imād al-Dīn seized him] when he encamped before it, in rank treachery towards Khīr-Khān, its lord, and having imprisoned him, plundered his tents and baggage, and put him in chains, he demanded that Hims should be surrendered to him. Khīr-Khān wrote to this effect to his lieutenants in the city and to his son, but they paid no heed to his letter and refused to consent

¹ Some words have been omitted owing to haplography on the part of the copyist (waqabdihi . . . waqabadahu): cf. Sibṭ in R.H.C. III, 569.

to his request. The Atābek remained before the city for a long time, engaging its defenders and prosecuting the siege with the utmost vigour, but he was unable to gratify his desire for it or to achieve his object. He set out thence towards Mosul, taking with him Sawinj b. Tāj al-Mulūk and the officers of the 'askar of Damascus, and kept the remainder in confinement at Aleppo. A correspondence ensued in regard to the liberation of the prisoners, but the Atābek refused [to release them] and demanded a ransom of fifty thousand dinars for them, which Tāj al-Mulūk consented to find and to pay.

A.H. 525

(4th December, 1130, to 22nd November, 1131)

When the news of the disaster and destruction which God had decreed for and caused to light upon the Bātinīya reached their fellows at Alamūt, they were filled with sorrow for them and distress at what had befallen them, and set about spreading the nets of their wickedness and setting the snares of their foul perfidy and deceit. They deputed emissaries from amongst the ignorant members of their brotherhood and their murderous gang to seize Tāj al-Mulūk unawares and assassinate him, and their choice fell upon two simpletons from Khurāsān, to whom they gave instructions to devise some means of gaining access to Tāj al-Mulūk and to kill him in his palace when an opportunity should offer. These two men reached

Damascus in the guise of Turks, wearing the *qaba* and the *sharbush* (high triangular cap), and made their way to some acquaintances of theirs amongst the Turks, whose good offices they asked to enable them to enter the employment [of the amīr] and have a regular salary assigned to them. Having thus deceived them—for the Turks had no suspicion of their purpose—they gradually progressed by insinuation and deceit until they found a place in the body of Khurasanian troops organized as a cortege for the protection of Tāj al-Mulūk. They were regularly employed in this service, and were thought to be completely trustworthy, since they had been guaranteed. They watched for an opportunity to strike down Tāj al-Mulūk until, on Thursday 5th Latter Jumādā 525 (7th May, 1131), when he had been to the bath and come back, and had reached the gate of his palace in the citadel of Damascus, all the members of his cortege, Khurasanians, Dailamites, and gens-d'armes, who were guarding him dispersed and left him, and they leapt upon him. One of them struck him with a sword, aiming at his head, but only dealt him a wound in the neck which did not penetrate into it, and [the other] struck him in the flank with a knife, the blade passing between the flesh and the skin. Tāj al-Mulūk at once threw himself from his horse, and escaped with his life, while the men-at-arms mustered in increasing numbers against the two assassins and hacked them to pieces with swords. Physicians and surgeons skilled in curing wounds were sent for, and both wounds were treated. One of them, that at his head, healed, but that in his flank formed a running sore. Thereupon normal conditions were restored and he rode out again, and for some time he kept up the usual custom of receiving the high officers, 'askarīs, and troops in his audience hall to present their salutations and to drink.

In this year also the report was brought from the village of Maktūm b. Hassān b. Mismār, that the amīr Dubais b. Sadaqa b. Mazyad [1] had arrived before the village, having fled from al-'Irāq with his household officers and ghulāms in fear of the Caliph al-Mustarshid billāh, Commander of the Faithful. He had lost his way, since he had with him no guide familiar with the roads and waterpoints. The object of his journey was the village of Mirā b. Rabī 'a,[2] but most of those who were with him had perished, and after a number had died of thirst his party broke up, and he had arrived in this village [of Maktūm] like a solitary wanderer with but a few of his companions. Tāj al-Mulūk dispatched a troop of horsemen thither to fetch him, and they brought him to the citadel at Damascus on the night of Monday 6th Sha 'bān 525 (6th July, 1131). He gave orders that he should be lodged in an apartment in the citadel and shown honour and respect, and that he should be given food and drink of refined and exquisite kinds ; he sent him also such clothing and appointments as befitted his rank and his dignity, and kept him confined in honourable, not dishonouring, confinement. He transmitted a report of these events to the Noble Court of the

---

[1] See above p. 76 n. 1.
[2] The chief of the Tayy Arabs, see above p. 130.

Caliph al-Mustarshid, and received a reply bidding him secure his person and take precautions against his escape pending the arrival of an officer to take him into custody and conduct him to Baghdād.

When 'Imād al-Dīn Atābek Zankī, lord of Mosul, learned of this, he dispatched an envoy to Tāj al-Mulūk, requesting him to deliver up Dubais to him, for which he would remit in return the fifty thousand dinars fixed for the ransom of his son Sawinj and the rest of the troops of Damascus who were kept in detention. Tāj al-Mulūk having given his assent to this, an agreement was reached upon the terms proposed. It was further agreed that the 'askar of 'Imād al-Dīn should proceed to the district of Qārā,[1] bringing with him the prisoners, that the amīr Dubais should be sent thither also with the 'askar of Damascus, and that when the latter received the prisoners they would surrender Dubais to Zankī's officers. They set out with him from Damascus accordingly and brought him to Qārā, and having received the prisoners from 'Imād al-Dīn's 'askar handed over Dubais to them on Thursday 8th Dhu'l-Qa'da of this year (2nd October, 1131). Each of the 'askars returned to its own quarters, and Sawinj with the rest of the party arrived at Damascus, to the joy and relief of Tāj al-Mulūk.

In this year the report arrived from Sarkhad of the death of its governor, Fakhr al-Dawla Gumushtagīn, the freedman of Tāj al-Mulūk, in Latter Jumādā (May). He was upright in conduct, enjoyed a good reputation, and was assiduous in

---

[1] A large village on the Damascus–*Hims* road, to the north of Nebk.

religious exercises, and loyal in observance of his duties.[1]

In Dhu'l-Qa 'da (September to October) of the same year Sadīd al-Dawla Ibn al-Anbārī, the secretary of the Caliph al-Mustarshid billah, Commander of the Faithful, arrived [at Damascus] as an envoy from him to treat of various matters which had necessitated his coming, and also to press for the surrender of the amīr Dubais to the officer who was to conduct him to Baghdād. Although it was too late for that, Tāj al-Mulūk entertained him honourably and was rejoiced at his arrival. Having accomplished the objects of his mission, and been presented with the gifts due to his rank and station, the envoy set out to return to Baghdād. On the way he was encountered in the neighbourhood of al-Rahba by the cavalry of the amīr 'Imād al-Dīn, who seized him, plundered all his baggage, and killed some of his guards. He suffered great hardships from imprisonment and ill-usage before he was freed and returned to Baghdād.

On Thursday 26th [2] Latter Jumādā of this year (28th May), Tāj al-Mulūk assembled a company of the amīrs, officers, courtiers, leaders of the troops, secretaries, jurists, and principal citizens in his audience-chamber, and having announced to them his premonitions of his approaching death, as the result of his wound, proposed as his successor

---

[1] lit. " praiseworthy in his aims."
[2] The reading in the text (" three nights past ") must be corrected to " three nights remaining," see above p. 203.

his eldest son Abu'l-Fath Ismā 'īl.[1] They replied "The command is thy command, which is not disobeyed nor discarded, and the decision thy decision ; it is not for us to depart therefrom. Our obedience to thee in thy life is as our obedience to thy son after thy death. May God give thee extension of years and graciously bestow upon thee fulness of health and hasten thy recovery." He was gladdened by their words and thanked them for these sentiments which bore witness to the nobility of their character. Thereupon he formally designated his son as his successor, and exacted a promise from them to act in obedience to him and carry out his commands, and bestowed upon him magnificent robes of honour, befitting one in his lofty station. On the same day the prince rode in these robes to his residence in the citadel in great pomp and state, in the midst of the amīrs, commanders, Khurasanian troops, ghulāms, armour-bearers, mace-bearers and heralds.[2] Their pleasure and joy were thereby redoubled and all the troops inclined towards him, and were assiduous in paying service and presenting their greetings to him every day.

A.H. 526

(23rd November, 1131, to 11th November, 1132)

In this year the news arrived from the quarter of the Franks of the death at 'Akkā, on Thursday

[1] This is the substance of his address, which is given in full in the text.
[2] *maqra 'dārīya wa jāwushīya.*

25th Ramadān, of Baldwin the Little, king of the Franks and lord of Jerusalem.[1] He was an old man whom time had worn down[2] with its hardships, and who had suffered many rigours of fortune from its vicissitudes and calamities. On many occasions he fell into the hands of the Muslims as a prisoner, in times both of war and of peace, but he always escaped from them through his famous devices and historic stratagems. After him there was none left amongst them possessed of sound judgment and capacity to govern. His place was taken after him by the new Count-King, the Comte d'Anjou,[3] who came to them by sea from their country, but he was not sound in his judgment nor was he successful in his administration, so that by the loss of Baldwin they were thrown into confusion and discordance.

In this year also the illness of Tāj al-Mulūk caused by his wound became aggravated and his recovery was despaired of. It dragged on until he grew weary of life and longed for death ; his weakness and the wastage of his body and strength increased, his end drew nigh, and his hopes of restored health were disappointed. He was called to the forgiving mercy and indulgence of God after the passage of one hour of the day of Monday 21st Rajab of this year (6th June, 1132), and all hearts were filled with sorrow at his loss

---

[1] This is obviously placed under the wrong year. 25th Ramadān was a Thursday in 525 = 20th August, 1131, in 526 it was a Monday or Tuesday = 8th or 9th August, 1132.
[2] or " had rendered experienced " ('arakahu).
[3] The text has al-Kund Ayjūr or Anjūr, which apparently stands for this title.

and all eyes with tears at the fate which had
befallen him.

> When death with claw-like nails
> Strikes at her prey, no amulet avails.

PART II

THE REIGN OF SHAMS AL-MULUK ABU'L-FATH ISMA 'IL SON OF TAJ AL-MULUK BURI SON OF ZAHIR AL-DIN ATABEK

When the amīr Tāj al-Mulūk Būrī, son of the Atābek (God's mercy upon him), passed in bliss from this transient world to the everlasting abode, bearing an honoured name and the glory of martyrdom, and his son Shams al-Mulūk Abu'l-Fath Ismā 'īl ruled in his stead, according to the testament made in his favour by Tāj al-Mulūk before his death, he showed himself beneficent in his rule and his conduct and single-minded in his actions and secret motives. He spread abroad justice amongst his subjects and multiplied his gifts to all the troops and 'askarīs. He confirmed the fief-holders in possession of their lands, and the recipients of state-pensions in their appointments, and increased the distribution of largesse. He confirmed his father's wazīr in the wazirate, and maintained the cadres of governors and officials as they were. He gave the decision and control of affairs into the hands of the chamberlain Yūsuf b. Fīrūz, the military governor of Damascus, and relied upon him in all matters of importance, and showed complete confidence in him both openly and in secret. His first act of government was to give attention to the conditions of his subjects and of the artisans and husbandmen. He relieved them of the quotas of the tax called *fai'a* which had been exacted from them annually, abolished the practice and forbade it to be levied, recompensing from other sources those whose pensions were charged to this head of revenue. This was in Rajab 526 (beg. 18th May, 1132), and in all parts of his dominions men praised him and blessed his name. He displayed also a gallantry, vigour, courage, boldness, and resolution, which none had ever imagined him to possess, and the instances of this which we shall relate in due course will by their vividness dispense with the necessity of description.

An example of this was afforded in the first place by his capture of the castles of al-Labwa and al-Ra's,[1] which had been in the hands of officers who were deputed to hold them on behalf of his father Tāj al-Mulūk and whom he had confirmed in their appointments.

Shams al-Mulūk received information that his brother, Shams al-Dawla Muhammad, lord of Ba 'albek, had taken measures against them and having forced them to surrender these castles to his authority, had sent confidential officers and governors of his own staff and choosing to hold them [on his behalf]. Shams al-Mulūk, displeased and exasperated at such an action directed against

---

[1] Labwa (Lebona) and Ra's Ba 'labakk (" the Source of Ba 'albek," i.e., of the river Orontes), both in the Biqā', to the N. of Ba 'albek.

himself, wrote to his brother, rebuking him in friendly terms, pointing out the folly of adopting such an attitude, and requesting him to abandon his pretensions to [1] the two castles and restore them to their former condition. His brother refused to consent to this demand. Shams al-Mulūk then paid no further heed to the matter, not even referring to it in speech, for a long time, but nevertheless made all preparations for delivering an attack upon the two castles, though no one was aware of his determination or the object which he was seeking. When at length he set out from Damascus with the 'askar and war equipment, in Dhu'l-Qa 'da (beg. 13th September, 1132) of this year [526], he let it be thought that he was going north, but he subsequently turned back along another road and made westwards instead of eastwards. Before the garrison of the castle of Labwa were aware of his approach, he had encamped before it and immediately delivered an assault with a decision and vigour which could not be resisted. The governor, foreseeing defeat as the inevitable end of such violent fighting, and aware that under no circumstances could he count upon a deliverer, sent on the same day to ask for quarter. His request was granted and his hopes fulfilled, whereupon he issued from the castle and surrendered it to Shams al-Mulūk, who put a garrison in it and appointed an officer on whose ability and energy he could rely to hold it. As soon as he had finished at Labwa he marched to the castle of al-Ra's, whose governor acted in

---

[1] The text has *an-nuzula 'alaihimā*, " to besiege them," but *'alaihimā* is probably an error for *'anhumā*.

precisely the same way, so that he took possession of it also and appointed a governor to hold it.

He marched thence and encamped before Ba'albek, whose lord, his brother, had made preparations and called up levies, and had in addition the support of a great host of peasants from the Biqā' and the mountains, as well as other bands of ravaging brigands. He besieged and blockaded them in the city and assaulted them with his horse and foot. The fighting men in Ba'albek came out against him in a body, and some were killed and a great many were wounded, as well as many of those on the wall. A few days later he made a vigorous attack on the outer town, which they had filled with men, distributing the 'askar around it so as to make the assault from all sides at once. He thus captured it and the 'askar occupied it after the greater number of those who were in it were killed and wounded. He now set up catapults against the city and the castle, and made persistent assaults upon them. When the lord of the city saw the vigour of his action and that he was set upon remaining there and prosecuting his attack, he sent a message promising obedience and loyalty, and asking that he might be confirmed in the possession of what he had enjoyed in the days of his father. Shams al-Mulūk, moved by brotherly affection to bear with what had happened and to overlook the past, consented to his petition and graciously granted him what he had requested. A settlement was reached between them on this footing, and Shams al-Mulūk returned with the 'askar to Damascus joyful and victorious at the beginning of Muharram (middle of November).[1]

A.H. 527

(12th November, 1132, to 31st October, 1133.)

In Muharram reports were received from the quarter of the Franks that a dispute had arisen amongst them—though a thing of this kind was not usual with them—and fighting had taken place between them, in which a number of them were killed.

In the same year a force of Turkmens encountered the lord of Zaradnā with his cavalry, and defeated him, killed him and those with him, and seized all their horses and animals. It is said too that Ibn Dānishmand [2] defeated and destroyed a considerable party which had come out of Constantinople, and killed the Greeks and others who composed it.

On 17th Latter Jumādā (25th April, 1133), the amīr Sawār made a raid with his horsemen from Aleppo upon Tell Bāshir. The Frankish knights who were in the city came out to meet him, and about a thousand of them, horse and foot, were killed and their heads taken to Aleppo.

When Shams al-Mulūk returned from Ba 'albek, after coming to the settlement with his brother, its lord, as related above, there reached him from the quarter of the Franks information regarding their

---

[1] The text adds " of this year."   [2] See above p. 50 n. 1.

evil intentions and their determination to violate the treaty established by mutual agreement. Certain of the merchants of Damascus complained to him that the lord of Bairūt had seized from them a number of bales of linen to the value of a considerable sum of money. He wrote therefore to the commandant of the Franks, requesting them to return them to their owners and restore them to those who had most right to them, but notwithstanding a prolonged interchange of letters on the subject, they failed to produce what he desired. Anger and resentment bade him retaliate for this act by the like, but he concealed it within himself, and revealing his purpose to none of his household officers or intimate courtiers, turned his attention and determination to making preparations to besiege Bānyās and to snatch it from the hands of the accursed ones who had seized possession of it. He set out thither towards the end of Muharram of this year, and having encamped before it on Sunday 1st Safar (11th December), led the 'askar in an assault upon it. It was garrisoned by a considerable body of horsemen and footsoldiers, but they were filled with alarm when he came upon them thus suddenly, and became downcast and disheartened. He approached their wall with vaulted shields,[1] accompanied by the Khurasanians[2] and wall-breakers, and at the moment when he dismounted from his horse the Turks likewise dismounted in a body, and discharged a hail of arrows at the defenders upon the wall. These concealed themselves, and not a man of them

---

[1] ad-daraq al-jafatiyāt.
[2] i.e., sappers; cf. Usāma (ed. Hitti) p. 73, trans. p. 102.

showed his head upon it again because of the multitude of archers. Shams al-Mulūk then fixed the vaulted shields against a part of the wall which he had seen to be weak, and the tunnellers bored there until they pierced right through the wall, when they rushed through the breach and entered the town in ever-increasing numbers. The Franks who were in the town took refuge in the citadel and the bastions, where they defended themselves and resisted all assaults. Meanwhile, Shams al-Mulūk took possession of the town, opened the gate, and killed or took captive every Frank who was encountered in it. When the troops who had fled to the citadel and the bastions saw what had befallen them, that the town was captured and that they themselves were objects of attack, and that there was none to help them or to hinder the enemy from attacking them, they asked for quarter, and on their request being granted surrendered and were all made prisoners. Shams al-Mulūk, having sacked the town and established in it a garrison of valiant men to defend and protect it, set off from it with the 'askar, carrying the prisoners and the heads of the slain, the women-folk and children of the former governor, and much war equipment, and reached Damascus on Thursday 6th Safar of this year.[1] The people came out of the city to meet him and to gaze at the quantities of prisoners in ropes and of heads on lances. The spectacle refreshed their eyes and rejoiced their hearts and strengthened their loins, and they were gladdened by it and gave abundant

[1] An error has crept into this date, which must be either Thursday 5th or Friday 6th Safar (15th or 16th December).

thanks to God Most High for this glorious victory and striking success which He had vouchsafed. The report of it spread amongst the Franks and filled them with awe and alarm that such a thing should have happened. Their hearts were filled with fear and terror, and they were greatly astonished that Bānyās should have been taken with such ease and in so short a time in spite of the strength of its fortifications and the number of its defenders ; they grieved also over those of the knightly horsemen and footsoldiers who had been killed.

In this year, Shams al-Mulūk Ismā 'īl determined to make for Hamāh in order to besiege it and recover possession of it from the hands of those who had seized it. He had concealed this design from all, and set about making preparations towards it and for the march thither, but news of his determination came to the ears of its commander, who displayed the utmost energy in strengthening its fortifications and preparing to defend it, and made ready for that purpose all the requisite equipment. The report of this was brought to Shams al-Mulūk, but he took no account of all this activity and was not deflected from his design. On the contrary, he moved out during the last ten days of the month of Ramadān of the year 27 (end of July, 1133). There was not one of the principal amīrs and courtiers but advised him not to make this movement and sought to restrain him from it, but he paid no heed to what anyone said nor was he ever heard to answer any speech. He was urged to postpone the march until the conclusion of the fast of the latter days, but few in number, of the blessed month [1] and the celebration of the feast [at the close of it], and to set out to his objective thereafter. But he would not hearken to this advice from any one nor act according to the counsel of any man, and held fast to the project of marching on it when its population and garrison would be off their guard, secure in the belief that no one would move during these days but would wait until after the feast, when the troops had finished holiday-making. Thereupon he set out at once on the march thither, and by moving with speed encamped before it and made an assault upon its inhabitants on the feast day itself (1st Shawwāl = 5th August). They were terror-stricken at the disaster which threatened them, and when he straightway advanced against them with a considerable and fully-armed force, they defended themselves in the alleys and buildings and bravely faced the hail of arrows. That day the 'askar returned [to its camp] after inflicting severe losses upon them in killed and wounded and in plunder and booty. Next day Shams al-Mulūk opened the attack upon them in the early morning with both horse and foot, and having distributed them around the city [so as to engage the defenders simultaneously] from all sides, he led the assault with his personal guard of Turkish ghulāms and a considerable force of foot-soldiers and horsemen. He selected a weak spot in the defences of Hamāh, and directing himself towards it, aimed at forcing his way into the city

[1] The month of Ramaḍān is observed annually as a fast by all Muhammadans.

through it. The vigour of his attacks upon the men and archers who were defending the place drove them off before him and he forced an entrance in person at that point. The citizens took refuge in asking for quarter and a body of the garrison came to him offering to surrender if their lives were spared. He not only spared them, but bestowed robes of honour and gifts upon them. He also made proclamation that none should lay hands upon them, and forbade any molestation of the citizens and restored what had been plundered from them. The greater number of troops in the citadel came out to him in consequence to beg for quarter, and he bestowed robes upon them and spared them also. When the governor saw this and realized his powerlessness to hold out against him, he too begged that he would guarantee him safety, and Shams al-Mulūk gave him his promise. The governor then surrendered the citadel with all that it contained to him, so that it fell into his hands along with the city with the greatest ease and in the shortest time. Having furnished it with a garrison under the command of a trust-worthy and reliable governor, he set out thence and made towards Shaizar, and encamping before it gave orders to devastate and lay waste its neigh-bourhood. He remained in this position until he was conciliated, and his goodwill won over by what was brought to him, when he set out to return to Damascus, into which he entered joyful and triumphant in Dhu'l-Qa'da of this year (September, 1133).

In this year the amīr al-Muntadī Abu'l-Fawāris

Waththāb b. Musāfir al-Ghanawī arrived on a mission from Egypt, on Saturday 26th Dhu'l-Qa 'da (30th September), with the reply to a letter emanating from Shams al-Mulūk. He presented the gifts which he had brought with him, magnificent robes, chests of Egyptian stuffs, horses and a sum of money, and the letter which had come by his hand was read. He remained at Damascus until all was made ready for his journey, and set out to return to Egypt on Saturday 28th First Rabī' of the year 28 (27th January, 1134).

In Dhu'l-Hijja (October) news was received of the arrival of a considerable military force of the Turkmens in the northern district, and that they had made raids upon Tarābulus and the Frankish castles in its provinces, had killed and taken captive a great host of the Franks and acquired a vast quantity of booty and animals. It was said that the lord of Tarābulus, Pons, son of Bertram of St. Gilles,[1] came out against them with the forces which he mustered from his provinces and engaged the 'askar of the Turkmens, but they routed him, and God gave them the victory over his broken muster and forsaken assembly. The greater number of his men and the main body of his defenders and knights were killed, and he fled with a small party from the castle known as Ba 'rin [2] and they took refuge in it and held out behind its walls. The army of the Turks [3] encamped before it and remained besieging it for so

---

[1] *Buns* (the text has *Bund*) *Talūlā ibn Badrān* a*s-Sanjīlī.*
[2] Mons Ferrandus, to the N. of Rafanīya.
[3] *al-Atrāk.*

long that the supplies of provisions and water in the castle were exhausted and the greater number of their men and horses perished. The Franks then devised a stratagem and seized an opportunity when the Turkmens were neglecting their watch to make their way out of the castle. Those who came out were about twenty men in all with their leader, and they made good their escape to Tarābulus. The king Pons (Talūlā), lord of Tarābulus, wrote to the king of the Franks at 'Akkā, imploring aid of him and of the Franks in his territories, and urging them to assist him. A great host of the Franks assembled to join him, and they marched against the Turkmens in order to make them raise the siege of Ba 'rin, and to rescue those of their own men who were still in it. The Turkmens, on learning of their determination and purpose, moved forward to meet them, slew a great number of them, and were on the point of inflicting a total disaster upon them had they not retired in a body to Rafanīya. Thereafter word was brought to them that the Franks had departed from there and were returning by the coast road, and in distress at this and sorrow at the booties which had escaped them, they separated to their own districts.

In Safar of this year, the lord of Jerusalem, king of the Franks, marched with his horsemen to the frontiers of the province of Aleppo and arrived at a place called Nawāz.[1] The amīr Sawār, who was [Zankī's] lieutenant in Aleppo, marched out against him with the 'askar of Aleppo and some

---

[1] S.W. of Athārib. The printed text has Nawār.

of the Turkmens, who joined his forces. The two armies met, and engaged in fighting and skirmishing until they came to the territory of Qinnasrīn, when the Franks made an attack upon the Muslims and drove them in a disastrous rout, in which they killed about a hundred of the Muslim horsemen, including several leaders of name and reputation. Of the Franks themselves more than that were killed. The routed army reached Aleppo, while the Franks continued their advance to Qinnasrīn and thence successively to al-Muqāwama and to Naqira.[1] The amīr Sawār again marched out against them from Aleppo with what remained of the ʿaskar and the Turks. They met a party of the Franks and fell upon them, drove them in flight, and killed of them about a hundred horsemen. The Franks withdrew defeated to their own lands and the Muslims returned with the heads of the slain and their prizes to Aleppo. Thus the sorrow of the first reverse was removed by the bestowal of the second favour. The king came to Antioch and news was brought to Sawār of the movement of the cavalry of al-Ruhā. On hearing this, he and Hassān al-Ba ʿlabekkī marched out, fell upon them in the north country, and exterminated them to the last man, and took captive all who came into their lands alive. Thereafter they returned to Aleppo, victorious and safe, bringing the prisoners and the heads.

[1] Naqira, one stage N. of Maʿarrat an-Nuʿmān. The text has *Naqira al-Ākharīn* (?)

A.H. 528

(1st November, 1133, to 21st October, 1134.)

In this year, Shams al-Mulūk Ismā'īl b. Tāj al-Mulūk marched out with his 'askar to Shaqīf Tīrūn, which is in the mountains overlooking the coastal zone of Bairūt and Sidon, and obtained possession of it on Friday 24th Muharram (24th November) seizing it from the hands of Dahhāk b. Jandal al-Tamīmī who had made himself master of it.

In this year also, Shams al-Mulūk went out in the latter part of First [1] Rabī' (end of January) to the hunting ground in the neighbourhood of Saidnāyā and 'Asāl.[2] On Tuesday 9th Second Rabī' (6th February), as he was separated from his guards and personal officers, one of the Turkish mamlūks of his grandfather Zahīr al-Dīn Atābek, named Ilbā, seizing the opportunity when they were alone together, rushed at him with his sword and aimed a terrible blow at him, intending to strike off his head. But God Most High decreed his safety and the sword fell from the mamluk's hand before he had accomplished anything. He at once threw himself to the ground and struck a second blow at the prince, which fell on the neck of his horse and dispatched it. The prince got between him and his horse and kept him until the guards came up to him in increasing numbers, when the man fled. He sent off a troop of horse-

---

[1] The text has "Second Rabī'," which conflicts with the date immediately following.
[2] 15 to 20 miles N. of Damascus.

men in pursuit of him, in order to track him down and seize him, and himself returned to the city. When the report of this occurrence spread abroad, there was some excitement and concern for him, but tranquillity was restored when he was seen to be safe and sound. The horsemen and guards who had been dispatched to pursue the assassin made a vigorous search for him in the mountains, high-ways, and paths, until they found him, and even then he wounded many of them by arrows before they captured him. When they brought him to Shams al-Mulūk, he put him to the question and asked him " What moved you to this action ? " He replied, " I did it solely to gain the favour of God Most High by slaying you and giving the people relief from you, for you have oppressed the poor and weak, the artisans, workers, and culti-vators, and have wronged both the troops and the civil population." He also mentioned the names of several innocent members of the guard whom he charged with complicity in this crime. The prince arrested them, included them in the charge with him, and had them all put to death at once in cold blood. The people blamed him for thus killing these guards on the bare word of this malefactor without the establishment of any proof or the production of any evidence. Even the unjust execution of these men did not satisfy him ; indeed he suspected his brother Sawinj b. Taj al-Mulūk and put him, though he was the elder brother of Sawinj, to a horrible death by starvation in a chamber. He went to excess in these evil and tyrannical actions and stopped at no limits.

In Dhu'l-Qa 'da of this year (began 23rd August, 1134), reports reached Shams al-Mulūk from the quarter of the Franks of their determination to break the terms of the armistice and denounce the friendly relations established between them, and of their preparations for assembling their forces and raiding and ravaging the provinces of Damascus. On receiving news of this Shams al-Mulūk began gathering his men-at-arms and summoned to his aid the Turkmens from all the provinces. Word was brought to him that the Franks had set out in the direction of Hawrān, whereupon he moved out with the 'askar and proceeding towards them, encamped over against them. The Franks set about devastating the principal cultivated estates of Hawrān, and some skirmishing took place between the two forces. Now the Franks had a host of horse and foot so vast that they besieged the Muslims in their camp, and neither horseman nor footsoldier could venture forth without being riddled with arrows and snatched to his death. This archery duel between the two sides had continued for some days, when Shams al-Mulūk threw them off their guard and marched out, unperceived by them, with a considerable body of the 'askar. Making for their towns of 'Akkā, Nazareth, and Tiberias and their environs, he seized an uncountable quantity of cattle, beasts of burden, women, children, and men, killing all whom he encountered, enslaving all who were in his path, burning everything that he found, and the hands of the Turkmens were filled with their booty. When the news of this reached the Franks, they were dismayed and disquieted, and they at once withdrew in disorder from their camp, making for their own territories. Shams al-Mulūk, learning of this, withdrew to his camp by way of al-Sha'rā,[1] himself and all his force unharmed, victorious and booty-laden. When the Franks reached their districts and saw what had happened to them and the disaster that had befallen their people, they were grieved, dispirited and dis-heartened, their unity was dissolved, and they were humbled and besought [Shams al-Mulūk for] the establishment of peace between them. Shams al-Mulūk returned joyfully to Damascus at the end of Dhu'l-Hijja of this year (middle of October).

In the same year news was received that the amīr 'Imād al-Dīn Atābek and the amīr Husām al-Dīn Timurtāsh, son of Il-Ghāzī b. Ortuq, had joined forces in an attack on the territories of Dā'ud b. Sukmān b. Ortuq. Dā'ud marched against them with his 'askar, and the two forces met at the gate of Āmid ; Dā'ud was put to flight, his 'askar scattered, several of his children cap-tured, and a number of his officers killed. This happened on Friday the last day of Latter Jumādā (27th April). 'Imād al-Dīn encamped before Āmid, besieged it, and cut down its trees, but he gained no success therefrom and withdrew. News was received also that 'Imād al-Dīn Atābek had encamped before the castle known as al-Sūr and had captured it after a siege in Rajab of this year (28th April–27th May). In this year too a succes-sion of reports was received from the neighbour-

---

[1] A common place-name in Syria ("the bush") ; here probably the district N. of Lake Huleh and Qunaiṭra.

hood of the amīr 'Imūd al-Dīn Atābek to the effect
that he had determined to make preparations for
an advance on the city of Damascus, in order to
besiege and blockade it, and that he was devoting
his attention to preparing for this purpose.

A.H. 529

(22nd October, 1134, to 10th October, 1135)

In this year reports spread among both the
officials and the general public in Damascus
concerning its lord, the amīr Shams al-Mulūk
Abu'l-Fath Ismā 'īl. It was said [1] that he went
to every excess in the indulgence of immorality
and in the doing of acts which, being prohibited
by religion, indicated the corruption of his
intelligence, his love of injustice, and the trans-
formation in his character from the impetuous zeal
for the interests of the Faith which formerly
marked him, and the eagerness to prosecute the
Holy War against the heretical foe. He set about
sequestrating the property of the officials and
governors, and bringing malignant and slanderous
charges against the employees in the provinces.
He took into his service a certain Kurd who came
to him from Hims known as Bertram the Infidel, a
man who was ignorant of Islām and its principles
and of the Faith and its tenets, and who disre-
garded without scruple every obligation undertaken towards any Muslim, and employed him to
extract the property of those officials and men of

[1] This paragraph has been abridged in translation.

reputable character who were made liable to confiscation, by evil methods of torture which he devised and various abominable forms of threatening and abusive language. In addition to this wicked way and outrageous behaviour, Shams al-Mulūk showed increasing avarice and a constant inclination towards low and unworthy actions, such as behaving in a hostile and tyrannical manner towards humble and contemptible persons. . . . Over and above these blameworthy actions and abhorrent qualities, he secretly proposed to confiscate the property of his confidential secretaries and of his domestic officers and personal attendants among the amīrs and chamberlains. He decided to make a beginning first of all with the chamberlain Saif al-Dawla Yūsuf b. Fīrūz,[1] who had enjoyed the highest esteem of his father formerly and of himself subsequently. His purpose became known, and Yūsuf b. Fīrūz fled from him to Tadmur, considering the greatest prize to lie in his distance from the prince's malevolence and relief from his supervision. In the midst of this disorder and disturbance, Shams al-Mulūk wrote to the amīr 'Imād al-Dīn Atābek, on learning of his determination to proceed to Damascus to undertake the siege and blockade of the city and of his desire to possess it, urging him to make haste to come thither in order that he might surrender the city to him of his own freewill and enable him to wreak vengeance upon all the commanders, amīrs and notables with whom he was displeased by

---

[1] The *Shihna* or military governor of Damascus. He had acquired Tadmur (Palmyra) as a fief from Tāj al-Mulūk and had strongly fortified and provisioned it, and fled thither on 1st Muḥarram of this year.

putting them to death, seizing their property, and expelling them from their dwellings. All this was due to some imaginary cause and some unbalanced design which he had conceived in his mind. He kept sending letters to him urging him to make all speed and to avoid lingering and delay, and would say to him in the course of such a parley " If there should chance in this matter any neglect, inadvertence, or delay, I shall be compelled to summon the Franks from their territories and shall surrender Damascus with all it contains to them, and the sin of the blood of its inhabitants shall be upon his [*i.e.*, 'Imād al-Dīn's] neck." He concealed this design, however, revealing it to none of his principal officers or courtiers, for his letters to this effect were written with his own hand. He also set about transferring money, vessels, and garments from his treasury to the castle of Sarkhad, until the entire contents had been removed thither, with the idea that he would turn it all to his own profit and put all his courtiers to death afterwards.

When this began to appear plainly and his secret motives became known, and he set about [1] arresting his officers, secretaries, and officials, as well as citizens of Damascus and intendants of estates,[2] the amīrs, commanders and leaders of the former guard of the atābek, together with all the 'askarīs and the citizens, were exasperated at his action and afraid of their own destruction should this objectionable plan succeed, knowing as they did what the conduct of 'Imād al-Dīn Atābek would be if he should capture the city. They

---

[1] Reading *washara 'a* for *shara 'a*.   [2] *muqaddamī 'ddiyā'*.

therefore discussed the matter between themselves and represented the situation regarding the prince to his mother, the Khātūn Safwat al-Mulk. She, in distress at this state of affairs and abhorrence of his action, summoned him and upbraided him in strong terms. Her benevolence, sound spirit of religion, and well-balanced intelligence moved her further to consider how this evil might be excised and the wellbeing of Damascus and its inhabitants restored. She therefore examined the position with a firm and prudent eye and sound judgment, and found no cure for the ill wrought by him save relief from him and the excision of the causes of the ever-augmenting disorder due to him. The leaders and chief officers of the guards advised her to this action, supported her judgment, and urged her to carry it out with all speed, before it should be divulged and the opportunity lost, adding that nothing was of any avail for him and no warning of any effect upon him. She turned her attention in consequence to the carrying out of her plan, and watched for an opportunity to present itself when he was alone. When at length the desired object was rendered possible at a moment when he was without his guards and armour-bearers, she ordered her guards to kill him without delay, showing neither mercy for him nor sorrow at his loss, because of his evil actions, the corruption of his mind, his vile conduct, and blame-worthy behaviour. She gave orders to carry out his body when he was killed and to lay it in a certain part of the palace in order that it might be seen by his guards. Everyone was rejoiced at his overthrow and pleased to be rid of him, and gave abundant thanks to God Most High for granting the opportunity whereby he was made away with, and multiplied blessings and praise upon her. This took place in the forenoon of Wednesday 14th Second Rabī' 529.[1]

Now the person known as Bertram the Infidel (may God curse him) had, on the Tuesday preceding the Wednesday on which the prince was killed, left his presence after he had secretly instructed him as to some evil which he should carry out for him. When he reached his home at noon on that day, God sent upon him a terrible disease which seized his breath, and his tongue swelled until it filled his mouth, and he perished forthwith. The other event followed on the next day, and all the people exerted themselves to the utmost in praising God Most High and thanking Him for this glorious sign and outstanding act of power.

Proclamation of allegiance was at once made to the brother of Shams al-Mulūk, the amīr Shihāb al-Dīn Mahmūd, son of Taj al-Mulūk b. Atābek. He sat in his brother's seat, in the presence of his mother, the Khātūn Safwāt al-Mulk, and the amīrs, chief representatives of the troops, and notables among the citizens presented themselves and saluted him with the amīrate. They were sworn to render obedience to him and to his mother, to be loyal in their service, to aid their partisans and strive against their enemies, and every man of

[1] The calendar date corresponding to this is Friday 1st February, 1135, but it is clear by comparison with the dates below that the Damascus reckoning was at least one day in advance of the astronomical calendar.

them took the oath in gladness of heart and fulness of hope. The joy manifested by all, both high and low, at this happy event and these laudable doings is beyond description, for they made sure of their escape from the dread which overshadowed them, and public affairs were set in order and hopes realized.

During this time a succession of letters was received from all parts with news of the advance of 'Imād al-Dīn with his 'askar and of his crossing of the Euphrates in all haste in order to receive possession of Damascus from its lord Shams al-Mulūk. His envoys arrived [shortly afterwards] in order to draw up the protocol of surrender,[1] only to find that the state of affairs was quite otherwise and the plan of action to the contrary. Nevertheless they were received with honour and respect, generously entertained, and sent back with a most polite and friendly letter in reply, and 'Imād al-Dīn was informed of the true facts of the case and of the unanimity of the population in the defence of the dynasty and protection of its inheritance, together with exhortations to show a friendly regard and return to an attitude of sincere sympathy.

When this reply reached him and he learned its contents, 'Imād al-Dīn refused to pay heed to it, lured on by the desire to possess himself of Damascus and imagining that the amīrs and leaders of the guards were divided by factional strife. Now the position was exactly contrary to what he imagined. He continued to prosecute his march and to hasten on his advance until he

---

[1] *litaqrīri 'l'amri.*

reached the outskirts of Damascus and encamped in the area extending from 'Adhrā' to al-Qusair[1] in the early part of First Jumādā 529 (began 16th February, 1135). Preparations to meet his attack had been actively made on receipt of the news of his determination. The outlying estates were abandoned in panic, and their population came into the city. Everything was in readiness to engage him in battle when he took up his siege positions, and all were united in the purpose of opposing him and driving him back. This situation of affairs remained unchanged and the firm stand made against him never relaxed in its temper. All minds were inspired through the greatness of their zeal and their resolution in combat with the desire to meet him in battle and to prepare themselves for his advance and approach to the city. Meanwhile he had moved from 'Adhrā' and encamped below the southern Pass.[2] Again and again he brought up his 'askar, which he had distributed between a number of points, like so many cavalcades,[3] until they were close to the city, when the sight of the multitudes who issued from the city, of the 'askars and town bands bristling with weapons, and of the Musallā and other places filled [with troops] and ambushes laid on all the roads, would inspire him with fear and deter him from making any further advance. Every day too a considerable number of deserters from his 'askar would come in on receiving promise of safety, in addition to [the losses which he

[1] About 10 miles N.E. of the city.
[2] al 'Aqaba al-qiblīya, see above p. 177 n. 1.
[3] Reading kalmawākibi for kalmarākibi (" like vessels "), unless the latter is used in the sense of the former.

suffered] by the plundering of their horses and seizure of booty from their horsemen.

When day after day went by and his efforts met with no result and his object was no nearer attainment, he sent an envoy to ask for peace and recognition of his suzerainty, and requested that the amīr Shihāb al-Dīn Mahmūd, son of Tāj al-Mulūk, should come out to his camp to pay homage to the Sultan's son, who had accompanied him, promising to bestow upon him robes of honour and to give him safe return to his city. He couched his letter to this effect in friendly language and made fair promises, but his request that Shihāb al-Dīn should go out was refused, and it was agreed that his brother Tāj al-Mulūk Bahrām-Shāh, son of Tāj al-Mulūk, should go out [in his place].

It happened at this juncture that the ra'īs Bishr b. Karīm b. Bishr arrived as an envoy from the Caliph al-Mustarshid Billāh, Commander of the Faithful, to 'Imād al-Dīn Atābek bearing robes of honour specially designated for him and an order to retire from Damascus and abandon all interference with it, and to come to al-'Irāq in order to take over its government and assume control over its affairs, and commanding also that the name of the Sultan Alp-Arslān who was living at Mosul, should be mentioned in the Khutba.[1] This envoy, with the qādī Bahā al-Dīn Ibn al-Shahrazūrī,

---

[1] See above p. 137 n. Alp-Arslān, the "Sultan's son," referred to in the preceding paragraph, was the son of Mughīth al-Dīn Mahmūd (reigned 1117-1131), and nephew of the reigning Sultan of 'Irāq, Ghiyāth al-Dīn Mas'ūd b. Muhammad (1133-1152). The Caliph Mustarshid was on the point of a quarrel (which cost him his life) with the Sultan Ghiyāth al-Dīn.

entered Damascus in order to draw up an agreement and see to the due observance of the order at the Friday service on 28th First Jumādā (15th March). An agreement was drawn up and the oaths were sworn, and the two envoys, after attending the cathedral mosque for the Friday prayer, when the Sultan Alp-Arslān was proclaimed from the pulpit by order of the Commander of the Faithful, returned to the Atābek's camp. Bahrām-Shāh went out and was received with honour by Zankī, and sent back with the utmost courtesy. The Atābek set off on his return journey on Saturday, the morrow of that day, and the fear felt in all hearts was replaced by security, all minds were restored to tranquillity after distress and panic, and unceasing gratitude and abundant praise were rendered to Him.

On his arrival at Hamāh the atābek became displeased with its governor, Shams al-Umarā al-Khawāss, on account of some action of his which came to his notice [1] and of the increasing volume of the complaints made by its inhabitants against his officers and representatives, and having removed him from his governorship appointed in his place another person of his own choice.

The amīr Shujā 'al-Dawla Bazwāj and the amīr Mu 'īn al-Dīn Unur both distinguished themselves during these operations by the capacity they had shown and the satisfactory way in which they had handled the regular troops and levies [of Damascus] during the dispositions for battle, and they were thanked and praised for their services.

[1] Reading *zahara* for *'azhara*.

A.H. 530

(*11th October, 1135, to 28th September, 1136*)

In the month of First Rabī' (began 9th December) the amīr Shihāb al-Dīn Mahmūd, son of Tāj al-Mulūk, received possession of the city and citadel of Hims.   When the sons of Khīr-Khān b. Qarāja, who were in Hims and its citadel, and Khumārtāsh, who governed it on their behalf, saw how the amīr 'Imād al-Dīn Atābek persisted in his siege of the city and with what energy he prosecuted his ambition to seize it and hold it, how he had taken the neighbouring town of Hamāh, and the vigour with which he attacked it, weakened its defenders, and directed constant raids against it, and when they realized that they were powerless to hold the city because of the scarcity of food and provisions in it, they sent envoys to Shihāb al-Dīn requesting him to dispatch an officer of his own choice to take possession of Hims and to give them in exchange for it whatsoever he might judge to be suitable.   The chamberlain Saif al-Dawla Yūsuf b. Fīrūz, who had undertaken to arrange this matter, from a desire to occupy Hims and transfer thither from Tadmur, since it is a well fortified place and a formidable fortress, acted as mediator and asked for permission to come to Damascus for discussion and the formulation of an agreement to this effect. Permission being granted to him, he came to Damascus and a prolonged interchange of views took place, leading to the conclusion that Hims and its fortress should be surrendered to Shihāb al-Dīn, and that Tadmur should be given up to Khumārtāsh in exchange for it. These conditions were endorsed and their observance secured by oath. Shihāb al-Dīn marched out of Damascus with the 'askar and proceeded thither. On his arrival Khumārtāsh, together with the sons and family of Khīr-Khān, evacuated the citadel with their possessions, and delivered it up to him. He took possession of it on Sunday 22nd First Rabī' 530 (29th December, 1135), occupied it, and established a garrison in it, entrusting the governorship of it to the chamberlain Yūsuf b. Fīrūz, on the understanding that his position in it was that of lieutenant of the amīr Mu'īn al-Dīn Unur al-Atābekī, as had been arranged. Shihāb al-Dīn also wrote to the various districts to dispatch foodstuffs to it and strengthen it with provisions, and after setting its affairs in order he returned to Damascus.

The amīr Sawār, lieutenant of 'Imād al-Dīn in Aleppo, and the atābek's governor in Hamāh set about making raids upon the districts and cornlands of Hims. In consequence of this an interchange of envoys and letters took place, which resulted in an armistice and the maintenance of amity and peaceful relations for a stated period, to such effect that the causes of conflict were eliminated and matters were set on a sound footing on both sides.

On Saturday 13th Sha'bān (16th May) reports arrived from the north that the amīr Mas'ūd Sawār had marched from Aleppo with a body of Turkmens who had joined him into the Frankish provinces, that they had taken possession of the greater part of them, and that their hands were filled with the spoils that they had gained. Confirmatory reports of this success were received from all quarters, magnifying and exaggerating it. A letter was received from Shaizar conveying the glad tidings of this event and giving an exact account of it, and its contents have therefore been set down in this place in order to confirm the report and corroborate the descriptions and accounts given of it. It ran as follows :

The latest news received by us in this neighbourhood is something which we are bound for the sake of the Faith to make known and to congratulate all Muslims upon. The Turkmens (God multiply them and succour them !) assembled to the number of three thousand horsemen, forming a fully-equipped force, and set out suddenly for the towns and districts of al-Lādhiqīya when they were not expected and little had been done to guard against their attack. They returned from this raid to Shaizar on Wednesday 11th Rajab (15th April), carrying with them more than seven thousand captives, men, women, boys and girls, and a hundred thousand head of livestock, consisting of cattle, sheep, goats, horses and asses. The area which they covered and devastated[1] exceeded a hundred villages large and small. They have been coming in successive batches,[2] and all Syria is filled with captives and beasts. Such a calamity as this has never befallen the northern Franks. Moreover not one prisoner amongst them will

---

[1] Read *ijtāhuhu* for *ihtājuhu*.   [2] *wahum mutawāsilūna.*

be sold except at his proper value, and no reduction will be made on the price first asked. They are taking them to Aleppo, Diyār Bakr, and the Jazīra.

At the close of the day on Wednesday 24th May,[1] there came up over Damascus black clouds which darkened the world, so that the day became like night. Thereafter there came up red clouds which lit up the world, so that those who saw them might imagine that they were burning fire. Prior to this a violent and tempestuous wind had sprung up which damaged many of the trees. It is said that at the same time and hour large hail and violent rains fell in Hawrān, so that the riverbeds ran with them, and during the night there was a great storm of rain bringing another fall of hail of such size as had never been seen.

A.H. 531

(29th September, 1136, to 18th September, 1137)

In this year news was received that Emanuel (?)[2] king of the Greeks, had emerged from Constantinople in Dhu'l-Qa'da of the year 30 (began 1st August) or, according to a contradictory report, on 1st Muharram 531. He reached the island of Antākiya (?) and remained there until his warships arrived with the heavy baggage, provisions, money,

---

[1] When he speaks of weather or crops, the author usually gives the date according to the Syrian (solar) calendar.

[2] The text has *Kiyālyānī*, which may perhaps be a copyist's perversion of *Imānyāl*.

and war-equipment on 10th April. He then besieged Nicæa and captured it (or, according to another account, its inhabitants came to terms with him) and advanced to the marches, where he gained possession of Adhana and al-Massīsa and other places, and forcibly captured 'Ain Zarba [1] after a siege. He captured also Tell Hamdūn, the lord of which was Ibn Haitham the Armenian, and removed its population to the island of Cyprus, then he restored the port of al-Iskandarīya (Alexandretta), and thence proceeded to Antioch and encamping before it blockaded its inhabitants at the end of Dhu'l-Qa 'da (middle of August). A reconciliation was effected between him and its lord, Raymond, son of ————,[2] and he set out to return to the Gates, and having captured all the castles that remained in the hands of the son of Leo the Armenian, he wintered there.

In Rajab of this year (began 25th March) the amīr Bazwāj marched with a considerable force of Turkmens from the 'askar of Damascus towards Tarābulus. Its Count came out to meet him with his army, and they engaged in battle. Bazwāj routed him and killed a considerable number of his men, and captured the castle of Wādī Ibn al-Ahmar amongst others.

In Rajab also Ibn Salāh, the governor of Hamāh, marched with his men-at-arms to the castle of al-Khariba[3] and captured it.

---

[1] Anazarbus of the Crusaders, afterwards Nawarza, between Sīs and al-Massīsa (Mamistra).

[2] The reading of this name is uncertain ; perhaps for *bīdafīn* = Poitevin (?), or the first part may be Kund = Comte, the latter part having been corrupted.

[3] See Dussaud, *Topographie*, 145-7.

In Sha 'ban (began 24th April) a report was received that 'Imād al-Dīn Atābek, son of Āq-Sunqur, had set out with his 'askar from Mosul and crossed the Euphrates during the first ten days of the month. He marched on Hims, preceded by Salāh al-Dīn with the advance-guard of the 'askar, and they encamped before it and besieged it. The governor, Mu 'īn al-Dīn Unur, who was in the town, on receiving his summons to surrender it, refused, on the ground that it belonged to the amīr Shihāb al-Dīn and that he was the latter's lieutenant in it. The Atābek thereupon opened hostilities against it and besieged it for some days, but his efforts were of no avail and he retired on 20th Shawwāl (11th July) and encamped before the castle called Ba 'rīn, in order to wrest it from the hands of the Franks. When they learned of this, they assembled their forces and encamped in the neighbourhood, in order to defend it and to support their men who were in it. 'Imād al-Dīn, on receiving news of their approach, laid an ambush for them. When the two armies met, a party of the Turks turned to flight before the Franks, and they killed a considerable number of them [1] on their return to the site of their encampment. 'Imād al-Dīn then came out upon them with those who had lain in wait to ambush them, and he mowed down the footsoldiers and seized their baggage and train. When the Franks approached the encampment and witnessed the disaster which had befallen them, they were disheartened and overcome with dismay. The 'askar of 'Imād al-Dīn now charged upon them, routed them, and wiped out the whole force by

[1] The pronouns may refer to either side.

killing and capture. An enormous quantity of booty in animals, baggage-train, and furnishings fell into their hands and ʿImād al-Dīn returned to the castle of Baʿrīn, whither their king, the Count of Anjou, had fled with those of the leaders of the Franks who accompanied him, in the extremity of weakness and fear. ʿImād al-Dīn therefore encamped over against them and besieged them in this castle, and they remained thus, suffering his blockade and his attacks, until the provisions which were with them were exhausted and they ate their horses. All the rest of the Franks in their territories and strongholds assembled together and joined the son of Joscelin and the lord of Antioch, and having collected their levies they set out to come to the aid of the forsaken and sorely-pressed garrison of Baʿrīn and to deliver them from the distress, fear, and destruction to which they were exposed. When they drew near the Atābek's camp and the news of their approach was confirmed to him, it became necessary under the circumstances to grant the besieged their liberty, and he made an agreement with them upon the condition that they acknowledged his suzerainty, and stipulated for a sum of fifty thousand dinars, which they should pay to him forthwith. He then set them free and took possession of the castle from them, and the forces which had assembled to aid them returned.

News was received [1] from the north that the amīr ʿImād al-Dīn Atābek left Aleppo with his

[1] This and the following paragraph are repetitions, with some additional details, of the events already described above.

'askar on Friday 16th Ramadān (27th May) of this year and encamped before Hims, set up his tents, and engaged in operations against it. The envoy of the king of the Greeks reached him [there].

On 4th Rajab of this year (28th March) the amīr Bazwāj marched towards Tarābulus with the 'askar and with those of the Turkmens whom he had mustered and collected. Its lord came out against him with his Frankish horsemen, but he laid ambushes for them in a number of places, and when the Franks reached the place known as al-Kūra, the men in ambush came out against them and drove them in flight. Most of them were put to the sword, and only a few escaped. Bazwāj then made an assault upon the castle which is at that place and plundered it, killing the leaders and followers who were in it. He captured also a number of persons who paid much money for their ransom, and both he and his 'askar gained large sums.

In Shawwāl (began 22nd June) an armistice and friendly agreement was established on a sound footing between 'Imād al-Dīn and Shihāb al-Dīn, lord of Damascus.

In Dhu'l-Qa 'da news was received of the withdrawal of the king of the Greeks with his army from Antioch towards Ba 'rīn, in its province,[1] on the 24th of the month (13th August), and he sent his envoy to 'Imād al-Dīn Atābek. The amīr Sawār, the atābek's lieutenant in Aleppo, overtook with a considerable squadron a number of the

---

[1] This seems to be an error; perhaps Ba 'rīn is by mistake for Baghrās (Pagrae).

Greek troops, killed some and captured others, and brought them to Aleppo.

In this year also the people of Aleppo set about fortifying it, digging out its trenches, and making themselves secure in it against the Greeks, because of their proximity to the city.

A.H. 532

(19th September, 1137, to 7th September, 1138)

The first day of Muharram of this year was Monday 20th September.

During this month the chamberlain Hasan, who had been sent to the king of the Greeks, arrived in company with the envoy of the king 'Imād al-Dīn Atābek.

On 14th Muharram (3rd October) the atābek arrived with his 'askar at Hamāh, and set out thence in the direction of the Biqā'. He captured the castle of al-Majdal [1] from the Damascenes, and Ibrāhīm b. Turghut, the governor of Bānyās in the province of Damascus, acknowledged his suzerainty.

A report was received that the lord of Antioch had arrested the Frankish patriarch there and had plundered his house. The reason for this was said to be that the king of the Greeks, when peace was established between him and Raymond, lord of Antioch, had stipulated as one of the conditions of peace that he should set up in Antioch a patriarch for the Greeks, as had been the custom of old, but had lapsed in later years. Raymond, lord

---

[1] Majdal 'Ainjar, see above p. 134.

of Antioch, went out to the king of the Greeks, who was in camp with his army at Marj al-Dībāj, and having negotiated an armistice and agreement with him returned to Antioch.

In Second Rabī' (began 17th December) 'Imād al-Dīn Atābek withdrew from [the province of] Damascus to Hamāh and after encamping before it marched to Hims and encamped before the city, besieging it.

In this year the Franks broke the armistice agreed upon between them and 'Imād al-Dīn Atābek, manifesting rebellion and stiff-neckedness, and creating evil and disorder, in spite of his good offices to their leaders and his withholding his hand from them when God gave them into his power, and they arrested a number of the Muslim merchants and men of Aleppo and traders, about five hundred men, in Antioch and the coast towns in Latter Jumādā (began 14th February).

In this year the sultan Mas'ūd wintered in Baghdād and his envoy came to the Atābek at Hims. The king of the Greeks wintered in the marches and the Pylæ and encamped at Marj al-Dībāj [in the outskirts of al-Massīsa].

On Sunday 15th [First] Jumādā (30th January) the amīr Bazwāj set out from Damascus with his 'askar for the quarter of the Franks. His relations with Shihāb al-Dīn, lord of Damascus, had become strained owing to his overbearing manner and his audacity in evil measures, and he was proscribed in consequence of the corruption of his ways, the evidence of his treachery and deceit, his barbarity, and his outrageous conduct. He remained in the outskirts of the city for some time, until a reconciliation was effected, when he re-entered the town and set about living in an upright manner and to the utmost satisfaction of all hopes. Shihāb al-Dīn however, plotted against him and killed him in the citadel of Damascus by the hands of the Shamsīya [1] on Monday 6th Sha 'bān (18th April). The cause of this was that Shihāb al-Dīn bore a grudge against him on account of certain actions which he disapproved and which inspired him with an aversion towards him ; moreover Bazwāj played fast and loose with the moneys of the revenue, squandering them in gratuities and largesses. He therefore devised a plot to kill him, and maintained a friendly and reassuring attitude towards him until the opportunity of killing him should present itself. It came about that Bazwāj visited him in the Rose Pavilion in his palace in the citadel. Now Shihāb al-Dīn had detailed a party of the Armenian Shamsīya, who were members of his cortège, to deal with him and had given them instructions to kill him. When they were able to overpower him in the absence of his attendants, they killed him and carried him out wrapped in a cloak to the tomb built for his wife, and he was buried there.

On Sunday, 17th Sha 'bān [2] Shihāb al-Dīn bestowed robes of honour on the amīr Mu'īn al-Dīn Unur [3] and appointed him to the office of Isfah-

---

[1] *Sibt* (ed. Jewett, p. 99, l. 20) reads *as-Sumanīya* ("Buddhists") but the Shamsīya were the Armenian sun worshippers (*Arevordik* "sons of the sun ") who were to be found in Mesopotamia down to the XVIIIth century ; see Conybeare, Cat. of Armenian MSS. in B. M., p. 181b ; W. Brandt, *Elchasai* (Leipzig, 1912), pp. 124 ff.

[2] Probably by error for Sunday 19th Sha 'bān (1st May).

[3] This appears to be the correct reading of the name, usually read as Anar.

sallār (commander-in-chief), with the title of Atābek. He also restored the office of Chamberlain to the Amīr-Hājib Asad al-Dīn Akiz, and having shown them marks of confidence, committed to them the control and disposal of all the provinces and of all matters of state.

In this month also, news was received from the north of the descent of the king of the Greeks with his army upon Shaizar, in order to besiege and blockade it. He set up a number of catapults against it, and battle was hotly joined between him and its garrison. A number of Muslims in the city were killed, so that it was on the point of destruction, notwithstanding the zealous efforts of the amīr 'Imād al-Dīn Atābek to reinforce it with men, weapons, and war material, and his occupation of a position opposite the Greeks, patrolling their flanks with his cavalry and killing all those of them who fell into his hands. Both sides remained in this situation until the Greeks wearied of their stay before the town and despaired of attaining their object in regard to it ; news came of their withdrawal from Shaizar towards Antioch, and the people rejoiced at their departure empty-handed and broken—to God Most High be the praise for this bounty everlastingly.

After this mention of the Greeks and their activities at this time, an account may be given of the beginning of their movements. They appeared first from the direction of the town of al-Balāt [1] on the great Thursday of their fast [2] and encamped

---

[1] An unidentified place north of Athārib, where the Crusading castle of Tell 'Aqibrīn was situated, a little over 20 miles W. of Aleppo.

[2] i.e. Thursday before Easter, 31st March, 1138.

unexpectedly before the castle of Buzā 'a in the Wādī on the Sunday, their festival.[1] Their cavalry raided the fringes of Hamāh on 19th Rajab (3rd April). A number of infidel Turks [2] fled for protection from them to Aleppo and warned those in Aleppo of the [approach of the] Greeks. They profited by the warning, brought in their outlying posts,[3] posted watchmen, took measures to defend themselves, made everything ready, and were on the alert a night before the attack. This warning by the refugees was a blessing and a favour from God. After these measures of defence and precautions had been taken, the Greeks seized, as was their practice, a considerable number of the people of Aleppo and its neighbourhood. The men of Aleppo dispatched a group of their notables to 'Imād al-Dīn Atābek at his encampment before Hims, appealing to him for aid. He dispatched to their assistance all the horsemen, footsoldiers, and archers whom he could spare, together with a quantity of equipment, and the party reached Aleppo on 27th Rajab (10-11th April).

News arrived that these Greeks captured the castle of Buzā 'a by capitulation on Saturday 25th Rajab (9th April), after besieging and blockading it and engaging it with catapults. After receiving its surrender [the king] acted treacherously with its people and violated his oaths to them. He assembled those whom he had deceived and numbered them, and it is said that they were five

---

[1] Reading '*idihim* for '*indahum*.

[2] *jamā 'atun min kāfiri turkin*. This curious phrase occurs again on p. 275, l. 9 (*alwaq 'atu . . . baina's-sultāni Sinjara wa-baina kāfiri turkin al-wāsili min nāhiyati's-sīni*) and p. 277, l. 8.

[3] *dammū atrāfahum*.

thousand three hundred souls. The qāḍī of Buzā 'a turned Christian, together with a number of the respectable citizens and others, about four hundred in all. The king remained in his place thereafter for ten days, smoking out some caves in which a number of persons had hidden themselves, and they were captured by means of the smoke.

On Sunday,[1] 5th Sha 'bān (17th April) the Greeks descended on the land of al-Nā 'ūra [2] and set out thence on Monday 6th and marched by Aleppo, accompanied by the army of Antioch, and the son of Joscelin. They encamped before Aleppo, and pitched their tents by the river of Quwaiq and the land of al-Sa 'dī. On the following day the king attacked with his horse and foot on the south and west of the city at the angle of the Burj al-Ghanam. A considerable force of the town bands of Aleppo made a sortie against them, fought with them and gained the victory over them, killing and wounding [3] a number. Amongst the casualties was a noted commander of the Greeks, who retired confounded to their camp. They remained before Aleppo for a very few days and withdrew on the morning of Wednesday, 8th Sha 'bān, in the direction of Salda'. The garrison of the fort of al-Athārib fled from it in panic on Thursday, 9th Sha 'bān (21st April), having first thrown fire into its magazines. This became known to the Greeks and a detachment of them marched

---

[1] The text has Wednesday, which is obviously an error ; similarly " Monday 6th " in the next line has been corrected from " Thursday 8th " in the text.

[2] A few miles east of Aleppo.

[3] Reading *faqatalū* (*fīhim*) for *faqutilū*, which seems impossible in syntax.

to the fort, descended before it, seized it, and took possession of its contents. They drove the captives and prisoners whom they had taken from the castle of Buzā 'a into the suburb and trench of al-Athārib. The amīr Sawār, the lieutenant in Aleppo, on learning of this and of the retirement of the Greeks from the city, marched out with the 'askar of Aleppo, overtook them at al-Athārib, and after inflicting a severe defeat upon them freed the prisoners and captives, all save a few. This took place on Saturday, 11th Sha 'bān, and the men of Aleppo were greatly rejoiced at this victory.

On Thursday, 9th of the same month, 'Imād al-Dīn Atābek marched from Hamāh to Salamīya, and having dispatched his heavy baggage to al-Raqqa remained behind with his cavalry as a light detachment. On the Monday, the king of the Greeks set out from the town of al-Ma 'arra and all the local troops who were posted in Kafr Tāb fled in fear of their lives. A number of confirmatory reports were received that the army of the Turkmens had crossed the Euphrates towards Aleppo under the son of the amīr Dā'ūd [grand-] son of Ortuq, in order to make an expedition against the Greeks, and had encamped at Majma al-Murūj. A considerable detachment of the 'askar of Damascus also went out to join the expedition in the service of 'Imād al-Dīn Atābek. The cause of the retirement of the Greeks empty-handed from Shaizar was the receipt of this news of the arrival of the Turkmens and the junction of the armies. The length of their stay before it was twenty-three days, and the date of the king's arrival at Antioch on his return was Sunday, 8th Ramadān (22nd May). A number of reports were subsequently received of the continued withdrawal of the Greeks to their own country, and all hearts were set at rest after their distress and fear.

In this year, repeated messages were sent from the amīr 'Imād al-Dīn Atābek to the amīr Shihāb al-Dīn, proposing a contract of marriage between him and the prince's mother the Khātūn Safwat al-Mulk Zumurrud, daughter of the amīr Jāwalī. His proposal was at length accepted and an agreement was drawn up. Envoys were sent from Damascus to make the contract on her behalf in the Atābek's camp at Hims on Monday, 17th Ramadān. The agreement provided for the surrender of Hims to him, and he took possession of it and its citadel accordingly. Its governor, the amīr Mu'īn al-Dīn Unur, received the castle of Ba'rīn in compensation for it. The Khātūn Safwat al-Mulk, mother of Shihāb al-Dīn, left her palace to proceed to the camp of 'Imād al-Dīn Atābek in the vicinity of Hims and Hamāh, in company with the officers of 'Imād al-Dīn who had been deputed to escort her to him, about the end of Ramadān (early June).

A.H. 533

(8th September, 1138, to 27th August, 1139)

The first day of Muharram of this year was Friday [9th September].

In this month, the amīr 'Imād al-Dīn Atābek met the Khātūn Safwat al-Mulk, mother of Shihāb al-Dīn, outside Hims, where there was assembled with him a great company of envoys from the Caliph, the Sultan, Egypt, the Greeks, Damascus, and elsewhere. In the same month the Franks made a raid in the neighbourhood of Bānyās. Shihāb al-Dīn went out with the 'askar to pursue them, but failing to overtake them returned to the city.

On the morning of Friday 23rd Shawwāl (23rd June), there was made known the plot directed against the amīr Shihāb al-Dīn Mahmūd, son of Tāj al-Mulūk, son of Zahīr al-Dīn Atābek, and his assassination while he was asleep in his bed during the preceding night, by the hands of his accursed slaves, Albaghash (?) the Armenian, to whom he had shown special favour and on whom he relied in all his occupations, the eunuch Yūsuf, whom he trusted to sleep by him, and al-Kharkāwī, the groom of the bed-chamber, who used to sleep in proximity to him. . . . These three accursed malefactors used to sleep round about his bed. When this thing was agreed upon with them, they lay down in their places as usual, and at midnight, when they were assured that he was asleep, they attacked and killed him in his bed upon his couch. Another groom who was with them called out and they killed him too. They planned out their course of action, concealed their secret, and so got out of the citadel. When the assassination became known, search was made for Albaghash, but he had fled and his house was plundered. The other two were seized and crucified on the wall over the Jābiya gate. Letters were sent to his brother the amīr Jamāl al-Dīn Muhammad, son of Tāj al-Mulūk, lord of Ba 'albek, acquainting him with the state of affairs. He came in haste to Damascus, without losing a moment, and took the place of Shihāb al-Dīn. He was formally invested with authority, and the oath of allegiance and loyalty was taken by the amīrs, commanders, and notables. Matters were thus settled and calm restored.

When the news reached the Khātūn Safwat al-Mulk, mother of the amīr Shihāb al-Dīn (God's meicy upon him) she was troubled and distressed, grieved at his loss, and indignant that such a fate should have befallen her son. She wrote to the amīr 'Imād al-Dīn Atābek, who was at Mosul, acquainting him with what had happened, and spurring him on to march without delay to take vengeance. On learning this news, he was moved with the utmost detestation of the crime and was not one to be content with the continuance of such actions. He therefore devoted his attention to making preparations for the task to which she had invited him, and having mustered his forces for this purpose, bent the reins of his determinations towards Syria, marching with all speed upon Damascus in order to attain every object of his ambition. A series of reports brought confirmation of this purpose to Damascus, where all precautions were taken and preparations made to guard the city against him. This was followed by news of his descent upon Ba 'albek on Thursday, 20th Dhu'l-Hijja, with a numerous army and vast host.

Prior to his arrival before it, the town had been garrisoned by men-at-arms and supplied with all equipment, and the appointment of its commander left to Mu 'in al-Din Unur, whose position had become firmly established in the kingdom, in which he held the highest rank and his commands and injunctions were executed. The atābek set up a number of catapults against the city, engaged the garrison in constant attacks, and rigorously blockaded it. It is said that the number of catapults mounted against it were fourteen, by which it was bombarded in turn night and day, until the inhabitants were on the verge of destruction. This went on until news arrived that it had surrendered on terms, owing to the greatness of the distress suffered by the inhabitants, the blockade and the breaching of the wall. The tower held out, defended by a party of the bravest of the Turks who had been specially deputed to protect it and prevent it from being captured, but when they despaired of help reaching them from Mu 'in al-Din [1] and of the arrival of any force to deliver them from the impending disaster, they surrendered it to 'Imād al-Din Atābek, after receiving from him solemn assurances, confirmed by his oath, of their personal safety. But when the fortress was in his hands he violated his pledge and went back on his guarantee of security, owing to a personal grudge and irritation against its defenders which he nursed in secret. He ordered them all to be crucified and none of them escaped except those whose destiny guarded them. The

[1] There is a play of words in the original on the name *Mu 'in al-Din* " Helper of the Faith."

people were horrified at his action and at such an unheard-of breach of oath on his part.

Prior to this, news had been received of 'Imād al-Dīn Atābek's capture of the castle of al-Athārib, on Friday, 1st Safar (7th October), of this year.

In Ramadān of this year (May) the report was received that the amīr al-Afdal Rudwān b. al-Walakhshī, the holder of power in Egypt, had left the country on account of a certain matter which had put him in fear of his lord the [Fātimid] Imām al-Hāfiz li-Dīn Allāh, Commander of the Faithful. He came to Sarkhad, and it was reported that its governor, Amīn al-Dawla Gumushtagīn al-Atābekī, had received him with honour and the greatest respect. He stayed for some time enjoying his hospitality and generosity, and thereafter left him to return to Egypt in pursuit of a plan which he had devised and a purpose upon which he had decided. When he arrived in Cairo, this plan miscarried with him, and he failed to attain what he had set his mind upon, and was placed in honourable confinement in the palace.

A.H. 534

(28th August, 1139, to 16th August, 1140)

The first day of Muharram of this blessed year was Tuesday [29th August].

In this month news was received that 'Imād al-Dīn Atābek, having completed his reorganization of the defence of Ba 'albek and its tower, and repaired the breaches in its fortifications, was engaged in making ready for his descent upon the city of Damascus. Subsequently news arrived of his departure thence with the 'askar and of his arrival in the Biqā' in the month of First Rabī' (began 26th October).

He dispatched an envoy to the amīr Jamāl al-Dīn Muhammad, son of Tāj al-Mulūk Būrī b. Atābek, lord of Damascus, demanding that he should surrender the city to him and receive in compensation for it whatsoever might be dictated by his choice and suggestion. On the rejection of his demand, he moved from the Biqā' and encamped at Darayyā,[1] in the outskirts of Damascus, on Wednesday, 13th Second Rabī' (6th December). As he was encamping at Darayyā the advance guards had become engaged with one another ; he captured a number of them, and the remainder fled to the town. Thereafter on Friday, 28th Second Rabī', he advanced to the town with his 'askar in fighting formation on the side of the Musallā. He defeated a considerable number of the armed bands of the town and the Ghūta, and put them to the sword ; some of them suffered death or captivity, others returned to the town either wounded or unharmed. On this day the town was on the verge of destruction, had it not been for the mercy of God. The Atābek returned to his camp with those who had been captured over and above those who had been killed, and refrained from fighting for some days.

He continued to send messages and to try to wheedle [the prince] into surrendering the city and accepting instead Hims, Ba 'albek, and what

[1] A large township five miles S.W. of Damascus.

other places he might suggest. Jamāl al-Dīn Muhammad b. Tāj al-Mulūk inclined to give his consent to this proposal, on account of the guarantee which it offered for the establishment of peace, the sparing of bloodshed, the prosperity of the provinces, and the restoration of calm, but when he asked advice on the matter from others they refused to entertain it.[1] The Atābek continued to deploy his 'askar for attack on occasional days, but without putting vigour into the fighting or rigorously enforcing the blockade, in the desire to spare bloodshed, with the restraint of one who was desirous of peace and loth to engage in combats and despoiling. In First Jumādā (began 24th December) Jamāl al-Dīn fell a victim to a lingering disease, which was now more now less oppressive, coming and going, diminishing and increasing, until it became so aggravated that all hope of his recovery was lost. Neither medical skill nor the charms of sorcerers availed him against it, and he remained in this condition until he came to his predestined end and passed to the mercy of God on the eve of Friday, 8th Sha'bān (29th March), at the same hour in which his brother Shihāb al-Dīn Mahmūd b. Tāj al-Mulūk (God's mercy upon them both) was assassinated. The people marvelled at this coincidence of time and hour, and magnified God and hallowed His name. Jamāl al-Dīn was prepared for burial and buried in the mausoleum of his grandmother in al-Farādīs ("The Gardens ").

The leaders and holders of authority after his death took counsel together and agreed to fill the

---

[1] Reading 'abāhu for 'ibā'ati.

gap caused by his loss by setting up his son, the amīr 'Adb al-Dawla Abū Sa'īd Ābaq b. Jamāl al-Dīn Muhammad, in his place. Pledges of loyal obedience and faithful service, confirmed by the most solemn oaths, were duly taken to him in this capacity. Order and administration was established on a sound footing, dissension was brought to an end, disturbance was succeeded by tranquillity, and distress of mind by calmness. 'Imād al-Dīn Atābek, on learning of this turn of affairs, advanced with his 'askar towards the city, eager to take advantage of any dissension which might be caused between the leaders by his death, so that he might attain thereby the fulfilment of some of his demands. The case turned out to be contrary to his hopes and the reverse of his imaginings. From none of the troops or armed bands of Damascus did he meet with anything but determination to pursue the struggle and steadfastness in the charge and the combat. He withdrew therefore to his camp weakened in spirit, and downcast at this failure.

Meanwhile an agreement had been come to with the Franks to take common action and support one another, and to unite and join forces in driving off the Atābek and preventing the achievement of his aims. A formal treaty to this effect was signed with solemn oaths and a guarantee of loyal execution of their promise. In consideration of this the Franks asked for a stipulated sum of money to be paid to them forthwith, that it might assist them and strengthen them in their undertaking, and for a number of hostages to ensure their ease of mind. Their requests were granted ;

the money was paid to them and hostages sent from among the relatives of the commanders. Thereupon they began to make preparations to send reinforcement and to give support, and they wrote letters to one another urging them to assemble from all the castles and cities in order to drive off the Atābek and prevent him from attaining his ambition at Damascus, before he should become too firmly settled to be dislodged and his might should become invincible, and he should be victorious over the Frankish bands and attack their cities.

The Atābek, on his part, on learning the truth of the position in regard to this decision and to their assembling together to attack him in conjunction with the army of Damascus, retired from his camp at Darayyā on Sunday, 15th [1] Ramadān (4th May), and made for Hawrān, in order to oppose the Franks if they should approach him, and to pursue them if they should keep at a distance from him. He pursued this policy for some time, and then returned to the Ghūta of Damascus and encamped at 'Adhrā' on Wednesday, 24th Shawwāl (12th June). Having burned a number of farms in the Marj and the Ghūta as far as Harastā al-Tīn, he withdrew northwards on the following Saturday, on learning that the Franks had encamped with all their forces at al-Madān.

The terms of the treaty with the Franks provided, amongst the promises made to them, for the recapture of the frontier fort of Bānyās from Ibrāhīm b. Turghūt and its surrender to them. Now it happened that Ibrāhīm b. Turghūt, its

---

[1] The text has 5th, but this was in the middle of the week.

governor, had gone out with his party towards Tyre, in order to raid it, and there encountered Raymond, lord of Antioch, on his way to support the Franks in giving assistance to the men of Damascus. They engaged in battle, and Raymond routed Turghūt, who was himself killed in the encounter together with a few of his party. The remainder of them returned to Bānyās, fortified themselves in it, and mustered for its defence the men of Wādi'l-Taim and elsewhere, and all whom they could collect. The amīr Mu'īn al-Dīn marched thither with the 'askar of Damascus, encamped before it, and remained during the whole of Shawwāl (began 20th May), engaging it with catapults and besieging it with military operations of various kinds, accompanied by a considerable detachment of the army of the Franks. News was received that the amīr 'Imād al-Dīn Atābek had alighted before Ba'albek and had sent during Shawwāl to summon the Turkmens from their abodes in order to proceed to Bānyās and to drive off the besiegers from it. The troops continued operations in this wise until the end of this year. . . . The siege of Bānyās was prosecuted without intermission until the supplies in it were exhausted and the garrison were short of food. It was then surrendered to Mu'īn al-Dīn, and the commander who was in it was compensated with a fief and a benefaction which satisfied him. Mu'īn al-Dīn, having surrendered it to the Franks and carried out the terms of his agreement with them, set out thence to return to Damascus at the end of Shawwāl (middle of June), having achieved his hopes and stultified his labours.

On the morning of Saturday, 7th Dhu'l-Qa 'da [1] 'Imād al-Dīn Atābek appeared outside Damascus with his 'askar on a flying raid. He reached the Musallā and approached the city wall unperceived, as the people were still in the last moments of their sleep. When dawn broke and the news of his arrival became known, shouts and cries were raised and the people rushed to arms and assembled on the walls. The gate was opened and the cavalry and footsoldiers made a sortie. 'Imād al-Dīn had in the meantime dispersed his 'askar in detachments to Hawrān, the Ghūta, the Marj, and all the outlying districts for the purpose of raiding, while he himself remained with his personal guard facing the 'askar of Damascus, in order to prevent any of them from pursuing any of his raiding horsemen. Battle was joined between him and the 'askar of Damascus, and a considerable number of both sides were wounded.[2] He then withdrew from the engagement, owing to his preoccupation with the squadrons whom he had dispersed to carry out the raids. An innumerable quantity of horses at pasture, sheep and goats, cattle, and furnishings fell into their hands, as their raid was so unexpected and took everyone by surprise. The Atābek halted at Marj Rāhit [3] on the same day, until his men assembled with their spoils, and set off to return by the northern road carrying a prodigious quantity of booty.

---

[1] Calendar date 24th June ; probably Saturday 22nd June.
[2] Reading *juriha* for *kharaja* (" went out ").
[3] To the N.E. of the city.

A.H. 535

(*17th August*, 1140, *to 5th August*, 1141)

In Ramadān (began 10th April) of this year news was received of a sortie of the troops in Ascalon against the cavalry of the Franks which were raiding its territory ; a number of them [1] were killed and they retired broken and empty-handed.

In this year also, word arrived from the north of the seizure of the castle of Masyāth by the Bātinīs, by means of a stratagem.

A.H. 536

(*8th August*, 1141, *to 26th July*, 1142)

In this year, news was received from the north that the Turkish amīr Lajah, who had left Damascus for the service of the amīr 'Imād al-Dīn Atābek, had made a raid upon the country of the Franks, and had gained a victory over their cavalry and done so great execution amongst them that the number of their slain was said to be about seven hundred men.

In this year also, word arrived of the death of the amīr Sa 'd al-Dawla, lord of Āmid,[2] and of the succession of his son Mahmūd . . . also of the death of the amīr the son of al-Dānishmand [3] (God's mercy upon him) and the succession of his son.

[1] Presumably the Franks, but the pronouns are ambiguous.
[2] Aigildi, see above p. 99.
[3] Muhammad b. Gumushtagīn, lord of Sīwās.

A.H. 537

(27th July, 1142, to 15th July, 1143)

In this year, news was received of the sortie of the lord of Antioch towards Buzā 'a, and that the amīr Sawār, the lieutenant charged with the defence of Aleppo, headed him away from it and prevented him from attacking it. Reports were received also that the king of the Greeks had appeared on the Marches for the second time. The lord of Antioch went out to him, did homage, and having reached an accommodation with him and set his mind at ease, left him and returned to Antioch.

In this year also a report was brought that the amīr 'Imād al-Dīn Atābek had captured the citadel of Āshib, which was famous for its strength and impregnability.[1]

In Ramadān (began 20th March) news arrived of the death of the king of the Greeks.

A.H. 538

(16th July, 1143, to 3rd July, 1144)

In this year news arrived of the capture of the citadel of Hīzān [2] by the amīr 'Imād al-Dīn.

On 3rd First Jumādā (13th November) the amīr and chamberlain Asad al-Dīn Akiz was arrested, his property seized, his eyes put out, and

---

[1] This place was afterwards known as 'Imādīya, from Zankī's title. It was situated above 75 miles N.E. of Mosul.

[2] In Armenia, S.W. of Lake Van. The district was previously in the possession of Ya 'qūb, son of Qilij Arslān I, Saljūqid Sultan of Anatolia.

he himself placed in confinement, and his party deserted his cause.

In this year also came the news from the neighbourhood of the Franks of the death of the Count of Anjou, king of Jerusalem, from an illness which befel him and proved fatal. His minor son and the boy's mother were appointed to the kingship in his place ; the Franks were satisfied with this and his position was established.

A.H. 539

(4th July, 1144, to 23rd June, 1145)

In Second Rabī' (October) word arrived of the issue of an 'askar against a considerable detachment of Franks which had entered the district of Ba 'albek in order to ravage it and dispatch raiding parties over it. Battle was joined and God gave victory to the Muslims over them, and they killed the greater number of them and seized all that they had with them. The hands of the Muslims were filled with their spoils and they returned safely to Ba 'albek, rejoicing and booty-laden. The residue of the Franks returned to their own place broken, dejected, and empty-handed.

In First Jumādā (began 30th September) word was received from the north that the 'askar of Aleppo had seized a considerable detachment of merchants, troops, and others, who had come out of Antioch to make their way to the country of the Franks, carrying much money, animals, stuffs and furnishings. They fell upon it, seized all that was in it, and killed all the Frankish horsemen who were escorting it for protection, and returned to Aleppo with the money, captives, prisoners, and animals.

In this year also reports were received from the north that the amīr 'Imād al-Dīn Atābek had captured the city of al-Ruhā by the sword, notwithstanding its strength and impregnability and its capacity to withstand and defend itself against the assaults and sieges of mighty armies, and that it had come about in this wise. The amīr 'Imād al-Dīn Atābek had long been desirous of it, ambitious to possess himself of it, and on the watch to seize any opportunity against it. The thought of it never ceased to revolve within his mind and his ambition for it was ever present in his memory. At length he learned that Joscelin, its lord, had left it with the bulk of his men-at-arms and with the chief men of his garrison and his most stalwart warriors, for some cause which, by reason of that which was decreed and doomed to befall, necessitated his absence from it. As soon as he received confirmation of this report, he made speed to march thither and hastened to encamp before it with a numerous 'askar in order to blockade it and bring pressure to bear upon its inhabitants. He wrote to the tribes of Turkmens, calling upon them to give support and assistance against it and to carry out the obligation of the Holy War, and a great host and vast multitude of them joined him, so that they surrounded the city on all sides and intervened between it and those who sought to bring supplies and foodstuffs to it. Even the birds could scarce approach it, in fear of their lives from the unerring shafts and watchfulness of the besiegers. He set up mangonels against its walls, and while these unceasingly bombarded the city, he engaged in constant and persistent fighting [1] with its people. The men of Khurāsān and of Aleppo who were familiar with the technique of sapping, and bold in carrying it out, set to work and made saps at a number of places which they selected as suitable for their operations.[2] They continued thus to push on with their sapping and to dig through the belly of the earth until they reached below the foundations of the bastions of the wall. They then shored these up with stout timbers and special appliances, and when they had made an end of that nothing remained but to set fire to them. They asked 'Imād al-Dīn Atābek for instructions on this matter, and after he had entered the sap and seen in person what had been done and expressed his admiration he gave them their orders. When fire was applied to the shoring it caught the timbers and destroyed them, and immediately the wall fell down. The Muslims forced their way into the city, after a great number on both sides had been killed over the ruins ; so many of the Franks and Armenians were killed and wounded that they were compelled to abandon the town and the Muslims took possession of it by the sword in the early forenoon of Saturday, 26th Latter Jumādā (23rd December, 1144). The troops set to pillaging, slaying, capturing, ravishing and looting, and their hands were filled with such quantities of money, furnishings,

---

[1] Reading *musirran* for *mudirran* and supplying some such verb as *wāsala*.

[2] Literally " of whose condition they were aware and of whose strength or weakness they satisfied themselves."

animals, booty and captives as rejoiced their spirits and gladdened their hearts. 'Imād al-Dīn Atābek, after giving orders to cease killing and plundering, set to work to rebuild what had been destroyed and patch up what had been damaged, detailed a select force to control its affairs, defend it, and make every effort on behalf of its interests, and reassured the citizens, giving them promises of good treatment and of the dispensation of justice to all of them, near and far. He then marched on towards Sarūj, from which the Franks had fled, and captured it, and there was not one place or stronghold by which he passed and before which he encamped but was immediately delivered up to him.

Proceeding to the castle of al-Bīra in those parts, which is of the utmost impregnability and difficulty of attack, 'Imād al-Dīn encamped before it and set about engaging and besieging it, and cut off from it all who sought to bring to it food, supplies, assistance or support. He continued thus besieging, engaging, and blockading it until it grew weak and the supplies it contained were exhausted. As he was on the point of gaining possession of it, he was disquieted and troubled by the news that his lieutenant in Mosul, the amīr Jaqar b. Ya 'qūb, had been attacked and slain,[1] and this brought about his withdrawal from it in order to investigate the conditions which had arisen in Mosul.

In First Jumādā [2] (began 30th October) word was brought that the amīr 'Imād al-Dīn Atābek, on the receipt of news that the men of al-Hadītha

---

[1] On 8th Dhu'l-Qa 'da (2nd May).
[2] i.e., before the expedition to Edessa.

and 'Āna [1] had thrown off their allegiance and revolted against him, dispatched against them a considerable detachment from his 'askar, which proceeded thither, and after fighting with them and blockading them captured them by the sword, slew the greater number of their inhabitants, and plundered them.

In the month of Ramadān news arrived from the north that the army of the Franks which had assembled at Antioch from all their districts and castles in order to succour the men of al-Ruhā . . . [2] 'Imād al-Dīn Atābek had dispatched a corps of considerable strength, made up of Turkmens and levies, to deal with it. They made a sudden attack upon it and fell upon all whom they found on its fringes and outskirts, and did such execution upon it that it retired immediately, not before the Turkmens had killed or captured many of the Franks and had seized a large number of their animals. Most of the footsoldiers were put to the sword, and they dispersed to their districts and castles, broken, disappointed of victory, and empty-handed.

A.H. 540

(24th June, 1145, to 12th June, 1146)

In First Jumādā of this year (began 20th October) a number of confirmatory reports were received from the neighbourhood of the amīr 'Imād al-Dīn Atābek that he was giving his attention to gathering equipment, making prepara-

---

[1] A populous district on the westerly bend of the Euphrates, about 150 miles N.W. of Baghdād.
[2] lacuna in the MS.

tions and mustering levies for the purpose of the Raid and the Holy War, and stories were circulated about him to the effect that he would probably march into the territories of Damascus and besiege the city. There was a continuous stream of reports about this, and about his activities in preparing a prodigious number of mangonels and appliances of war and materials required for the subjugation of strong and impregnable places of every kind. This went on until the beginning of Sha'bān (began 17th January), when news arrived that his determination had been diverted from this project and the guiding-strings of his thought turned in another direction, and that the mangonels had been sent back from Ba 'albek to Hims. It was said that word had reached him from al-Ruhā that a number of the Armenians had formed a plot against it and were seeking to destroy all those who were garrisoning it, that their hidden secret had been revealed, and that the guilty parties were seized, hunted out, and requited therefor with the punishments, such as slaying, crucifying, and scattering throughout the land, which are meted out to those who go to and fro in the earth to create mischief.

A.H. 541

(13th June, 1146, to 1st June, 1147)

The narrative already given of the activities of 'Imād al-Dīn Atābek in the latter part of the year 540, of his encamping before the castle of

Dawsar [1] at a moment unexpected by its garrison, his attack upon and plundering of its suburb and seizure of its people, renders it unnecessary to repeat or to describe these events in detail.[2]   He was continuing to blockade the fortress and to engage in operations against its garrison in the month of Second Rabī' of the year 541 when news arrived that one of his attendants, for whom he had a special affection and in whose company he delighted, a man of Frankish origin known as Yaranqash,[3] who nursed a secret grudge against him on account of some injury previously done to him by the Atābek, had, on finding an opportunity when he was off his guard in his drunkenness, and with the connivance and assistance of certain of his comrades amongst the attendants, assassinated him in his sleep on the eve of Sunday, 6th Second Rabī' (night of Saturday, 14th September). Although the Atābek had taken the utmost precautions by surrounding himself with armed men and weapons, and had a strong guard posted around the enclosure of his tent, he slaughtered him upon his bed after a number of effective blows had been dealt upon his vital parts, and no one knew anything about them until the attendant who slew him had escaped to the fortress of Dawsar, known at that time as Ja 'bar, the lord of which was the amīr 'Izz al-Dīn 'Alī b. Mālik b. Sālim b. Mālik. . . . The armies of the Atābek dispersed

---

[1] This was the old name of the castle generally known as Qal'at Ja'bar, on the left bank of the Euphrates, a little above Raqqa.
[2] The section referred to is not contained in this MS., being replaced by a long digression of the author on the pompous absurdity of royal titles in his age.
[3] The pronunciation is quite uncertain.

like the bands of Saba,[1] his stores of money and rich treasuries were plundered, and he himself was buried there without enshrouding until his body was removed, so it is said, to a mausoleum near al-Raqqa. The Sultan's son who had been under his guardianship went with those who accompanied him or who attached themselves to him towards Mosul, and along with him went Saif al-Dīn Ghāzī, the son of 'Imād al-Dīn Atābek (God's mercy upon him). The governor in Mosul, 'Alī Kūchak, resisted their entry for some days until an agreement was reached between them, when he opened the gate and the Atābek's son entered, assumed control, and took his father's place.

Meanwhile the amīr Saif al-Dawla Sawār and Salāh al-Dīn [al-Yāghīsiyānī] returned to Aleppo, and along with them went the amīr Nūr al-Dīn Mahmūd, son of 'Imād al-Dīn Atābek. As soon as he entered Aleppo, he set about assembling troops and disbursing money to them, and his control was established, and public order restored. The amīr Salāh al-Dīn, however, separated from him and returned to his own governorship of Hamāh, in distrust and fear of his life lest he should be the victim of a plot. Nevertheless all the towns were in confusion, the roads became unsafe, after enjoying a grateful period of security and a noteworthy respect for authority, and the hands of the Turkmens and [Arab] brigands[2] were set free to do mischief and robbery in the outlying places and in all the country districts.

When the report of the Atābek's death was brought to Mu'īn al-Dīn, and he learned the

---

[1] See above p. 117 n.   [2] *al-harāmīya ;* see above p. 115, n. 2.

position of affairs, he set about making preparations to proceed to Ba 'albek and to seize the
opportunity of recovering it, with instruments of
war and mangonels. He advanced speedily
towards it, and having encamped before it,
blockaded it and engaged in battle with its
defenders. Not more than a few days passed ere
the deficiency of water in the place compelled
them to submit to his authority. Its governor [1]
was a man of resolution, intelligence and knowledge
of affairs, and having stipulated for the grant of a
fief to himself amongst other matters, he surrendered both town and citadel to him. Mu 'īn
al-Dīn carried out the terms of the agreement
made with him, and took over all the grain-stuffs
and war material in the city during the month of
First Jumādā (began 9th October). He corresponded also with the governor in Hims and an
armistice and friendly arrangement was concluded
between them, which conduced to the general
well-being and prosperity of the provinces. A
correspondence took place also between him and
Salāh al-Dīn at Hāmah, and a similar agreement
was come to between them. Thereafter he led his
forces back to Damascus, after completing his
business at Ba 'albek and establishing a garrison
in it for its protection, and entered the city on
Saturday, 18th Latter Jumādā of this year.[2]
Here he found the attendant Yaranqash, the
murderer of 'Imād al-Dīn Atābek (God's mercy
upon him), who had left the castle of Ja 'bar, in

[1] He was Najm al-Dīn Ayyūb b. Shādhī, father of Saladin.
[2] Apparently Saturday 23rd November (calendar date 16th Latter
Jumādā), unless 18th is an error for 8th, i.e., Saturday 16th November
(calendar date 9th Latter Jumādā).

fear lest its lord should be summoned to give him up, and had come to Damascus in the confident belief that he would be secure there, openly putting forward his action as a claim to consideration, and imagining that he would be made welcome.[1] He was arrested and sent to Aleppo under the escort of a guard, and after some days there was carried to Mosul, where, it is said, he was put to death.

Meanwhile, during Latter Jumādā, news arrived that the son of Joscelin had assembled the Franks from all quarters and had attacked the city of al-Ruhā unexpectedly with the connivance of the Christians who were living there, and had entered it, taken possession of it, and slain all the Muslims who were to be found within it. The breasts of all men were anguished on hearing these disagreeable tidings. On the heels of this came the news that the amīr Nūr al-Dīn, lord of Aleppo, on hearing this report, had set out with his 'askar, preceded by Saif al-Dawla Sawār and reinforced by the Turkmens who assembled from all quarters, so that they formed a great host of about ten thousand horsemen. They marched with all speed, night and day and in the early hours of morning, so that the horses dropped by the roadsides from the fatigue of the march, and arrived at the town after the son of Joscelin and his associates had occupied it. The Muslims attacked them and put them to the sword; a number of the Armenians and Christians of al-Ruhā were killed, and the defenders were driven back to a fort called the

[1] Literally "in the belief that the state of affairs was as he imagined it to be."

Water-Tower, which was occupied by the son of Joscelin with about twenty of his bravest knights. The Muslims surrounded them on all sides and set to work to undermine the fort, and in less time than it takes to tell it fell down upon them. The son of Joscelin made his way out and escaped from it secretly with his companions. The remainder were captured and the sword blotted out of existence all those of the Christians of al-Ruhā upon whom the Muslims laid hands. Those of the Muslims who had been made prisoner were released and a great quantity of riches, furnishings, and captives were taken in plunder from the town. All men's spirits were rejoiced by this victory after sorrow and prostration, and their hearts were strengthened after they had lost courage and felt their cause forsaken. The Muslims returned with the spoils and the captives to Aleppo and the other districts.

In Shawwāl of this year (began 5th March) envoys and correspondence were exchanged between the amīrs Nūr al-Dīn Mahmūd son of 'Imād al-Dīn Atābek, lord of Aleppo, and Mu 'īn al-Dīn Unur, until an agreement was concluded between them on the most friendly and cordial footing. A marriage was contracted between Nūr al-Dīn and the daughter of Mu 'īn al-Dīn, and a firm settlement was reached on the basis of the proposals made by each party. The contract was drawn up in Damascus on Thursday, 23rd Shawwāl (30th March) in the presence of the envoys of Nūr al-Dīn, and the bridal outfit having been made ready the envoys set out to return to Aleppo, accompanied by the daughter of Mu 'īn al-Dīn and a company of his household officers on Thursday, 15th Dhu'l-Qa 'da (17th April).

Mu 'īn al-Dīn, having acquired implements of war and mangonels, and having assembled all whom he could assemble of horse and foot, set out towards Sarkhad and Bosra. He had concealed his design in order the more effectually to attain his object, and encamped unexpectedly before Sarkhad. It was then held by the person known as Altūntāsh, the ghulām of its former governor Amīn al-Dawla Gumushtagīn al-Atābekī. This person in his folly had deluded himself with the belief that he could withstand whosoever should become master of the city of Damascus and the hope that the Franks would help him to attain his object, together with whatsoever reinforcement and assistance he desired, and that they would support him in his proposed activities of raiding and sowing disorder. He had, in accordance with the predestined decree, left the castle of Sarkhad to proceed to the Franks in order to seek aid of them and draw up with them an agreed plan for their mischievous works, not knowing that God does not prosper the acts of evildoers, and ignorant of Mu 'īn al-Dīn's plans to crush him by speedy action and to counter his hopes by besieging [his city]. The latter cut off his return to either of the two castles [Sarkhad and Bosra] and for a long time fighting went on continuously between the garrison of Sarkhad and the besiegers, saps were prepared, and letters were repeatedly dispatched from the Franks to Mu 'īn al-Dīn seeking to move him to restore peace by all manner of soft-speaking and by promises, threats and menaces, should he not agree to his request, while he for his part clung to a policy of dissimulation and evasion. In the meantime he learned of their mustering together and preparing to move against him, in order to disquiet him and cause him to abandon the siege, and this news compelled him to correspond with Nūr al-Dīn, lord of Aleppo, requesting of him the assistance of himself and his 'askar against the infidel antagonists. Nūr al-Dīn consented to his request, and as, by a fortunate contingency, he was already in marching order with his 'askar outside Aleppo, he directed the reins of his advance towards him, and marching with all speed reached Damascus on Wednesday 27th Dhu'l-Hijja.[1] He encamped at 'Ain Shuwāqa, and after staying for a few days proceeded towards Sarkhad. No finer 'askar than his was ever seen, in appearance, equipment, and numbers.

When the two 'askars united, the garrison in Sarkhad sent to them, offering to surrender, and asking for a delay of a few days before giving up the place, but this was only dissimulation and guile on their part until the Frankish troops should arrive and force their besiegers to retire. But God, for the perfecting of his bounty to the Muslims and the advantage of the Faithful, decreed the arrival of one who brought news of the assembling and mustering of the Franks and of their advance with all speed with both horse and foot towards Bosra. Now there was at Bosra a large detachment of the 'askar investing the town, and immediately on receipt of this news the 'askar set out for Bosra

---

[1] Wednesday 28th May (calendar date 25th Dhu'l-Hijja), unless it is a textual error for 17th Dhu'l-Hijja (Wednesday 21st May).

like falcons to their prey and hawks towards their partridges. By this means they reached Bosra before the Franks and blocked their way to it. The combatants drew up eye to eye, and their ranks closed up to one another, and the 'askar of the Muslims gained the upper hand over the polytheists. They cut them off from watering-place and pasture ground, they afflicted them with a hail of shafts and death-dealing arrows, they multiplied amongst them death and wounds, and set on fire the dried herbage on their roads and paths. The Franks, on the verge of destruction, turned in flight, and the Muslim knights and horse-men, seeing a favourable opportunity presented of exterminating them, made speed to slay and to engage in combat with them. Mu 'īn al-Dīn, however, endeavoured to restrain the Muslims and prevent them from attacking and pursuing the Franks on their retreat, for fear of a rally on their part and a counter attack upon the Muslims. Thus the Franks returned homewards on their tracks, defeated and disheartened, and encompassed by death and destruction. All hope of deliverance at their hands was lost, and Bosra was surrendered to Mu 'īn al-Dīn, after an arrangement was come to with its garrison and they were conceded possession of the fiefs which they proposed. Thence he marched back to Sarkhad, the surrender of which to him was carried out under the same conditions. The two 'askars returned to Damascus, reaching it on Sunday, 27th Muharram of the year 42 (29th June, 1147), and Nūr al-Dīn stayed in the Atābek's palace and set out to return to Aleppo on Wednesday, 30th Muharram of that year.

At this time, Altūntāsh, who had gone from Sarkhad to the Franks in his ignorance and folly, arrived at Damascus from the land of the Franks, without a guarantee of security or permit granting his right of entry, imagining that he would be received with honour and taken into service after his odious evildoing and treachery to Islām. He was at once placed in confinement, and his brother Khutlukh having brought a suit against him for the injury which he had done him by putting out his eyes, a tribunal was assembled to decide their case. It was attended by the qādīs and jurists, who declared for his brother's right of retaliation against him, and he was blinded in consequence, as he had blinded his brother. He was then permitted to reside in a house belonging to him in Damascus, and stayed there.

A.H. 542

(2nd June, 1147, to 21st May, 1148)

In Safar (July) of this year the chamberlain and civil secretary Mahmūd returned from Baghdād with the reply to the letters from Mu'īn al-Dīn [1] which had been sent by his hand, and accompanied by two envoys [2] from the Caliph and the Sultan. With them they brought the diploma of investiture and robe of honour for Mu'īn al-Dīn. [3] They invested him with it and he appeared in public [4]

---

[1] Reading *al-mu'īnīya* for *al-mu'aiyina*.

[2] The printed text has *rasūlan*, which should be amended to *rasūlā'l-khalīfati*.

[3] Literally *Zahīru'l-Dīn waMu'īnuhu* "Upholder and Helper of the Faith."

[4] Reading *zahara* for *zaharā*.

wearing it on Saturday, 18th First Rabī'[1] (16th August). They remained for some days and returned with the replies to the letters they had brought.

On Thursday, 21st Second Rabī' (18th September), an envoy from Egypt arrived at Damascus bringing a diploma of investiture and a gift of horses and money for Mu 'īn al-Dīn in accordance with established custom in similar cases.

In Latter Jumādā (began 28th October), the governorship of the fortress of Sarkhad was confided to the amīr Mujāhid al-Dīn Buzān b. Māmīn, on his undertaking to furnish a quantity of money and grain and entering into and observing certain conditions and promises made on oath. He set out thither and occupied it in the middle of the same month, to the joy of all the inhabitants of that district, on account of his generous and upright character, strict observance of the principles of religion, and personal scrupulousness, after his predecessors, who observed their duties towards God neither in matters of belief nor worship nor equitable dealing nor purity of heart nor generosity of action.

In this year a succession of reports was received from Constantinople, the territories of the Franks, Anatolia, and the neighbouring parts, of the coming of the king of the Franks from their lands, amongst them being Almān and [the son of] Alphonso,[2] with a company of their nobles in

---

[1] The text has Second Rabī', which conflicts with the calendar and the date immediately following.

[2] *Almān wa Alfunsh.* The former is evidently taken as the proper name of Conrad, Emperor of Germany, the latter is Bertram, son of Alphonso Jourdain, and grandson of Raymond of Toulouse.

number innumerable and equipment incomputable.
They were said to be making for the land of Islām,
having issued a summons throughout their lands
and strongholds to set out on expedition thither
and hasten towards it and to leave their own
territories and cities empty and bereft of protectors
and defenders. They brought with them amounts
beyond reckoning of their moneys, treasuries and
weapons, until it was said by some that their
numbers amounted to a million horse and foot, and
by others to be even more. They seized the
dependencies of Constantinople and its king was
obliged to humour them, maintain peace with
them, and bow to their will. When the news of
their approach became known and their purpose
was bruited abroad, the governors of the neighbouring lands and of the Islamic territories in their
proximity began to make preparations for warding
them off and to muster their forces for engaging in
the Holy War with them. They repaired to their
outlets and mountainous defiles which hindered
them from crossing and debouching on the land of
Islām, and assiduously launched raids upon their
fringes. Death and slaughter commingled with
the Franks until a vast number of them perished,
and their sufferings from lack of foodstuffs, forage
and supplies, or the costliness of them if they were
to be had at all, destroyed multitudes of them by
hunger and disease. Fresh reports of their losses
and of the destruction of their numbers were
constantly arriving until the end of the year 542,
with the result that men were restored to some
degree of tranquillity of mind and began to gain
some confidence in the failure of their enterprise,

and their former distress and fear were alleviated in spite of the repeated reports of the activities of the Franks.

A.H. 543

(22nd May, 1148, to 10th May, 1149)

The first day of this year was Friday 21st May, the sun being in Gemini.

In its early days several reports were received from different sources of the arrival of the ships of the aforementioned Franks at the sea coast, and of their landing on the shores of the coastal fortresses of Tyre and 'Akkā and their junction[1] with those of the Franks who were in these parts. It was said that after all that had perished of them by killing, disease and hunger, they still numbered about a hundred thousand men. They repaired to Jerusalem, and carried out the obligation of their pilgrimage, after which a number of them returned to their own country by sea. A great host of them had perished by death and disease, including some of their kings, but Almān, who was their greatest king, remained with some others of lesser rank. There was a divergence of views amongst them as to which of the lands of Islām and Syrian cities they should proceed to attack, but at length they came to an agreed decision to attack the city of Damascus, and their malicious hearts were so confident of capturing it that they already planned out the division of its estates and districts. This news arrived in a series of reports, and the governor

---

[1] Reading *ijtimāʿ* for *ijmāʿ*.

of the city, the amīr Mu 'īn al-Dīn Unur, set about making ready equipment and preparing to engage them and to counter their malice, fortifying the places where their attack was feared, setting men to guard the roads and passes, cutting off the movement of supplies to their stations, filling up the wells, and effacing the watering places.

The Franks directed their march towards Damascus with their host, their might and their armoury, in numbers estimated at fifty thousand horse and foot, and accompanied by such quantities of baggage train, camels and cattle, as swelled their forces to a surpassing number. They approached the city and made for the site known as Manāzil al-'Asākir,[1] but finding no water there, since the supply had been cut off from it, they proceeded to al-Mizza,[2] owing to its proximity to water, and advanced on the town with their cavalry and foot-soldiers. The Muslims drew up in face of them on Saturday, 6th First Rabī' (24th July) and battle was joined between the two forces. A great multitude joined in the struggle with them, composed of the levies and the death-dealing Turks, the town bands, volunteers and *ghazis*,[3] and death was scattered abroad among them. The infidels gained the upper hand over the Muslims owing to the superiority of their numbers and equipment. They gained control of the water, spread throughout the orchards, and encamped in

[1] " The camps of the Regiments," located by Dussaud (*Topographie historique*, p. 315), beyond the Wooden Bridge, to the south of the city (see above p. 196).

[2] A large village to the S.E. of the city.

[3] The *ghāzīs* (*ghuzāh*) or " Holy Warriors " were bands of irregular troops who moved to any part where fighting was proceeding against the infidels.

them. They moved close up to the town and occupied a section of it which no troops either in ancient or recent times had succeeded in holding. On this day the Mālikite jurisconsult and imām Yūsuf al-Findalāwī (God's mercy upon him) found martyrdom by the water near al-Rabwa, owing to his stand in face of the Franks and refusal to retire before them, in steadfast obedience to the commands of God in His Holy Book.[1] A similar fate befell the ascetic 'Abd al-Rahmān al-Halhūlī (God's mercy upon him).

The Franks now set about cutting down trees and building stockades with them, and destroying the enclosures.[2] The night passed in this wise, with all the people discouraged and straitened in spirit through fear because of the horror of what they had witnessed. They made a sortie against the Franks early on the following morning, which was Sunday, and after charges by each side against the other, the Muslims gained the upper hand over them and multiplied death and wounds amongst them. The amīr Mu'īn al-Dīn distinguished himself in combat with them, and displayed a valour, steadfastness and gallantry such as was never seen in any other, never wearying in repelling them nor taking respite from the struggle against them. The mill of war ceased not to grind between them, with the infidel horsemen ever delaying to make their famous onslaught until the opportunity

[1] Qur'ān IX, 112 : " Verily God hath purchased from the Believers their lives and their goods in return for their possession of Paradise ; they shall fight in the Path of God, and they shall slay and be slain— a promise binding upon Himself, true."

[2] Reading probably *hazā'ir* (cf. MS. and Abū Shāma), for which the editor has substituted *qanātir* (" sluices ").

should be offered them, until at length the sun inclined to its setting, night drew nigh, and men's souls sought for rest. Each side returned to its own place, but the regular troops passed the night in the field facing the Franks, and the citizens in watch and sentry duty on their walls, with the enemy in full view close to them.

Meanwhile letters had been dispatched to the governors of the outlying districts with appeals for assistance and reinforcement. Parties of Turkmen cavalry and of footmen from the outskirts were constantly arriving, and [next morning] the Muslims made an early attack upon the Franks, with their confidence renewed and their fears dissipated. They held their ground in face of the Franks and discharged upon them shafts of fate and arrows of wounding, which fell without intermission upon footman or knight, horse or camel, in their camp. During this day there arrived from the Biqā' and elsewhere large numbers of bowmen, by whom the numerical strength [of the Muslims] was increased and their military equipment redoubled. Each side separated from the other and retired to the position which it had established [at the end of] this day. In the early morning of the following day, Tuesday, the Muslims advanced to attack them with the swiftness of hawks swooping on mountain partridges, and having encompassed them in their camp and surrounded their sleeping quarters, they made havoc of the barricades which they had constructed with trees from the orchards, by a hail of arrows and bombardment of stones. The Franks on their part declined to come out, in fear and discouragement, and not one man of them showed himself. It was thought that they were planning a ruse and preparing a stratagem. None of them appeared save a few horsemen and footsoldiers by way of skirmishing and keeping off the enemy in case the latter should attack [1] before they found either a clear field for their own charge or some device to secure their escape. Not a man of them could approach [the Muslims] without being thrown prostrate by a shower of arrows or a lance thrust. A large number of footsoldiers of the town bands and men of the villages became emboldened against them, and made a practice of lying in wait for them on the roads, when they suspected no danger,[2] and killing all those whom they captured, and bringing in their heads to claim rewards for them. A large number of heads were brought in.

Meanwhile reports reached the Franks from several quarters of the rapid advance of the Islamic armies to engage in the Holy War against them and of their eagerness to exterminate them, and they became convinced of their own destruction and of the imminence of disaster. Having taken counsel of one another, they found no way of escape from the net into which they had fallen and the abyss into which they had cast themselves save to retreat in disorder at dawn on the Wednesday, the following day, and to flee, broken and forsaken. When the Muslims learned this, and the signs of the retreat of the Franks became clear to them, they moved out to attack them on the

---

[1] Reading *almuhājima* for *almuhājina*.
[2] This is the reading of the MS. (*'aminū*), for which the editor has substituted *inthanaw* (" turned back ") : cf. Abū Shāma (*R.H.C.* IV, 58).

morning of the same day and hastened towards them, pursuing them with arrows, so that they slew a large number of men, horses, and other animals in their rear files. In the remains of their camps, moreover, and along their highroads there were found such uncountable quantities of burial pits of their slain and of their magnificent horses, that there were stenches from their corpses that almost overcame the birds in the air. They had also burned down al-Rabwa and al-Qubba al-Mamdūdīya [1] during that night. The people rejoiced at this mercy which God had bountifully bestowed upon them, and multiplied their thanks to Him for having vouchsafed to them an answer to the prayers which they had offered up without ceasing during the days of this distress, and to God be praise and thanks therefor.

It came about after this mercy that Mu 'īn al-Dīn joined forces with Nūr al-Dīn, lord of Aleppo, on his approach to Damascus to succour it in the latter part of Second Rabī' (middle of September) of this year, and they proceeded together to the castle in the neighbourhood of Tarābulus which is called the Castle of 'Araima.[2] It was held by the son of King Alfonso, one of the Frankish kings mentioned above, who had perished at 'Akkā. With him were his mother and a considerable body of his personal attendants, knights and leaders of his men. The Muslims surrounded the castle and made an assault upon

---

[1] Suburbs of the city, al-Rabwa lying directly to the west of it. The site of al-Qubba ("The Long Pavilion") is uncertain.

[2] The name, which is missing in the MS., has been supplied by the editor from Ibn al-Athīr. 'Araima was about seven miles S. by W. of Sāfīthā.

it, the 'askars of Nūr al-Dīn and Mu 'īn al-Dīn having been joined by a detachment of about a thousand horse from the 'askar of Saif al-Dīn Ghāzī, son of the Atābek [lord of Mosul]. Both sides engaged actively in the struggle and most of the garrison were killed or made prisoner. The son of the king was captured, along with his mother, and all that the castle contained of war equipment, horses, and furnishings was plundered. The 'askar of Saif al-Dīn retired to its camp at Hims, Nūr al-Dīn returned to Aleppo, taking the king's son and his mother and the captives with him, and Mu 'īn al-Dīn withdrew to Damascus.

In the meantime there had arrived at Damascus the Sharīf and amīr Shams al-Dīn al-Husainī, the Naqīb.[1] He had come on from Saif al-Dīn Ghāzī, son of the Atābek, having been deputed as an envoy from the Caliphate to all the governors and to the tribes of the Turkmens, to urge them to assist the Muslims and engage in the Holy War against the polytheists. This was the reason for the fear of the Franks that continual reinforcements would join the forces opposed to them, and for their retreat in the manner described. He set out to return to Baghdād with the answer to his mission on Wednesday, 11th Rajab of the year 43 (24th November).

News arrived in Rajab from Aleppo that Nūr al-Dīn, its lord, had set out with his 'askar towards the Frankish territories,[2] and had captured a

---

[1] i.e., marshal and keeper of the register of the descendants of the Prophet. His full name has been omitted.
[2] Insert from Abū Shāma (R.H.C., IV, 60): " and made towards Afāmiya and taken possession of a number of Frankish castles and fortresses."

considerable number of Franks ; further that the lord of Antioch had assembled the Franks and in an attack [1] upon Nūr al-Dīn at a moment of heedlessness on his part had inflicted such losses on his 'askar, baggage-train, and animals as had been decreed by their destinies. Nūr al-Dīn himself and his 'askar retreated, and he returned safely to Aleppo, having lost none but a few of his 'askar and killed a fair number of the Franks. He remained for a few days in Aleppo making good the losses of his transport train and replenishing what he required in the way of weapons for the 'askar, then returned to his camp, or, according to other reports, did not return.

A.H. 544

(11th May, 1149, to 29th April, 1150)

The first day of this year was Wednesday, 11th May.

In view of the frequent instances of ill faith on the part of the Franks living in Tyre, 'Akkā, and the coastal ports after their retreat from Damascus, and their disregard of the terms of the armistice which they had agreed upon with Mu 'īn al-Dīn, by making ravages in the districts of Damascus, it became necessary for the amīr Mu 'īn al-Dīn to set out towards their territories with the 'askar of Damascus, in order to carry out raids and make devastations in them. In the latter part of 543 he encamped in Hawrān with the 'askar and

---

[1] Reading (with Abū Shāma) waqasadahu for fasaddahu.

corresponded with the Arabs, and unceasingly directed raids against their towns and outlying districts, day in and day out. He summoned also a considerable body of the Turkmens and gave them a free hand in plundering their territories and in slaying all those of[1] the [Arab] brigands and of the raiders and ravishers who might be seized in their districts. He did not cease from constricting them in this wise, and persisted in causing them vexation and distress, until he constrained them to ask for terms of peace and for the renewal of the agreement for an armistice and amicable relations on payment of a small annual tribute. Envoys went to and fro in order to draw up the treaty and define its terms, and the oaths of loyal observance of its stipulations were taken in Muharram of the year 544. The period of the truce was fixed at two years, and oaths were sworn to this effect. The strife ceased, and the population of both provinces were eased in mind, satisfied at its conclusion, and rejoiced at its provisions.

Simultaneously with this, letters arrived from Nūr al-Dīn, informing him that the lord of Antioch had assembled the Franks of his land, and had come out seeking to do mischief with them in the districts of Aleppo. He added that he himself had moved out with his 'askar to the environs of Aleppo in order to engage him and avert his malice from the provinces, and that there was pressing need for Mu 'īn al-Dīn's assistance by marching to join him in person with his 'askar that they might unite the forces of both their 'askars against him. The state of affairs made it necessary for the amīr

[1] *min* has apparently dropped out of the text before *al-harāmīyah*.

Mu 'īn al-Dīn to depute the amīr Mujāhid al-Dīn Buzān b. Māmīn with a considerable detachment of the 'askar of Damascus to set out towards him and to serve him with loyalty to the utmost of their abilities. The amīr set out on ―――― [1] in the first ten days of Safar (10th to 19th June), while Mu 'īn al-Dīn remained with the rest of the 'askar in Hawrān in order to investigate the condition of the Arabs, to protect their districts, and to encourage them to transport grain upon [2] their camels to Damascus, according to their usual custom.

In Safar of this year also there arrived from Nūr al-Dīn, lord of Aleppo, the glad tidings of 'the favour conferred upon him by God, to Him be the praise, in giving him victory over the deluded muster and broken host of the Franks, so that none of them escaped save a few to spread the news of their perdition and their sudden overthrow. When Nūr al-Dīn was reinforced by the cavalry which he had summoned from the Turkmens and from the outlying districts, as well as by the detachment of the 'askar of Damascus which joined him under the command of the amīr Mujāhid al-Dīn Buzān, his spirits were strengthened, his striking power became formidable, and the numbers of his host were swelled. He marched towards the position of the Franks in the province of Antioch with an army of nearly six thousand fighting horsemen, exclusive of followers and baggage-train, whereas the Franks numbered about four thousand horsemen armed with lances, and a thousand fighting men on foot, exclusive of followers. When they

[1] Left blank in the MS.   [2] Reading '*alā* for '*an*.

reached the place known as Inab,[1] Nūr al-Dīn moved towards them with the victorious 'askar. When they met eye to eye, the infidels made their famous charge upon the Muslims, but the Muslims split up into detachments which attacked them from various directions and swarmed over them. The two forces engaged in a hand-to-hand struggle, enveloped in thick clouds of dust, and the swords of Islām had the final word against them. When the haze was dispersed, God, to whom be the praise and thanks, had bestowed upon the Muslims the victory over the polytheists, and they lay upon the ground prostrate and dust-befouled,[2] bereft of the fruits of their warfare. None of them escaped save a few individuals, whom fate had respited or to whose hearts fear had given wings, to carry the news of their destruction and annihilation. The Muslims set about seizing their spoils and possessing themselves of their baggage-train, and their hands were filled with the booty and animals taken from the Franks. The accursed Prince,[3] their leader, was found stretched out amongst his guard and his knights ; he was recognized and his head cut off and carried to Nūr al-Dīn, who rewarded the bearer of it with a handsome gift. This accursed one was amongst the Frankish knights who were famed for their gallantry, valour, power of cunning, and great stature, and had acquired special repute by the dread which he inspired, his great severity, and excessive ferocity. This engagement took place on Wednesday, 21st Safar (29th June) of the year 44.

---

[1] 12 miles W. by N. of Ma 'arrat al-Nu 'mān.
[2] Reading *mu 'affarīna*.   [3] *al-balins*, i. e., Raymond.

Thereafter Nūr al-Dīn encamped with the 'askar at the gate of Antioch, which, though it had been emptied of its guardians and protectors, and had none left in it save the townspeople [was yet protected by] the numbers of these and the impregnability of their city. Negotiations were begun between Nūr al-Dīn and the citizens on his demand for the surrender of the city to him, in return for a guarantee of their safety and the inviolability of their lives and property, but they put forward the plea that this was a step which they could not take until after all hopes of the arrival of a deliverer and succourer against those who were attacking them should have been lost. They brought to him all the precious objects and money which they could collect, and besought a respite, which was granted to them and consent given to their petitions. Thereupon Nūr al-Dīn posted a detachment of the 'askar to remain on guard before the city and to prevent any from entering it, and himself marched with the rest of the 'askar to Afāmiya. He had already dispatched the amīr Salāh al-Dīn [al-Yāghīsiyānī] with a large section of the army to encamp before it and to engage in besieging it and in operations against it. When the garrison of the town learned of the destruction of the Franks, and lost all hope of means of reinforcement and succour, they asked to surrender on terms, and were promised that their lives should be spared. They then surrendered the town, and Nūr al-Dīn observed his word to them, and posted in it such a garrison as he considered sufficient to guard and defend it. This was on 18th First Rabī' of the year (26th July).

Nūr al-Dīn now withdrew with his 'askar towards Antioch . . .[1] in the direction of Antioch, to reinforce those who were in it. Nūr al-Dīn sought a favourable opportunity to attack and destroy them, but they refrained from venturing into his neighbourhood and feigned to be engaged in other operations. It became necessary to conclude an armistice and agreement with those in Antioch, on the stipulation that everything in the proximity of the territories of Aleppo should belong to him, and everything in the proximity of Antioch to them. He therefore withdrew from the latter in the opposite direction to the Franks, since in this campaign he had captured the castles, forts, and strongholds around Antioch, and had taken abundant booty from them. The amīr Mujāhid al-Dīn Buzān, with the 'askar of Damascus, separated from him, and arrived safely at Damascus with all his company on Tuesday,[2] 4th Second Rabī' of this year. In this engagement he and his party performed distinguished service and were gratefully remembered for their gallantry, courage, soundness of judgment, and knowledge of military tactics. It is from his own words and description that this narrative has been written, but with a view to abridgment and avoidance of prolixity.

It fell out in the meantime that Mu 'īn al-Dīn left his 'askar and came to Damascus during the last days of First Rabī' 544, on account of some matter which necessitated his presence. He ate a

[1] Insert from Abū Shāma (R.H.C., IV, 63) : " on hearing that a detachment of Franks was advancing from the coast."
[2] Apparently an error for Wednesday, the first of the month according to local reckoning having been Sunday 7th August.

hearty meal, as was his usual custom, and was seized thereafter by a loosening of the bowels. His zeal in the conduct of the business on which he was engaged moved him to return to the 'askar in Hawrān, though he was still suffering from this malady, which had in fact become aggravated and led to the weakening of his strength. From this resulted the disease known as dysentery,[1] which acts upon the liver ; it is a disease to be feared and one from which its victim scarcely ever recovers. Some alarm was felt for him, he lost strength, and it was necessary for him to return to Damascus in a litter to have it treated. He reached the city on Saturday, 7th Second Rabī' (14th August), but his illness and the fears for his life increased, his strength ebbed away and he breathed his last in the night preceding Monday, 23rd Second Rabī' of this year (night of Sunday, 28th August). He was buried in the arched recess of the Atābek's palace, in which he had resided, but was afterwards removed to the college which he had founded. After his burial was over, a meeting was held between Husām al-Dīn Bulāq, Mu'aiyid al-Dīn the prefect,[2] Mujāhid al-Dīn Buzān, and the leaders of the troops, in the chamber of Mujīr al-Dīn,[3] to whom the chief authority and precedence belonged, and matters were arranged between them as was most advantageous in the circumstances.

Word was brought from Mosul of the death of the amīr Saif al-Dīn Ghāzī, son of 'Imàd al-Dīn

---

[1] jūsantiryā.

[2] The ra'is or prefect seems to have been the chief civil official in the town.

[3] Abū Sa'īd Ābaq, the Būrid amīr of Damascus, see above p. 259.

Atābek (God's mercy upon him), by reason of a prolonged attack of colic at the beginning of First Jumādā of this year (began 6th September), and that he had devolved his authority upon his brother [Qutb al-Dīn] Mawdūd b. 'Imād al-Dīn, under the control of the amīr 'Alī Kūchak.

News arrived of the movement of the Franks upon the provinces in order to devastate and create havoc in them,[1] and [the amīrs of Damascus] set about arming to ward off their attack. The report of the plundering and enslaving carried on by the Franks in the districts of Hawrān had been carried also to Nūr al-Dīn, who resolved upon arming to attack them, and wrote to those in Damascus informing them of his resolve to prosecute the Holy War, and demanding from them the assistance of a thousand horsemen, to be sent to him under the command of a reliable leader. Now they had made a treaty with the Franks to take joint action against any Muslim forces which should attack them, and therefore tried to put Nūr al-Dīn off with specious arguments and dissimulation. On learning this, however, he set out and encamped at Marj Yabūs, and posted some of his troops at Ya 'fūr.[2] When he approached Damascus, and those in the city were informed of his advance, without knowing whither he intended to proceed, they had sent news of him to the Franks and exacted a promise from them to send support

[1] In consequence of internal rivalries and factional struggles which had broken out at Damascus, the details of which are omitted here.

[2] Marj Yabūs was on the main road from Damascus to the Biqā' and Ba'albek, about 18 miles N.W. of the city ; Ya'fūr 14 miles due W. of Damascus.

against him. The Franks had set out towards the district of Ascalon, in order to rebuild Gaza, but [on receipt of this message] their advance guards arrived at Bānyās. Nūr al-Dīn was informed of their approach, but he paid no heed to them, saying " I shall not turn aside from engaging them in Holy War." Meanwhile he restrained his troops from plundering and doing injury in the villages, and adopted a benevolent attitude to the cultivators, alleviating the distress [caused by the presence of his army], and prayers were continually being offered up for him by the people of Damascus and its provinces, and all the cities and their districts. Prior to this the rains had been withheld from Hawrān, the Ghūta, and the Marj so long that the majority of the people of Hawrān had abandoned it on account of the scarcity and severe distress, the exhaustion (?) [1] of their flocks and herds, and lack of drinking water. When Nūr al-Dīn reached Ba 'albek, it happened by the predestined decree and celestial mercy that the heavens opened their fountains with rains, dews, outpourings, and heavy showers lasting from Tuesday, 3rd Dhu'l-Hijja 44 (4th April) until the following Tuesday. The watercourses overflowed, the pools of Hawrān were filled, the mills turned, and the crops and plants that had been withered up were restored to fresh green shoots. The people clamoured with blessings upon Nūr al-Dīn, saying " This is due to his blessed influence, his justice, and his upright conduct."

Nūr al-Dīn then moved from his camp on the

---

[1] The text has *tarwi'* : one would expect some such phrase as " the difficulty of watering " (su *'ūbat tarawwi*).

A 'waj[1] and encamped by the Wooden Bridge [at the place] known as Manāzil al-'Asākir [2] on Tuesday, 26th Dhu'l-Hijja (25th April). He sent a message to Mujīr al-Dīn and the *ra'is*, in which he said : " It is not my purpose in occupying this encampment to seek to engage in warfare with you nor to besiege you. I have been prompted to this action solely by reason of the frequent appeals of the Muslims of Hawrān and the Arab cultivators whose possessions have been seized, whose women and children have been scattered by the hand of the Franks, and who have none to succour them. It is not possible for me, in view of the powers with which God, to Him be praise, has endowed me in order to bring help to the Muslims and to engage in the Holy War against the polytheists, together with abundance of wealth and of men, neither is it lawful for me, to withhold my hand from them and from giving assistance to them, since I am aware of your inability to guard and protect your dominions, and of the remissness which has led you to call upon the Franks for assistance in fighting against me, and of your bestowal upon them of the moneys of the poor and weak amongst your subjects, whom you thus rob and defraud of their due. This is displeasing in the sight of God and of every Muslim, and there is no alternative but that you shall lend the aid of a thousand horsemen, all pretexts being put aside, who shall be dispatched with a commander whose courage may be relied

[1] The ancient Pharpar, flowing from Mt. Hermon and to the south of the city.

[2] See above p. 283, n. 1. The reading *al-'Āsir* in the text should be corrected accordingly.

upon in order to deliver the port of Ascalon and other places." [1]

The answer to this letter was in these terms : " Between us and thee there is naught but the sword, and a company of the Franks is even now on the way to aid us to repel thee, shouldst thou advance upon us and beleaguer us." When the envoy returned to him with this answer and he read it, he was filled with intense astonishment and indignation at it, and determined to advance against the city and attack it on the morrow of that day, which was Wednesday, 26th [2] April. But thereafter God sent heavy and continuous rains which prevented him from carrying out this purpose, and diverted him from it.

A.H. 545

(30th April, 1150, to 19th April, 1151)

The first day of this year was Monday [1st May].

In Muharram peace was concluded between Nūr al-Dīn and the rulers of Damascus. The cause of this was that Nūr al-Dīn was loth to shed the blood of the Muslims [as he would do] if he were to continue to attack the city and to besiege it ; moreover he was brought certain reports which moved him to this course. It happened also that they promised to recognise his suzerainty, and to insert his name in the allocution from the pulpit at Damascus after those of the Caliph and the Sultan,

---

[1] Abū Shāma (p. 66) reads " Ascalon and Gaza."
[2] The text has 25th.

and also on the coinage. Oaths were duly taken to this effect, and Nūr al-Dīn bestowed on Mujīr al-Dīn a full robe of honour with a collar, and escorted him back to the town with every mark of honour and respect. His name was read from the pulpit of Damascus on Friday 12th [1] Muharram (12th May). Thereafter the ra'īs was summoned to the camp, made the recipient of a full robe of honour also, and escorted back to the town. A company of the troops and domestic officers went out to visit him at the camp, and conversed with him. He made generous gifts to all the mendicants, the poor, and the distressed, so that none who sought him returned empty-handed, and none who begged of him was disappointed of a reward. He left his camp on the eve of Sunday to return to Aleppo, having fully carried out his purposes and plans.

News arrived from Aleppo on 5th Muharram that its 'askar of Turkmens had captured the son of Joscelin, lord of A 'zāz, with his company, and that he was now securely confined in the citadel of Aleppo. All the people rejoiced at this success. Word was brought also that the king Mas 'ūd [2] had arrived with his 'askar in order to attack Antioch. He encamped before Tell Bāshir and blockaded it at some time during the month of Muharram. Nūr al-Dīn also, after his withdrawal from Damascus and the confinement of the son of Joscelin in the citadel of Aleppo, set out with his 'askar to A 'zāz, the town of the son of Joscelin.

---

[1] The text has 14th.
[2] Mas 'ūd I son of Qilij-Arslān, Saljūqid Sultan of Anatolia, reigned 1116–1156.

He encamped before it, blockaded it, and persevered in hostilities against it until God facilitated his capture of it by capitulation, though it was exceedingly impregnable, difficult of access, and lofty. After taking possession of it and establishing a trustworthy garrison in it, he set out to return to Aleppo joyful and triumphant, during the month of First Rabī' (began 28th June). Concerning Tell Bāshir the report arrived on Friday 1st Second Rabī' (28th July) that after blockading it and engaging in hostilities against it, Mas 'ūd had withdrawn from it for certain reasons which necessitated this course, and most of its defenders [subsequently] arrived in it.

Word was brought of the arrival of Mankūbars with a company of Turks and Turkmens in the region of Hawrān and of his junction with the amīr Sirkhāl, governor of Bosra, for the purpose of raiding and devastating the villages of Hawrān. It was rumoured that this was done with the consent of Nūr al-Dīn. They sought to create havoc and destruction at Sarkhad, and to besiege the town, and thereafter withdrew to other districts in order to make mischief and drive the cultivators from the fields.

In Rajab of this year (began 24th October) reports were received from Nūr al-Dīn concerning his victory over the army of the Franks who were encamped in face of him near Tell Bāshir, that their losses and slain were enormous, and the hands [of the Muslims] were filled with spoils and captives, and that he had captured the castle of Khālid,[1] which he was engaged in besieging and blockading.

---

[1] On the Sajur river, S.E. of Tell Bāshir.

During the last ten days of Rajab, word was received from Hawrān that the amīr Mankūbars had encountered al-Hājī and his men from the 'askar of Damascus at the place known as————,[1] and had defeated and mortally wounded him.

A.H. 546

(20th April, 1151, to 7th April, 1152)

The first day of this year was Friday [20th April].

On Wednesday, 13th [2] Muharram (2nd May) the advance guard of the 'askar of Nūr al-Dīn encamped on the land of 'Adhrā in the territory of Damascus, and in the neighbouring parts. On the following Thursday, a considerable detachment of them repaired to al-Saham and al-Nairāb,[3] and laid an ambush by the hill for the 'askar of Damascus. When the 'askar came out of the city to oppose them, they received warning of the ambush from one who came to them in haste, and the ambush having been disclosed, the troops retired to the city, and escaped from disaster without loss, except for some of their rear files, who were wounded.[4] On the following Friday, Nūr al-Dīn arrived with his 'askar and encamped at 'Uyūn Fāsarīya, between 'Adhrā and Dūma, and extending into these localities. On the following Saturday they advanced from that place and

---

[1] The reading of the MS. and text is uncertain.
[2] The text has 10th by error.
[3] Al-Nairāb was at the point where the Baradā and its canals issue from the mountains W. of the city.
[4] Reading juriha for kharaja.

encamped in the lands of Hajīrā and Rāwiya [1] and those parts, in an immense host and vast numbers. The undisciplined elements in the Damascene 'askar, and the robbers and despoilers amongst the mob, made themselves free of the people's crops, which they harvested and uprooted, and of their fruits, which they destroyed without meeting prevention or opposition. Their owners were thereby reduced to bitter distress, the prices were affected, the movements of traders were interrupted and there was general concern. Equipment was issued and preparations were made to guard the city and the wall. Nūr al-Dīn's envoys brought the following message from him to the authorities in the town : " I seek nothing but the good of the Muslims and to make war against the Franks, and to rescue the prisoners who are in their hands. If you will support me with the 'askar of Damascus, and we aid one another in waging the Holy War, and matters are arranged harmoniously and with a single eye to the good, my desire and purpose will be fully achieved." The reply which was sent to him, however, was not of a nature to satisfy him or to coincide with his object.

On Saturday the 23rd of this month (12th May) Nūr al-Dīn moved his troops from the last-mentioned camp and descended in the district of the mosque al-Qadam [2] and the vicinity east and west of it. The number of tents was so great that they reached to the New Mosque, south of the

[1] Both a few miles S.S.E. of the city.
[2] A sanctuary, about two miles S. of the city, greatly venerated on account of a stone showing footprints said to have been made by Moses.

city. This site had never in all previous years been selected for an encampment by commanders of armies. A number of skirmishes took place between the advance guard of Nūr al-Dīn's 'askar and some who went out against it from the city, each side returning thereafter to its own place, but the 'askar itself persistently abstained from advancing upon the city and opening the attack upon its inhabitants, from a desire to avoid the slaying of souls and the disablement by wounds of large numbers of the troops. As a result the evil-doers on both sides were given a free hand to rob, to harvest the cereal-crops in the Marj, the Ghūta, and the outlying districts of the city, to demolish the houses in the villages, and fetch the materials obtained from their demolition into the city or the camp. The losses suffered by their owners, the husbandmen and peasants, were increased, and the appetite of the baser sort and the mob steadily mounted to an outrageous degree of plundering, without any control being exercised over them or measures taken to stop them. The supply of straw for the horses' fodder gave out in all parts, the price rose, and a serious situation came about. Meanwhile reports were received and confirmed of the mustering and assembling of the Franks to come to the aid of the people of Damascus, and all believing and right-minded men were filled with distress of mind and increasing aversion to such a hateful and repulsive state of affairs. No change took place in this uncomfortable situation, and skirmishes went on every day without any regular attack or fighting, until Thursday 13th Safar (31st May).

Thereafter the 'askar of Nūr al-Dīn moved from this camping-station and halted in the districts of Fadhāyā, Halfabaltain,[1] and al-Khāmisain, in the vicinity of the city, and no armies in former times were ever known to have ventured to approach these places. An engagement took place on the day mentioned ; a large number of the cavalry and footsoldiers of the city were wounded, and the livestock of the peasantry and the poorer classes were seized, together with the animals of the humble citizens [2] and the personal property of the peasants of the Ghūta, the Marj, and the outlying districts. On Thursday, 20th [3] Safar (7th June) Nūr al-Dīn moved back from there to Dārayyā, on receiving from several sources the alarm that the Frankish army was approaching the city to bring it relief. This action was taken in order that he might be close to their lines of advance and was dictated by the firmness of his resolve to engage them and the fullness of his preparations for battle with them. For the 'askar of Nūr al-Dīn had reached a number beyond computation for multitude and strength, and was in a state of continual increase by reason of the detachments which came in one after the other from the districts and the Turkmen tribes. Yet in spite of this he would not allow any of his 'askar to press forward into an engagement with any of the Muslims, whether troops of the city or its lower classes, owing to his scruples against shedding blood where it would not serve his ends, since it was only folly and vanity which moved them to

---

[1] These names should be corrected accordingly in the text.
[2] *almuta 'alliqati mina'l-balad.*   [3] Text : 10th.

rush out and display themselves, and they always returned with the worst of the bargain and driven in defeat. After remaining thus for some days he moved to the neighbourhood of al-A 'waj, in view of the proximity of the Frankish army and their determination to attack him. He then judged it necessary to withdraw to al-Zabdānī [1] in order to lure on the Franks, but sent a detachment of his 'askar, numbering about 4,000 horsemen, with several of the leaders, to join the Arabs in the districts of Hawrān, with the objects of seeking out and attacking the Franks and of keeping observation upon their arrival and the issue of the 'askar of Damascus to unite with them, and ultimately of cutting them off.

It fell out that the Frankish army reached the A 'waj after his withdrawal and alighted there on 3rd First Rabī' (20th June) and a large body of them came to [2] the town [of Damascus] in order to supply their wants. Mujīr al-Dīn and Mu'aiyid al-Dīn [3] went out with their domestic officers and a considerable number of the citizens and held a meeting with their king and his domestic officers, but they found them in numbers and strength far short of what they had imagined.

It was agreed between them that the two armies should encamp before the castle of Bosrā, in order to take possession of it and draw the revenues of its territories. Thereupon the army of the Franks marched to Ra's al-Mā[4], but the 'askar of Damas-

---

[1] At the headwaters of the Baradā in the Anti-Lebanon.
[2] Abū Shāma (p. 71), reads *dakhala* (" entered ") for *wasala*.
[3] i.e., the *ra'īs* or prefect Ibn as-Sūfī.
[4] A camping-ground in *H*awrān, near Dilli, and about 20 m. N. of Dar 'ā.

cus was not in a condition to go out to join them, owing to the weakness and mutual dissensions of the troops. The detachment of Nūr al-Dīn's 'askar which was in Hawrān, together with those of the Arabs who had joined with them, marched in great force towards the Franks in order to inflict signal chastisement upon them. The Frankish troops retired for refuge and self-preservation to the Lejāh of Hawrān. On news of this reaching Nūr al-Dīn, he set out and encamped at 'Ain al-Jarr in the Biqā', intending to return towards Damascus and to attack the Franks and the Damascene 'askar. Meanwhile the Franks, on joining forces with the 'askar of Damascus, had repaired to Bosrā, in order to besiege it and engage in hostilities against it. But they were unable to carry this out, and when the governor of the town, Sirkhāl, came out against them with his men, they retired before him discomfited. The Frankish army returned to its own territories between the 11th and 20th of First Rabī', and sent letters to Mujīr al-Dīn and Mu'aiyid al-Dīn demanding the residue of the tribute promised to them for causing the withdrawal of Nūr al-Dīn from Damascus and saying : " Had it not been for us driving him off, he would not have withdrawn from you."

At this time also news was received of the arrival of an Egyptian fleet at the coast towns in exceeding strength and plenitude of number and equipment. It was said that it numbered seventy ships of war laden with men, such a fleet as had never come forth in previous years, and there had been spent upon it a sum said to be in the neighbourhood of three hundred thousand dinars. It approached

Yāfā, one of the coast towns of the Franks, and [those on board] slew, and took captive, and burned whatsoever they laid hands on, besides seizing a considerable number of Greek and Frankish vessels. Thereafter they proceeded to the port of 'Akkā, where they did likewise and took possession of a considerable number of Frankish ships of war, and killed a great host of pilgrims and others. Having dispatched all that they could to Egypt, they proceeded to the ports of Tyre, Bairūt, and Tarābulus, and did likewise there. Nūr al-Dīn promised to march towards this fleet to give it his assistance in crushing the Franks, but it happened that he was preoccupied with the business of Damascus and of his return thither to prosecute its siege. He was in high hopes of taking possession of it, knowing its weakness, the sympathy felt towards him by the troops and citizens, and the reputation for uprightness and justice which he enjoyed amongst them. It is related that Nūr al-Dīn ordered his army to be paraded and counted, and that it reached fully thirty thousand fighting men. Thereafter he set out, and encamped at al-Dalhamīya in the Biqā'. Thence he proceeded towards Damascus, and encamped at Kawkabā, to the west of Dārayyā, on Saturday,[1] 21st First Rabī' (7th July). His cavalry raided the road leading from Hawrān to Damascus, and seized large quantities of camels, grain, and livestock. They raided also the Ghūta and the Marj and drove off all the animals which they encountered. On the Monday he moved from this encampment and halted near Dārayyā, towards the Wooden Bridge.

[1] Probably an error for Sunday (8th July).

A proclamation was made in the city summoning the troops and town-bands to go out against him, but none of them put in an appearance except a few who had gone out formerly. On Wednesday, 24th, he moved from this camp and halted at al-Qatī ʻa [1] and the neighbouring parts. Thence he approached the city until he came close up to it, and some skirmishing took place between the two parties, but without a regular assault being delivered or any vigour put into the fighting.

News was brought to Nūr al-Dīn that his lieutenant, the amīr Hassān al-Manbijī, had captured the city of Tell Bāshir by capitulation on Thursday, 25th First Rabīʻ (12th July). The drums were beaten and the trumpets sounded in his camp to celebrate the joyful tidings. The messenger [2] was accompanied by a party of the notables of Tell Bāshir who came to regulate the affairs of the city [with Nūr al-Dīn].

Nūr al-Dīn remained fixed in his decision not to make an assault upon the city nor to engage its people and troops, out of a scrupulous aversion to the slaying of Muslims, saying : "There is no need for Muslims to be slain by the hands of one another, and I for my part will grant them a respite that they may devote their lives to the struggle with the polytheists." In accordance with these sentiments, negotiations for the establishment of a treaty were carried on during the month of Second Rabīʻ upon certain conditions and proposals which were specified. The negotiations were carried on

---

[1] A southern suburb close to the city, near the " Mosque of the Footprint " (above p. 303, n. 2).
[2] Reading *al-mubashshir* for *al-masīr*.

by the jurist Burkhān al-Dīn ʿAlī al-Balkhī and the amīr Asad al-Dīn Shīrkūh and his brother Najm al-Dīn Ayyūb. The points of disagreement were gradually narrowed down, and negotiations continued, until an agreement was reached on the basis of acceptance of the conditions proposed. The oaths to observe it and the ratification of its terms were exchanged between both parties on Thursday, 10th Second Rabīʿ (26th July) of this year.

On the Friday, the morrow of that day, Nūr al-Dīn set out towards Bosrā in order to encamp before it and besiege it, and requested from Damascus such supplies as he required of war materials and mangonels. The reason for this expedition was that Sirkhāl, the governor who was in the town, was reported to have thrown off his allegiance and become a rebel, and had shown leanings towards the Franks and supported them, therefore Nūr al-Dīn, in displeasure at this conduct on his part, dispatched a considerable force from his ʿaskar against him.

On Thursday, 12th Rajab 546 (25th October), Mujīr al-Dīn, lord of Damascus, proceeded to Aleppo with his domestic officers. On his arrival, he was conducted before Nūr al-Dīn, lord of the city, who received him with honour and excelled in the munificence of his conduct towards him. After Mujīr al-Dīn had promised allegiance to him and to act loyally as his lieutenant in Damascus, he came to an agreement with him on certain matters which he laid before him. Mujīr al-Dīn then left him and returned, rejoicing at the honour and high consideration shown to him by Nūr al-Dīn, and arrived in Damascus on Tuesday, 6th Sha 'bān (20th November).

At the end of Sha 'bān (beginning of December) word arrived from Bānyās that a considerable body of Turkmens had raided its suburbs and, when the Frankish governor of the castle went out with his party to oppose them, had killed and captured a number of the Franks, of whom none escaped save the governor himself and a handful of others. When the news reached those in authority in Damascus they were displeased at such an action as this, in view of the agreement made for an armistice and peaceful relations, and sent out against them a detachment of the 'askar of Damascus. These fell in with some of the Turkmens who had fallen behind the rest of their party, and recovered the booty which was in their hands, and brought back three men of them.[1]

During the early days of Ramadān (began 12th December) a report was received that the greater part of the army of the Franks had proceeded to the Biqā' and, taking its inhabitants by surprise, had raided a considerable number of villages, seized all the men, women, elders, and children in them, and driven off their beasts of burden, livestock, and riding beasts. The news reached the governor of Ba 'albek, who sent out his men against them, and his forces were joined by a great host of the men of the Biqā'. They hastened straight towards the Franks and overtook them at a time when God had sent down upon them such repeated falls of snow as delayed and distracted them. Thereupon they killed the

---

[1] Reading ('ādū) bi-thalāthati nafarin in place of thalāthata.

greater number of their footsoldiers, and recovered those of the captives and animals who had not perished in the snow, but they were very few. The Franks returned in the most miserable conditions of discomfiture and distress, thanks be to God and gratitude for His aid to the Muslims.

A.H. 547

(8th April, 1152, to 28th March, 1153)

The first day of this year was Tuesday [8th April].

In Muharram word arrived from Nūr al-Dīn of his descent upon the castle of Antartūs with his ʿaskar and his capture of it. Those of the Franks who were in it were killed, and the remainder asked for and were granted security for their lives. Having placed a garrison in it, he withdrew and took possession of a number of other castles either by the sword, accompanied by the capture of prisoners, and destruction and burning, or by capitulation.

News arrived from Ascalon on Thursday 10th Muharram (17th April) of the victory of the men of Ascalon over the Franks in their neighbourhood at Gaza, when a great number of them perished and the remainder fled.

In the latter part of Safar (began 8th May), Mujīr al-Dīn set out with the ʿaskar, accompanied by the wazīr Muʾaiyid al-Dīn, towards the castle of Bosrā, and encamped before it in order to besiege its governor, Sirkhāl, and to blockade its population, on account of his disobedience to his commands and prohibitions, his tyranny and injustice to the population of the villages in Hawrān, and his imposition upon them of more than they could bear. In order to prosecute the siege Mujīr al-Dīn called for mangonels and other war equipment. It happened that he proceeded to Sarkhad [during the siege of Bosrā], in order to see it for himself, and having asked permission to this effect from its governor Mujāhid al-Dīn [1] the latter replied : " This place is under thy rule and I hold it on behalf of thee." He also sent instructions to his son, Saif al-Dīn Muhammad, who represented him in it, to make all preparations which were necessary. He received Mujīr al-Dīn with all due ceremony, coming out of the castle to meet him with a party of his officers and bearing the keys, and paying him the respect due to him, cleared the castle of his own men, and Mujīr al-Dīn entered it with his household officers. He was pleased at this, and marvelled at the action of Mujāhid al-Dīn, thanked him for it, and having presented to him the gift of horses and precious objects which he had made ready for him, left him and returned gratefully to his camp before Bosrā. He continued operations against it for a number of days, until a reconciliation was effected and the governor undertook to carry out his wishes, when he returned to Damascus.

[1] Buzān, see above p. 280.

A.H. 548

(29th March, 1153, to 17th March, 1154)

The first day of this year was Sunday [29th March].

On 26th Muharram (23rd April) news arrived from Egypt that al-'Ādil, known as Ibn al-Sallār, who had attained to lofty rank and whose position in the wazirate had become firmly established, so that he exercised absolute control over all functions of government,[1] had been assassinated in his bed by the son of his wife, the amīr al-'Abbās. He had just held a council to determine the expenditure on the manning of the fleet, in order to equip it for sailing to Ascalon with provisions to strengthen its garrison with money, men, and foodstuffs against the Franks who were encamped before it and blockading it with a vast assembly and mighty host, so that its people were on the verge of destruction,[2] and had risen from the council, according to his custom, to rest after his labours and refresh himself by a light slumber.[3] . . .

A succession of reports arrived from Nūr al-Dīn, Sultan of Aleppo and Syria, concerning the strength of his resolve to assemble the 'askars and Turkmens from all the provinces and cities in order to lead an expedition to bring destruction upon polytheism and rebellion against God, and to bring aid to the men of Ascalon against the

[1] Literally : " his commands to release and to seize, and his decisions in loosing and binding were executed."
[2] The wording of the original is rather confused ; I read *wahum* for *wahuwa* in the last line of p. 319.
[3] The further details of the assassination etc., are omitted.

Franks who were besieging it. They had reduced it to sore straits by bringing up to its assault the God-forsaken tower, in the midst of a great host (may God defend it from their malice). It became necessary for Mujīr al-Dīn, lord of Damascus, to proceed to join Nūr al-Dīn with the entire body of his 'askar, in order that they might support one another in the Holy War. He set out on Saturday, 13th Muharram [1] (11th April) and joined forces with him in the north. An agreement was reached between them and all the commanders, the amīrs of the provinces and the Turkmens, who had come with vast forces.

Nūr al-Dīn had just captured by the sword the castle known as Aflis,[2] in accordance with a decree ordained by God and brought to pass by His furtherance and expedition, though it was of exceeding natural strength and strongly fortified. The Franks and Armenians found in the castle were killed and the troops gained a great quantity of money and captives. They set out thereafter [in company], making for the frontier-castle of Bānyās, and encamped before it on Saturday, 19th Safar [3] (16th May), at a moment when it was emptied of its defenders and the opportunity of seizing it was presented. In the meantime, repeated summons were received from the men of Ascalon and appeals to Nūr al-Dīn for aid, whereupon God decreed that strife and slaughter should break out between the Muslim troops, who, though

---

[1] So in the MS., probably by error for 14th.

[2] Identified by Dussaud (*Topographie*, p. 237) with Afīs, on the road from Ma 'arrat al-Nu 'mān to Aleppo, about 20 miles N.N.E. of the former.

[3] The text has 29th, but possibly in error for 26th (23rd May).

they numbered approximately ten thousand horse and foot, retired from Bānyās in disorder before a single Frank had struck a blow at them or any Frankish troops had come up with them. They encamped at the camping-ground known as al-A'waj and determined to renew the siege of Bānyās and to capture it, but thereafter they reverted from this decision without cause or reason, and parted company. Mujīr al-Dīn returned to Damascus and entered it safe and sound, both himself and all his men, on Monday, 11th First Rabī' [1]; Nūr al-Dīn returned to Hims and encamped there with his 'askar.

News was received of the arrival of the Egyptian fleet at Ascalon. The spirits of its population were strengthened by the money, men, and food-stuffs [brought by the fleet], and they captured a considerable number of the vessels of the Franks at sea, while these for their part did not relax their siege and blockade of the city and constantly attacked it with the aid of the tower. . . .[2] They pressed upon it with attacks both morning and evening, until at length the way was opened to them to deliver an assault upon it at a certain point in the city wall. Having battered it down, they rushed into the town, and a great host were killed on both sides. Necessity and force of arms compelled [the men of Ascalon] to seek terms of surrender, which were granted to them, and all of them who could depart left the city and proceeded by land or sea to Egypt and elsewhere.

[1] So in the text, but the 11th must have been a Friday or Saturday (5th or 6th June); an emendation to 11th Second Rabī' (Monday, 6th July) scarcely fits in with the context.
[2] A paragraph relating to internal dissensions at Damascus is omitted.

It is said that in this captured frontier-city there were innumerable quantities of military stores, moneys, provisions, and grain-stuffs. When the news of its fall spread throughout the country, it was received with grief and distress, and the occurrence of such an event gave cause for redoubled anxiety—magnified by He whose irresistible decree cannot be withstood nor the execution of His foreordained command opposed.

In Dhu'l-Qa 'da (began 18th January, 1154) prices rose in Damascus owing to the absence of the usual grain convoys from the north, Nūr al-Dīn, lord of Aleppo, having issued orders preventing and prohibiting this traffic. This measure caused great distress among persons of humble condition and the poor and weak. The price of a sack of wheat reached twenty-five dinars and even more. A large number of persons withdrew from the town, and they suffered such hardship, distress and weakness that a great many died on the roadsides, and the supply of provisions was cut off on all sides. It was said that Nūr al-Dīn was determined to proceed to the siege of Damascus and hoped to capture it by this means, since it was difficult for him to break down its resistance owing to the strength of its sultan and the number of its troops and auxiliaries—we pray God for speedy release from distress and to look upon His creatures with compassion and mercy, as He hath ever shown goodness and bounty to them in the past.

A.H. 549

(18th March, 1154, to 6th March, 1155)

The first day of this year was Wednesday [17th March].

Between the 11th and 20th of Muharram the amīr and isfahsallār Asad al-Dīn Shīrkūh reached the outskirts of Damascus as envoy from Nūr al-Dīn, lord of Aleppo. He encamped by al-Qasab in the Marj with a body of troops numbering about a thousand. This action was resented and caused a feeling of hostility towards him ; Mujīr al-Dīn would not go out to receive him and refused to associate with him. Correspondence was exchanged as circumstances required, but resulted neither in the establishment of concord nor in any satisfactory arrangement.

The price of provisions rose owing to the interruption of the grain-convoys, and Nūr al-Dīn arrived with his 'askar to join Shīrkūh on Sunday, 3rd Safar (18th April). He encamped at 'Uyūn al-Fāsarīya by Dūma, and on the following day moved and halted on the lands of the estate known as Bait al-Ābār,[1] in the Ghūta. He advanced on the city from the east, and a large body of its troops and armed bands went out to oppose them. Some fighting took place between them, after which each party returned to its own quarters, but Nūr al-Dīn renewed the attack day after day. On Sunday, 10th Safar (25th April), by virtue of the predestined decree and effective command [of God],

---

[1] Located by Dussaud (*Topographie*, 312) immediately to the E. and S.E. of the city.

and for the good fortune of the king Nūr al-Dīn, and the people of Damascus, and all men together, Nūr al-Dīn, having mustered his troops and made preparations for a vigorous attack, advanced early in the morning. The 'askar of Damascus went out against him as usual and fighting began between them. Nūr al-Dīn's troops then attacked from the east at a number of points, and the Damascenes fell back before them until they were close up to the wall at the Gate of Kaisān [1] and the tannery to the south of the city. Owing to the bad management of the authorities and the foreordained decrees, there was not a breathing soul, either of troops or townsmen, upon the wall, save for a negligible handful of Turks, whose resistance could be discounted, on one of the towers. One [2] of the footsoldiers went forward to the wall, upon which there was a Jewish woman, who let down a rope to him. He climbed up and obtained a footing on the wall, unperceived by any, and was followed by a number of others. Nūr al-Dīn's troops then hoisted a standard, and planting it on the wall shouted *Ya Mansur,*[3] whereupon the troops and citizens ceased to make further resistance owing to the affection which they entertained for Nūr al-Dīn, and his justice and good reputation. One of the woodcutters hastened with his axe to the East Gate and broke its bolts ; the gate was thrown open, and Nūr al-Din's 'askar entered by it with ease and confidence, and proceeded swiftly through the main streets. Not one man put up

[1] At the S.E. angle of the wall, in the Jewish quarter.
[2] Read *ba'du* for *ba'da.*
[3] Literally " O victorious one."

any resistance to their advance. The Thomas Gate [1] also was opened, and the troops entered through it. Thereafter, Nūr al-Dīn himself and his domestic officers entered the city, to the joy of all the people, troops and 'askarīs, because of their sufferings from famine, the high cost of food, and fear of being besieged by the Frankish infidels.

Mujīr al-Dīn, perceiving that he was overborne and mastered, fled with his domestic officers to the citadel. A message was sent to him, with a guarantee of security for his life and property, whereupon he went out to Nūr al-Dīn, who reassured him and promised him favourable treatment, and himself entered the citadel on the Sunday already mentioned. He at once gave orders to proclaim an amnesty to the citizens and to prevent any of their houses from being plundered. A number of the baser sort and the rabble hastened to the 'Alī market and other markets, and rioted and plundered, but the lord the king Nūr al-Dīn sent to the citizens that which restored their tranquillity and removed their apprehensions. Mujīr al-Dīn removed all his possessions from his residences in the citadel, and all his treasuries of money, weapons, and furnishings, notwithstanding their quantity, to the Palace of the Atābek, the residence of his grandfather, where he stayed for some days. Nūr al-Dīn then gave him instructions to move to Hims, with all those of his intimates and followers who desired to remain with him. A diploma had previously been made out by Nūr al-Dīn assigning a number of the districts of Hims to him and his

[1] In the N.E. wall, leading into the Christian quarter.

troops as territorial holdings, and he set out thither according to the foreordained decision [of God].

On the day after the morrow of that day, the leading citizens amongst the jurists and merchants were summoned and addressed in terms which added to their satisfaction and joy, and a beneficent attention was given to measures which would promote their wellbeing and bring realization of their hopes, whereupon manifold blessings were invoked and praises bestowed upon him and thanks given to God for the disposition with which He had endowed him. This was followed by the abolition of the duties on the melon market and the vegetable market, and of the farming-out of the canals ; the decree to that effect was drawn up and was read from the pulpit after the Friday prayers, and the people rejoiced at this earnest of better times, and husbandmen, cultivators, women,[1] and journeymen raised their voices openly in prayer to God to grant him length of days and to give victory to him and to his standards.

In the last days of Muharram (middle of April) of this year the report arrived from Mārdīn of the death of its lord, the amīr Husām al-Dīn [Timur-tāsh] son of Il-Ghāzī b. Ortuq (God's mercy upon him) on 1st Muharram. He was possessed not only of nobility of station among the Turkmens, but also of sagacity and affection for men both of religious and profane learning, and was distinguished among his peers by the excellence of his character.

During First Jumādā (began 14th July), word

[1] So in the text, but al-huram is perhaps an error for [ahl] al-huraf, " artisans."

was received from Egypt that a considerable number of Frankish vessels from Sicily had sailed up to the city of Tinnīs while its inhabitants were off their guard, and had made an assault upon it, killed, captured, enslaved, and plundered, and retired with their booty three days later, leaving the place derelict. Later on those who had fled from it by sea after the disaster, and those who had escaped and concealed themselves, made their way back. There was general distress on hearing this abhorrent news.

A.H. 550

(7th March, 1155, to 24th February, 1156)

The first day of this year was Monday [7th March].

On 24th First Rabī‘ (28th May) terms of truce were agreed upon between al-Malik al-‘Ādil [1] Nūr al-Dīn, lord of Damascus, and the king of the Franks for the space of one year, and the convention remained in force upon these terms until the expiry of the specified period.

A few days later a royal command was issued by Nūr al-Dīn to arrest Dahhāk, the governor of Ba ‘albek. He demanded of him the surrender of the city, and on his consenting to do so the victorious ‘askar set out to take it over. It was surrendered on Thursday, 7th Second Rabī‘ [2]

---

[1] " The Just King." This is the first appearance in Syria of this type of semi-royal title, which apparently originated in Egypt some years earlier as the title of the omnipotent wazīrs, and was subsequently used by all the Aiyūbid and Mamlūk sultans.

[2] The text has First Rabī‘, which conflicts with the date given above.

(9th June), and Nūr al-Dīn entrusted its government and defence to the officer who received its surrender.

During Sha 'bān (began 30th September), news arrived from Egypt that the holder of the wazirate, the Knight of Islām, Ibn Ruzzīk, when he had established his authority, determined to come to terms with the Franks and make peace with them, and to induce them to withhold their malevolence by a bribe of money to be paid to them from the Treasury and from a tax levied on the revenues of the fiefs held by the commanders of the territorial forces. When, however, he took counsel of the latter in regard to this, they were indignant and rejected his proposal with horror, and determined to depose him and set up in his place a person in whom they had confidence. They chose a commander known as the amīr ————,[1] who was noted for gallantry, courage, and capacity for government, and approval was given to the appointment of a naval officer distinguished by his energy and of proved insight in naval operations to command the Egyptian fleet. This man selected a company of seamen who spoke the Frankish tongue, dressed them in Frankish dress, and sent them forth on a number of vessels belonging to the fleet. He himself went out to sea to investigate various places and hiding-places and the routes usually taken by the vessels of the Greeks, and to obtain information about them. Thereafter he repaired to the harbour of Tyre, on information which had come to him that there was a large Greek polacca there with many men

[1] lacuna in the text.

and a great quantity of riches. He made an assault upon it, seized it, killed those who were in it and took possession of its contents. After staying for three days, he burned the vessel and went out to sea again, where he captured some vessels with Frankish pilgrims, and having slain, taken prisoner, and plundered, returned to Egypt with his booty and his captives.

In the month aforementioned, news arrived from Aleppo of the outbreak of strife between the sons of the king Mas'ūd [son of Qilij Arslān] after his death, the sons of Qutulmish, and the sons of Qilij Arslān,[1] and that al-Malik al-'Ādil Nūr al-Dīn, lord of Damascus and Aleppo, intervened between them in order to promote peace and reconciliation and to warn them against a dispute which would strengthen their Greek and Frankish enemies and embolden them to attack the Muslim fortresses. He put out all his efforts to this end with admirable mediation and lavish gifts and gratifications, and peace was restored between them.

In the month of Ramadān (began 9th October), further news arrived that al-Malik al-'Ādil Nūr al-Dīn had descended with his 'askar upon the territories belonging to the King Qilij Arslān,[2] son of the King Mas'ud [b. Qilij-Arslān] b. Sulaimān b. Qutulmish, king of Qūniya and the neighbouring lands, and had captured a number of its castles and fortresses by the sword and by capitulation. The king Qilij Arslān and his two brothers,

---

[1] *i.e.*, the various branches of the Saljūqid house in Anatolia.
[2] Qilij-Arslan II, who succeeded Mas'ūd I in this year and reigned till 588/1192.

Dhu'l-Nūn and Dūlāb (?), were engaged in warfare with the sons of al-Dānishmand. It fell out that the sons of the King Mas'ūd were sustained with Divine aid against the sons of al-Dānishmand and granted victory over their forces in a battle fought near a place known as Āqsarā in Sha'bān 550 (began 30th September). When Qilij Arslān returned and learned of the action of al-Malik al-'Ādil Nūr al-Dīn in his lands, he considered it a detestable outrage in view of the treaty terms, truce, and marriage relations which existed between them, and wrote letters to him in a tone of censure, reprobation, menaces and threats. Nūr al-Dīn replied to him with polite excuses and smooth words, and the situation between them remained unchanged on this footing.

A.H. 551

(25th February, 1156, to 12th February, 1157)

The first day of this year was Friday [24th February].

After the arrival of the pilgrims [from Mecca] on Friday 6th Safar (30th March), al-Malik al-'Ādil Nūr al-Dīn set out towards Aleppo with a portion of his 'askar on Tuesday 24th Safar (17th April), on receipt of news of the plundering and devastation wrought by the Franks in the districts of Aleppo. He was met on the way by a courier bringing the glad tidings of the victory of his 'askar at Aleppo over the Franks who were ravaging near Hārim, and their slaughter and capture of a number of them. There arrived along with the courier a considerable number of heads of these Franks, and they were carried in procession round Damascus.

On the eve of Thursday, 9th Sha'bān 551, corresponding to 27th September, and at the second hour thereof, there befel a mighty quaking of the earth. . . . This quaking was repeated on the eve of Wednesday 22nd Sha'bān (10th October), and similar shocks took place both before and after. . . . News arrived from Aleppo and Hamāh of the destruction of many places and the collapse of one of the bastions of Afāmiya in these terrible earthquakes. . . . Further shocks took place during Ramadān and Shawwāl,[1] too many to be recorded. God Most High averted from Damascus and its environs the consequences which the people dreaded from the frequence and persistence of this quaking, out of His compassion and mercy towards them (to Him be the praise and thanks), but reports were received from Aleppo of the multitude of shocks there and the destruction of some of its dwellings. As for [2] Shaizar, the greater number of its houses fell down upon their inhabitants, so that a large number of them were killed, and at Kafr Tāb the population took to flight in fear of their lives. The same was reported from Hamāh, but it was not learned what happened in the other cities of Syria on this signal manifestation of the Divine power.

On Wednesday 21st Ramadān (14th November) the king Nūr al-Dīn (God increase him victorious) returned to his city of Damascus from Aleppo and

---

[1] The detailed account of many of these shocks is omitted.
[2] Reading *'amma* for *'illā*.

the provinces of Syria, after investigating and regulating their affairs, and safe and sound in person and host, after the establishment of friendly relations between him and the son of sultan Mas'ūd and lord of Qūniya, and the settlement of the conflict which had broken out between them.

During Shawwāl (began 17th November) terms of agreement and truce were agreed upon between him and the king of the Franks for the period of one full year beginning from Sha'bān (began 19th September), it being stipulated that the tribute paid to them from Damascus should be eight thousand dinars of Tyre. The protocol of agreement was written down to this effect, after it had been confirmed by binding oaths.

In Sha'bān news was received from Egypt of the scarcity and rise in the prices of grain there and the great distress caused thereby to the weak and poor and others. The governor issued orders couched in emphatic terms to the husbandmen and to those who were holding up large stocks of grain to sell what was surplus to their own food requirements to those who had little and were in need. Nevertheless, and notwithstanding the reported sufficiency of the Nile floods during this year, conditions tended only to become increasingly worse.

During the last ten days of Dhu'l-Hijja (3rd to 12th February), the Frankish infidels treacherously broke the terms of the armistice and treaty which had been concluded, by reason of the arrival of a considerable number of Franks by sea and the strengthening of their military force thereby. They marched to the district of al-Sha'rā, in the neigh-

bourhood of Bānyās, where there were assembled
at the time the grazing horses of the 'askarīs and
of the citizens, the beasts of burden of the peasantry of the villages, and the animals of the merchants and Arab cultivators,[1] in all a vast number
beyond computation, on account of the need of
pasturing them there and their reliance on the
armistice which had been concluded by agreement.
It happened that there was some neglect on the
part of the Turks who were charged with their
protection, and the Franks seized the opportunity,
drove off all that they found, and robbed their
owners of them, not to speak of the Turkmens and
others whom they took captive. So they returned
victorious, booty-laden, and sinning[2]—may God
in His wisdom take upon Himself the punishment
of them and the reversal of fortune against them,
" for to Him is that not difficult."

A.H. 552

(13th February, 1157, to 1st February, 1158)

The first day of this year was Wednesday
[13th February].

On the eve of Wednesday, 19th Safar[3] (3rd April),
there was a great earthquake shock just about
dawn . . . followed by another on the eve of the
Thursday following . . . and another after the
congregational prayer of the Friday following. A

---

[1] Abū Shāma (R.H.C., IV, 84), reads " Arabs and cultivators."
[2] Abū Shāma (l.c.) reads āminīn, "unmolested," instead of āthimīn.
[3] Either the day of the week or the date must be wrong ; this
Wednesday was probably 15th Safar.

series of reports was received from the north relating the terrible effects of these earthquake shocks, both the earlier and the latter ones, in the city of Shaizar, Hamāh, Kafr Tāb, Afāmiya, and the neighbourhood as far as places in the province of Aleppo.

At the same time a number of envoys came to Nūr al-Dīn from the lords of the provincial cities, castles, and districts to make preparations for an immediate attack upon the accursed enemies of God and the raiding of those who were opposed to him of the infidel antagonists, the sowers of disorder in the lands and breakers of their solemn oaths to maintain friendly and peaceful relations. Thereupon the lord Nūr al-Dīn gave orders to decorate the city in rejoicing at these circumstances and himself did on this occasion what it had never been the custom to do in the days of former governors. He commanded that the citadel and royal residence should be decorated by adorning their walls with weapons of war, such as cuirasses, breast-plates, shields, swords, spears, Frankish bucklers, lances, banners, flags, kettledrums, trumpets, and various kinds of instruments of music. Troops, citizens, and strangers all pressed to view this sight and expressed their admiration of the spectacle, which lasted for seven days— may God couple this with furtherance and success and the realization of the hopes for the abandonment of the lying and misguided infidels, by His goodness and bounty.

On Tuesday, 3rd First Rabī' [1] (16th April) the

---

[1] The text here has 13th and in the next paragraph 12th, which conflict with the dates given below.

lord Nūr al-Dīn (God prolong his days) set out for Ba 'albek in order to investigate its condition and attend to the organization of the garrison troops in it. Reports also reached him from Hims and Hamāh of the raiding of the accursed Franks upon those districts and of their setting their hands to plundering and disorder therein—may God grant a good reversal of fortune against them and speedily bring destruction upon them.

On Monday, 2nd First Rabī' (15th April) Zain al-Hujjāj (God bestow upon him safety) set out to proceed to Egypt as envoy from the lord Nūr al-Dīn in order to present to the governor there the letter which he carried with him. He was accompanied also by the envoy who had come from Egypt.

On Sunday, 15th First Rabī' (28th April) the messenger of good tidings arrived from the victorious 'askar at Ra 's al-Mā' with the news that Nusrat al-Dīn Amīr-Mīrān,[1] on receiving information that the accursed Franks had dispatched a numerous and well-equipped squadron of their best warriors to Bānyās to hold it and to strengthen it with weapons and money, had hastily marched out to meet them with the victorious 'askar. It was said that they numbered seven hundred horsemen of the bravest of the Hospitallers, the serjeantry and the Templars,[2] apart from foot-soldiers. Nusrat al-Dīn came up with them before they reached Bānyās, but after its defenders had gone out to join them, and he inflicted a crushing defeat upon them. He had placed some of his stoutest

---

[1] The brother of Nūr al-Dīn.
[2] *Al-isbitārīya wal-sarjundīya wad-dāwīya.*

Turks in ambushes at various points, and when the battle began between them, and the Muslims chanced to retire before the Franks in the first round, the men in ambush came out against them, and God sent down His aid upon the Muslims and withdrew it from the polytheists. The whetted swords were given power over their heads and necks with the terrible blows of destiny and death, the unerring lances and severing arrows seized upon their bodies, so that none of them escaped, save a few of those whom destiny had respited and to whose hearts fear had given wings. There was scarce a man in the whole company but was killed, or wounded, or despoiled, or taken captive or left abandoned on the ground, and there fell into the hands of the Muslims an uncountable booty in their horses, weapons, beasts, moneys and documents [1] and in the number of them taken prisoner and the heads of their slain. The main body of their footsoldiers, consisting of Franks and of the Muslims of the Jabal 'āmila who had attached themselves to them, were wiped out by the sword. This battle took place on Friday, 13th First Rabī' (26th April), and the prisoners, with the heads of the slain and the [captured] equipment, reached the capital on the Monday following. They were taken in procession round the city, when a great host and vast multitude assembled to see them, and it was a gratifying public holiday, whereat the hearts of the Believers and the bands of the Muslims were rejoiced. This was a recompense from God (exalted be His name) for the evildoing

---

[1] This is the usual meaning of *qarātīs*, but it may also mean " she-camels " and a number of other objects.

of the polytheists, for their shamelessness in violating their oaths to observe the armistice with the lord Nūr al-Dīn and breaking their agreement to maintain peace, and their raid upon the horses at pasture and the cattle of the merchants and cultivators who had been constrained to seek the pasturage in al-Sha 'rā, trusting to the security offered by the armistice and misled by the confirmation of the treaty of amity. A party of the prisoners taken from the polytheists were sent to the lord Nūr al-Dīn at Ba 'albek and he gave orders for their execution without respite—this is a humiliation for them in the present life, and in the life to come they shall have bitter chastisement, " and those who have done unjustly shall know with what reversal they shall be reversed." [1]

This brilliant victory was followed by a second joyful report from Asad al-Dīn [Shīrkūh], that a large number of the warriors of the Turkmens had joined with him, and that he had been victorious over a considerable squadron of the polytheists, which came out from their castles in the north. They were put to flight and the Turkmens despoiled all those of them whom they seized. Thereafter Asad al-Dīn arrived at Ba 'albek with the 'askar composed of the leaders and fighting men of the Turkmens, who had come in large numbers and a vast host to engage in the Holy War against the polytheists, the enemies of God. He met al-Malik al-'Ādil Nūr al-Dīn on Tuesday [2] 25th First Rabī', when the decision was taken to proceed to the territories of the polytheists in order to subjugate them and to carry out the obligation

---

[1] Qur'ān, XXVIII, 225.   [2] The text has Monday.

of the Raid and the Holy War against their inhabitants, and to make a beginning by descending on Bānyās and blockading it and endeavouring to capture it—may God further this by His grace and hasten its fulfilment by His aid ! [1]

On Thursday, 27th First Rabī' (2nd May) Nūr al-Dīn arrived in his capital in order to arrange for the issue of weapons and the despatch of them to the 'askar. After a stay of a few days he set out at once to join the assembled squadrons of the Turkmens and Arabs, to engage in the Holy War with the infidel antagonists. Immediately on his arrival he proceeded to carry out the business on which he had come. He gave orders to dispatch what mangonels and weapons were required to the victorious 'askar and [2] to make proclamation in the city calling upon those who had undertaken to engage in the Holy War and upon the volunteer bands from both the men of the city and strangers to equip themselves and prepare to wage a struggle with the Franks, the upholders of polytheism and heresy. He himself made haste to set out at once to the victorious 'askar, pressing on his journey without hesitation or delay, on Saturday, the last day of First Rabī', and he was followed up by a vast multitude, imposing in its numbers, of armed bands, volunteers, religious teachers, Sūfīs, and pious devotees.

On the following Saturday, 7th Second Rabī' (18th May), and after the descent of al-Malik al-'Ādil Nūr al-Dīn upon Bānyās with his 'askar and

---

[1] Similar expressions occur at intervals below, and have generally been omitted without remark.
[2] Reading *wa* before *bi'n-nidā'i*.

his siege of it with catapults, a carrier-pigeon arrived from the victorious 'askar in the outskirts of Bānyās with a letter publishing news of the arrival of a courier from Asad al-Dīn's camp with the Turkmens and Arabs at Hūnīn,[1] bringing a report to the following effect. The Franks (God forsake them) dispatched a troop of their principal leaders and warriors, numbering more than a hundred horse exclusive of followers, in order to fall upon this party, imagining that they were only a handful of men and not knowing that they were some thousands strong. When the Franks approached them, the Muslims leapt towards them as lions to their prey and overwhelmed them with slaughter, capture, and spoliation, and none but a few of them escaped. The prisoners, the heads of the slain, and their equipment of choice horses, bucklers, and lances arrived at the city on the Monday following the date mentioned, and were paraded through it, whereupon all hearts were rejoiced and multiplied thanks to God for this further bounty granted in succession to the previous one—may He hasten their destruction and overthrow. This mark of Divine favour was followed by the arrival of a carrier-pigeon from the camp at Bānyās on Tuesday, the morrow of that day, announcing the capture of the city of Bānyās by the sword after four hours [2] had passed of this same Tuesday, when, the sap having been finished and fire thrown into it, the tower which had been undermined fell down, the troops forced their way

---

[1] The site of the later Castellum Novum, at the junction of the northern road from Safad and the cross-road from Tibnīn to Bānyās.

[2] *i.e.*, from sunrise.

in through the gap, plied the sword in slaying its inhabitants and plundered its contents. Those who escaped fled to the citadel, but the siege of them was still proceeding and their capture would not long be delayed by the favour of God Most High—may God further it and bring it speedily to pass.

It befel thereafter, in accordance with the fore-ordained decrees, that the Franks assembled together from their fortresses, with the determination to rescue Humphrey,[1] lord of Bānyās, and his Frankish companions who were besieged along with him in the citadel of Bānyās. These for their part had come to the verge of destruction and had exerted themselves to obtain terms of capitulation from the lord Nūr al-Dīn, offering to surrender what they still held of the citadel and all its contents, if they might be released in safety, but he would not consent to their request and desire. When the king of the Franks arrived from the direction of the mountain with his host of horse and foot, taking by surprise the two armies, that which was encamped[2] before Bānyās to besiege it, and that which was holding the road in order to prevent access to it, policy necessitated their withdrawal from thence and the Franks reached the fortress and relieved [3] those who were holding it. When, however, they saw that the wall of Bānyās and the dwelling of its inhabitants were entirely in ruins they despaired of rebuilding it after such destruction. This was in the last ten days of Latter Rabī' (12th to 20th June).

---

[1] al-hunufrī.
[2] Reading an-nāzili for an-nāzilaini (cf. R.H.C., IV, 88).
[3] Reading istakhlasū.

On Wednesday, 9th First Jumādā (19th June), the pigeons arrived with letters from the camp of Nūr al-Dīn conveying information that al-Malik al-'Ādil Nūr al-Dīn, learning that the camp of the Frankish infidels was at al-Mallāha,[1] between Tiberias and Bānyās, set out with his victorious 'askar of Turks and Arabs and marched with all speed. When he was almost upon them and they, taken by surprise,[2] saw his standards overshadowing them, they made speed to don their armour and to mount, and dividing into four detachments they charged upon the Muslims. Thereupon the king Nūr al-Dīn dismounted and his stout warriors dismounted with him, and they smote them with arrows and spears, so that in less time than it takes to tell it, their feet slipped with them and death and destruction overwhelmed them. God, the Mighty, the Omnipotent, sent down His aid upon His faithful followers and His abandonment upon the stiff-necked infidels ; we overpowered their horsemen with slaughter and captivity, and the swords extirpated their footsoldiers. They were a great number and a vast assembly, but none of them escaped, according to the report of a reliable informant, save ten men whom destiny had respited and to whose hearts fear had lent wings. It was said that their king (God curse them) was amongst them, and it was said that he was one of the slain, but no information was obtained concerning him, though a vigorous search was made for him. Of the 'askar of Islām there were lost none but two men, one of whom was a noted warrior, who had

---

[1] Close to the N.W. corner of Lake Hulah.

[2] Reading *ghārrūna*.

slain four of the infidel braves, and was himself
slain at the arrival of his destined hour, the other
an unknown stranger. Each of them passed away
a martyr, rewarded and recompensed (God's mercy
upon them). The hands of the 'askarīs were filled
with an innumerable quantity of the horses,
equipment, beasts, and baggage furniture of the
Franks, and their church with its famous apparatus
came into the hands of the king Nūr al-Dīn. This
was a mighty conquest and manifest aid from God,
the Powerful, the Giver of victory—may God
increase thereby the might of Islām and abase
polytheism and its faction.

The prisoners and the heads of the slain reached
Damascus on the Monday following the date of the
victory. They had set the Frankish horsemen in
pairs upon camels, each pair being accompanied
by one of their standards unfurled, to which were
attached a number of skins of their heads with
their hair. Their leaders and the commanders of
their fortresses and provinces were set each one
upon a horse, each wearing his coat of mail and
helmet and with a standard in his hand, while the
footsoldiers—serjeants and Turcopoles [1]—were
roped together in threes or fours or fewer or more.
An uncountable number of the townsfolk—old
men, young men, women, and children—came out
to see what God (exalted is His Name) had granted
to the whole body of Muslims in this brilliant
victory, and they multiplied their praises and
glorification to God, and their fervent prayers for
al-Malik al-'Ādil Nūr al-Dīn, their defender and
protector.

[1] *ad-durkubūlīya.*

Nūr al-Dīn now set about delivering an attack upon their territories in order to take possession of them and subjugate them (may God aid and support him therein by His grace and favour). On Thursday, 25th First Jumādā (4th July) . . . and on the eve of Sunday, 4th Latter Jumādā (14th July) repeated earthquake shocks occurred.[1] Reports arrived from the north that these earthquakes were felt in Aleppo and likewise in Hims with a violence which terrified and distressed their inhabitants, and that several places were destroyed in them, and in Hamāh, Kafr Tāb, and Afāmiya. Amongst the places destroyed were some which had been rebuilt after their destruction in the former earthquakes. It was reported also from Taimā [2] that these earthquakes had done terrible damage to its dwellings.

Between the 11th and 20th of Latter Jumādā a series of reports were received of the arrival of [Qilij Arslān] the son of Sultan Mas'ūd,[3] with a great host in order to besiege Antioch. The circumstances made necessary the establishment of an armistice between al-Malik al-'Ādil Nūr al-Dīn and the King of the Franks, and letters passed to and fro between them with proposals and disputations, so that the matter went amiss and failed to lead to the desired conclusion of peace and a satisfactory and successful formula. Al-Mālik al-'Ādil (God increase him victorious) arrived with a portion of his 'askar at the seat of his authority on Saturday, 25th Latter Jumādā

---

[1] Details omitted. Further shocks are recorded below during Rajab (August).

[2] On the northern slopes of the Jabal Drūz.

[3] See above p. 324.

(3rd August), and kept the remainder of his 'askar and his officers, together with the Arabs, in the field, opposite the provinces of the polytheists (God forsake them). On Sunday, 3rd Rajab (11th August) he set out towards Aleppo and its districts in order to make a tour of inspection of them and supervise their defence, since the polytheists had ravaged them and the troops of the king Ibn Mas'ūd were in their immediate neighbourhood.

[After renewed earthquake shocks in the month of Rajab] reports arrived from the north with the horrifying and disquieting news that Hamāh, together with its citadel and all its houses and dwellings, had fallen down upon the heads of its inhabitants—old men, young men, children and women, a large number and vast assembly of souls—so that none escaped, save the merest handful. As for Shaizar, its suburb escaped, except for what had been destroyed earlier, but its famous castle fell down upon its governor, Tāj al-Dawla, son of Abu'l-'asākir ibn Munqidh (God's mercy upon him), and his followers, save for a few who were without. At Hims, the population had fled in panic from the town to its outskirts and themselves escaped, while their dwellings and the citadel were destroyed. At Aleppo some of the buildings were destroyed, and its people left the town. As for the more distant castles and fortresses as far as Jabala and Jubail, the earthquakes produced hideous effects on them ; Salamīya was ruined and all the places in succession therefrom as far as al-Rahba and its neighbourhood. Had not the mercy and goodness of God overtaken His creatures and the cities, there would have been a terrible disaster, and a serious and distressing situation.[1]

At the beginning of Dhu'l-Qa'da (began 5th December) news was received from Hims of the death of its governor, the amīr entitled Salāh al-Dīn [al-Yāghīsiyānī]. In his youth he enjoyed high favour in the service of 'Imād al-Dīn Atābek Zankī, lord of Aleppo and Syria (God's mercy upon him), and gained advancement with him by reason of his loyalty, his capacity, trustworthiness in acting on his behalf, and sureness of judgment. When he was stricken in years, his strength left him and forced him to give up active pursuits except for riding on horseback. Subsequently he was compelled of necessity to travel in a litter to settle affairs and inspect his districts, but down to the time of his death he suffered no diminution of bodily senses and intelligence with which fault could be found. He was succeeded in his rank and office by his sons.

Mention has already been made of the departure of al-Mālik al-'Ādil Nūr al-Dīn from Damascus with his troops towards the cities of Syria, on receipt of news that the factions of the Franks (God forsake them) were assembling together and proceeding against them, being emboldened to attack them by reason of the continuous earthquakes and shocks which had afflicted them and of the destruction wrought amongst the castles, citadels, and dwellings in their districts and marches. [Nūr al-Dīn therefore took measures] to

[1] Further shocks are related during Ramaḍān and Shawwāl (October to November), which were especially severe in Aleppo and Ḥamāh.

protect and defend them and to bring solace to those of the men of Hims, Shaizar, Kafr Tāb, Hamāh and elsewhere who had escaped with their lives, whereupon there assembled to join him a great host and vast numbers of men from the fortresses and provincial cities and from the Turkmens. He encamped with them in exceeding force opposite the army of the Franks in the neighbourhood of Antioch, and encompassed them so that not one horseman of theirs could set out to make a raid.

A few days after the beginning of Ramadān of the year 552 (began 7th October, 1157) al-Mālik al-'Ādil Nūr al-Dīn contracted a severe illness. When it grew worse and he feared that it might prove fatal, he summoned his brother Nusrat al-Dīn Amīr Mīrān and Asad al-Dīn Shīrkūh and the principal amīrs and commanders, and counselled them in accordance with what he judged to be necessary and most advantageous. He gave them instructions that his brother Nusrat al-Dīn should occupy his place after his death and fill the gap of his loss, owing to his reputation for gallantry and vigour, and that he should stay at Aleppo, and that Asad al-Dīn should hold Damascus as the lieutenant of Nusrat al-Dīn, and swore them all to the observance of these conditions. When this agreement had been confirmed, his illness became aggravated, and he set out in a litter for Aleppo and took up his quarters in the citadel. Asad al-Dīn proceeded to Damascus, in order to protect its territories from the ravages of the Franks and to attack the territories of the accursed, in the latter part of Shawwāl (ended 4th December).

A succession of alarming rumours was received after this concerning the king Nūr al-Dīn and there was general perturbation and anxiety ; the armies of the Muslims dispersed, the provinces were thrown into confusion, and the Franks were emboldened. They proceeded to the town of Shaizar, entered it by assault, and slew, took prisoner, and plundered. There assembled from various parts a great host of the men of the Ismā-'īlīya amongst others, and these defeated the Franks, slew a number of them, and drove them out of Shaizar.

It fell out that when Nusrat al-Dīn arrived at Aleppo, the governor of the citadel, Majd al-Dīn [Ibn al-Dāya], closed the gates in his face and refused to obey him. The town bands of Aleppo, however, rose and saying " This is our governor and king after his brother," marched to the gate of the city with their weapons and broke its locks, and Nusrat al-Dīn entered with his troops and occupied the town. The men of the town bands gave vent to reproaches, upbraiding, and threats against the governor of the citadel, and made a number of proposals to Nusrat al-Dīn, amongst them being the revival of their custom of inserting in the call to prayer the phrases " Hither to the best of works," and " Muhammad and 'Alī are the best of mankind." [1] He consented to their requests and gave them fair words and promises, and took up residence in his own house. The governor of the citadel then sent to Nusrat al-Dīn and the men of Aleppo saying : " Our master al-Mālik al-'Ādil

[1] Both were Shi'ite formulas, which were in use under the Fāṭimids, and had been abolished by Nūr al-Dīn a few years before.

Nūr al-Dīn is himself alive and conscious in his illness, and there was no necessity to do that which has been done." According to another account, the blame in this matter rests upon the governor. Secrecy was preserved, and a number of persons were admitted to the citadel and saw Nūr al-Dīn alive and with full understanding of what he said and what was said to him. He disapproved of what had happened and said : " This time I excuse the town bands for their mistaken judgment and do not blame them for their slip, since their only desire was to safeguard the interests of my brother and my appointed successor."

Reports and good tidings were subsequently spread abroad throughout the countries of the restoration to health of the king Nūr al-Dīn, and the hearts and souls of all men were cheered and rejoiced after the alarm, anxiety, and distress which they had felt. His health continued to improve, and attention was now turned to correspondence with the commanders summoning them to resume the Holy War against the accursed. Nusrat al-Dīn had in the meantime been appointed governor of the city of Harrān and its dependencies,[1] and had set out thither.

When confirmation reached Asad al-Dīn at Damascus of the reports conveying the glad tidings of the recovery of al-Mālik al-'Ādil Nūr al-Dīn and of his determination to summon the armies of Islām to engage in the Holy War against the enemies of God and those who were on campaign in Syria,[2] he made haste to set out from

---

[1] Reading *wamā 'udīfa* ('*ilaihā*) for *wa'udīfa* (cf. *R.H.C.*, IV, 24).
[2] ' Syria ' here, as always in this text, denoting the province of Aleppo.

Damascus to Aleppo. On his arrival there with his horsemen, he joined al-Mālik al-'Ādil Nūr al-Dīn, who received him with honour and praised his zeal, and they proceeded to take such measures for the defence of the provinces from the malice of the bands of infidelity and error as would lead to the general wellbeing—may God of His bounty and goodness further the attainment of these desires and hopes.

A.H. 553

(2nd February, 1158, to 22nd January, 1159)

The first day of Muharram of this year was Monday [3rd February].

In the early days of this month a series of confirmatory reports were received from the quarter of the Franks (God forsake them) who were on campaign in Syria, relating to their blockade of the castle of Hārim and their persistence in bombarding it with stones from mangonels, until its defences were weakened and it was captured by the sword. This success whetted their eagerness to dispatch raiding parties into the districts of Syria and to make free with their hands in devastations and ravages in its fortresses and villages, by reason of the dispersal of the armies of Islām and the dissensions which existed between them, owing to the distraction of al-Mālik al-'Ādil with the throes of the illness which had befallen him.

In Safar (began 4th March) the joyful news arrived by messenger of the departure of al-Mālik

al-'Ādil Nūr al-Dīn from Aleppo on his way to
Damascus. The accursed infidels were engaged
with unremitting cupidity in dispatching raiding
parties upon the districts of Hawrān and the
Iqlīm,[1] in setting their hands to ravaging, wasting,
burning and destroying in the villages, and in
plundering, taking captive and enslaving. They
advanced to Dārayyā and encamped there on
Tuesday, the last day of Safar (1st April), burned
down its dwellings and mosque, and spared no
efforts to destroy it. A large number of the
'askarīs and of the town-bands went out against
them, desirous of seeking them out and making all
speed to engage them and drive them off, but they
were prevented from carrying out their resolve
after they had approached the Franks. When the
infidels (God forsake them) saw the amount of
military equipment which was in the field [2]
against them, they departed towards al-Iqlīm at
the end of the same day. The king Nūr al-Dīn
reached Damascus and took up residence in its
citadel at dawn on Monday, 6th First Rabī'
(7th April), safe and sound, both himself and all
his company. He was welcomed with great pomp,
ceremony, and magnificence, and all the world
rejoiced at his fortunate arrival, diligently giving
thanks for his safety and recovery from sickness
and praying for length of days to him and victory
to his standards. He set about organizing the

---

[1] *Iqlīm* is a general term for *district* or *province*, but it is uncertain
which of the provinces of Damascus was called " The Iqlīm " without
qualification. The district which best fits the context is that along the
Nahr al-A 'waj (see above p. 298, n. 1), now called Iqlīm Ballān.

[2] In Abū Shāma (*R.H.C.*, IV, 27) " the large numbers who had come
out."

troops and making ready equipment for the Holy War—may God strengthen him with His aid and grant the attainment of all his aims.

At the beginning of First Rabī' of this year, word arrived from Egypt of the emergence of a considerable contingent of its 'askar to Gaza and Ascalon. They raided their districts, and those of the accursed Franks who were there came out against them. But God gave the Muslims victory over them by slaying and capture, so that none of them escaped save a few, and the Muslims took what they had seized as booty and returned safely and victorious. It was said that the commander of the Holy Warriors [1] on sea captured a number of vessels of the polytheists, laden with Franks ; an immense number of them were killed and taken prisoner, and he, having gained possession of riches, war material, and furnishings from them beyond computation, returned victorious and booty-laden.

On Sunday, 9th Second Rabī' (11th May) al-Mālik al-'Ādil Nūr al-Dīn went out from Damascus to the Wooden Bridge with his victorious 'askar, equipped with instruments of war, hastening to engage the polytheistic infidels. Prior to this, Asad al-Dīn, on his arrival with his company of Turkmen cavalry, had led them in a raid upon the districts of Sidon and its neighbourhood, and they had captured an excellent and abundant spoil. The Frankish horsemen and footsoldiers who were stationed there came out to engage them, but they laid an ambush for them and took them as spoil. Most of the Franks were killed and the remainder, including the son of the commander who was in

---

[1] *Ghuzāh*, see above p. 283, n. 3.

charge of the castle of Hārim, were captured. The Muslims returned safely with the prisoners, the heads of the slain, and the booty, having suffered no casualties other than one horseman lost— praise and thanks be to God therefor.

Word arrived from the royal camp that the Franks (God forsake them) had assembled together and marched against the victorious 'askar, that the lord Nūr al-Dīn had advanced with the 'askar forthwith, and battle was joined. It came about that the 'askar of Islām, owing to the failure of one of the commanders, gave way and dispersed, but Nūr al-Dīn stood fast in his place, facing the Franks with a small body of his bravest attendants and personal officers. They loosed arrows at them and slew a great number both of them and of their horses, until at length the Franks turned in flight, fearing lest an ambush had been laid by the Muslim cavalry and should come out upon them. Thus God (to Him be praise) delivered Nūr al-Dīn from their violence, by His aid and by his own great boldness, firmness of mind, and far-famed valour. He returned to his camp safely with his company and upbraided those who were the cause of his withdrawal before the Franks, while the Frankish host dispersed to their own provinces. He wrote to the king of the Franks,[1] expressing his desire for a reconciliation and armistice, and urged him thereto, but after the passage to and fro of correspondence between the two parties no agreement was reached between them. The victorious 'askar

---

[1] This is the more natural construction, but the words may also be read as " The King of the Franks wrote." In Abū Shāma (p. 99) the language is explicit in the latter sense.

remained in the field for some time thereafter, until the wise judgment of Nūr al-Dīn determined upon returning to his capital city, and he reached it on —— [1] Sha'bān (began 28th August) of this year.

On Tuesday, 11th [2] Ramadān (7th October), the chamberlain Mahmūd the *muwallad* [3] arrived from Egypt with the reply of its governor, al-Malik al-Sālih [Talā'i' b. Ruzzīk], to the letters which he had been charged to carry. [4] Accompanying him was one of the principal amīrs of Egypt in the capacity of an envoy, bringing a gift of money for the royal treasury of Nūr al-Dīn, together with various Egyptian stuffs, and Arab horses. A detachment of the Franks (God forsake them) came to blows with them [5] on the roads which they were traversing, but God gave the Muslims the upper hand over them, so that none of them escaped save a very few. Following on this, news was received from the Egyptian 'askar of its victory over a considerable body of Franks and Arabs, approximately four hundred horsemen or more, at al-'Arīsh, one of the watering-points [between Palestine and Egypt], when the Franks were overpowered by death, captivity, and despoiling. This was a great victory and highly esteemed success—to God be given the praise and thanks therefor.

---

[1] lacuna in the text.

[2] The text has 21st, which conflicts both with the calendar and with other dates given by the writer ; cf. also Ibn Muyassar in *R.H.C.*, III, 472-3.

[3] " Son of slave parents," *i.e.*, descendant of a Turkish ghulām.

[4] Reading *tahammalahu* for *tahammalnā* (" we were charged ") (cf. A.S., p. 102)

[5] Read *ilaihim* (A.S. *lahum*) for *al-muhimma*

A number of corroborative reports were received from Constantinople in Dhu'l-Hijja (began 24th December) of this year of the emergence of the king of the Greeks therefrom with a great host and vast assembly in order to attack the cities and fortresses of Islām, his arrival at Murūj al-Dībāj and encampment there, the despatch of his squadrons to raid the districts of Antioch and the neighbouring provinces, and that a force of Turkmens had gained the victory over a company of them. This was after he had captured in the territories of [the son of] Leo,[1] king of the Armenians, a number of his castles and fortresses. When news of this reached al-Mālik al-'Ādil Nūr al-Dīn, he set about writing to the governors of the cities and fortresses, informing them of the doings of the Greeks, and bidding them exercise vigilance and prepare to engage in the Holy War against them and inflict chastisement upon all of them who should fall into their hands.

A.H. 554

(23rd January, 1159, to 11th January, 1160)

The first day of this year was Friday [23rd January].

During the early days of Dhu'l-Hijja of the year 553 al-Mālik al-'Ādil Nūr al-Dīn had contracted an illness, which increased its hold on him to such an extent that it sapped his strength, and

---

[1] Read *min a 'māli Lāwīn* (as in A.S., p. 103) ; or possibly some words have dropped out (e.g., *mina 'l-a 'māli 'llatī li'bni Lāwīn*), as the passage refers not to Leo, but to his son Thoros.

alarmist rumours were set on foot about him by those who were envious of his fortune, and by mischief-makers amongst the lower classes of his subjects. The civil population and local troops were filled with dismay, and the dwellers in the frontier districts and lands were distressed, fearing lest any evil should befall him, more especially in face of the reports of the movements of the Greeks and the news concerning the Franks (God forsake them). When he became conscious of his own weakness, he gave instructions to his principal officers, saying to them : " I have resolved to deliver an injunction to you concerning what has come into my mind, so do ye give heed and obedience to it and abide by its conditions." They said : " We hear and obey thy command, and whatsoever thou dost enjoin of thy judgement and thy decree, we do accept it and shall act in accordance therewith." Then he said : " I fear for the subjects and all the Muslims lest there should come after me ignorant, evildoing and oppressive governors. As for my brother Nusrat al-Dīn Amīr Mīrān, in view of what I know of his character and evil deeds, I cannot consent to giving him authority over any of the affairs of the Muslims. Therefore my choice has fallen upon my brother the amīr Qutb al-Dīn Mawdūd, son of 'Imād al-Dīn, governor of Mosul [1], because of the intelligence, uprightness, piety, and true belief which appertain to him, to occupy my place after me and to fill the gap of my loss. Do ye then be obedient to his command after me and

---

[1] The text adds wakhawāssihi (" and his personal officers ").

hearken to his decree, and swear loyalty to him with sincerity of intention and heart and singleness of purpose and mind." They replied : " Thy command shall we obey and thy decision shall we execute," and swore binding oaths to act according to the provisions of his injunction and to execute its terms. He then dispatched his envoys to this brother of his to acquaint him with the condition of affairs, in order that he might be in readiness for it and prepared to carry out his part with speed. Thereafter God manifested his bounty upon him and upon all the Muslims by the beginning of his convalescence and the increase of strength in his mind and body ; he took his seat in the council-chamber to give audience [1] and receive salutations, and all men's hearts were rejoiced by this boon and their spirits strengthened by its renewal.

Now the amīr Majd al-Dīn, the lieutenant in Aleppo, had placed patrols on the roads to guard travellers upon them, and the resident at Manbij seized a certain man, a porter from Damascus, known as Ibn Maghzū, who had letters with him. He sent the man and the letters to Mujāhid al-Dīn, the governor of Aleppo, who, when he learned their contents, ordered the bearer of them to be crucified, and at once dispatched them to al-Mālik al-'Ādil Nūr al-Dīn. When he received them, on Thursday, 14th [2] Muharram of the new year (5th February), he found them to be from the intendant of his *diwan*, the governor of the citadel, and one of his chamberlains to his brother Nusrat al-Dīn Amīr Mīrān, lord of Harrān, informing him that the

---

[1] Read *lid-dukhūli* for *al-madkhūlu*.
[2] Literally " in the second decade of Muharram."

life of his brother al-Mālik al-'Ādil was despaired of, and urging him to come with all speed to Damascus in order that it might be given into his hands. On learning of this, Nūr al-Dīn showed the letters to their writers, who acknowledged them, and were confined by his orders. There was a fourth in their party, but he had had fears and fled two days before. Simultaneously, there arrived a letter from the lord of Qal'at Ja'bar with information that Nusrat al-Dīn had crossed, hastening towards Damascus. Nūr al-Dīn thereupon dispatched Asad al-Dīn with the victorious 'askar to drive him back and prevent his coming; subsequently word reached him of his return to his own place on learning of the recovery of his brother al-Mālik al-'Ādil, and Asad al-Dīn returned to Damascus with the 'askar.

The king's envoys arrived back from Mosul with the answer to the letters which they had been charged to carry to his brother Qutb al-Dīn. When they parted from him, he had already moved out with his 'askar to proceed to Damascus, but on leaving Mosul he received the news of the recovery of the king Nūr al-Dīn, and remaining where he was dispatched the wazīr Jamal al-Dīn to investigate the situation. The wazīr arrived at Damascus on Saturday, 8th Safar (28th February) in great pomp and state, and a great host went out to meet him. . . . He had a meeting with al-Mālik al-'Ādil Nūr al-Dīn, and certain negotiations and agreements were made between them, which ended in the return of the wazīr to whence he came after receiving due honour and consideration. Nūr al-Dīn sent with him for his brother Qutb al-Dīn and his household officers such a gratification as the existing circumstances required, and the wazīr *isfahsallar* Asad al-Dīn Shīrkūh and his household officers set out along with him on Saturday, 15th Safar (7th March).

In the meantime there arrived an envoy from the king of the Greeks, from his camp, bearing a choice gift which he had sent to al-Mālik al-ʿĀdil, consisting of brocade and other fabrics, with a friendly letter, and mules.[1] A similar gift was made in return, and he set out on his way back in the latter days of Safar. It was related concerning the king of the Franks (God forsake him) that a reconciliation and armistice had been established between him and the king of the Greeks—may God turn the malice of each of them back into his own throat, and cause him to taste the requital for his treachery and guile.

Between the 10th and 20th of Safar also the chamberlain Mahmūd al-Mustarshidī set out for Egypt in company with the returning envoys (God grant them safety), bearing the replies [2] from al-Mālik al-ʿĀdil to the letters which they had brought with them from al-Mālik al-ʿĀdil al-Sālih [Ibn Ruzzīk], its governor.

News arrived from the neighbourhood of the king of the Greeks, of his determination to march against Antioch and to attack the Islamic fortresses. Al-Mālik al-ʿĀdil Nūr al-Dīn made haste to proceed to the cities of Syria in order to relieve them of their fears from the malice of the Greeks

---

[1] Abū Shāma (p. 104) reads *fi ʿāl* (" action," i.e., courteous gesture) for *bighāl* (" mules ").
[2] Reading *bijawābāti* for *bijarāyāti*.

and Franks (God forsake them), and set out with the victorious 'askar on Thursday, 5th [1] First Rabī' of this year (26th March) towards Hims, Hamāh, and Shaizar, with the intention of continuing his march to Aleppo if [2] circumstances should demand it.

On 1st First Jumādā (21st May), a series of joyful reports were corroborated from the victorious 'askar of the king Nūr al-Dīn in the territories of Aleppo, to the effect that the amīrs, commanders and governors of the provinces had arrived one after the other with vast numbers and large forces, to engage in the Holy War against the parties of the misguided infidels, both Greeks and Franks, on account of their purpose to attack the territories of Islām and their covetous desire to possess themselves of them and make ravages in them, and in order to defend these territories from their malice and protect them against their guile. Then God, in the greatness of His bounty towards His creatures and of His loving kindness and compassion for His cities, willed to infuse into the determination of the king Nur al-Din such sureness of judgment and design, ability of management and decision, and purity of intention towards God and singleness of mind, in regard to the armistice and amicable arrangement established between him and the king of the Greeks, as had not been reckoned upon nor imagined by any. Thus, by the good judgment of the king of the Greeks and his knowledge of the evil results to which the

---

[1] The text has 3rd, but it is evident from dates quoted in other passages that First Rabī' began locally on Sunday, 22nd March.

[2] Reading 'in for 'ilā 'an.

effects of wars give rise and the difficulty of attaining the hoped-for end, a formal agreement was reached on this matter in consolidation of peace, after the passage of envoys to and fro with proposals for terms of settlement. The request of the king of the Greeks for the liberation of the Frankish leaders detained in the confinement of the king Nūr al-Dīn and their transference to his own camp was granted, and Nūr al-Dīn dispatched them all to him, together with the [other] demands which he had made. The king of the Greeks recompensed this generous act with gifts rivalling those of the greatest and most powerful sovereigns : magnificent brocade robes of various kinds and in large numbers, precious jewels, a brocade tent of great value, and a gratifying number of local horses.[1] Thereafter, between the 11th and 20th of First Jumādā 554, he departed from his camp with his army to return to his own land, having earned thanks and praise, and without injuring a single Muslim, and all hearts were restored to tranquillity and security after their distress, anxiety and fear.

News arrived after this that al-Mālik al-'Ādil Nūr al-Dīn had made a surpassing great banquet on Friday, 17th First Jumādā (5th June) for his brother Qutb al-Dīn and his 'askar, and for those commanders and governors and their troops who had come with him to engage in the Holy War against the Greeks and the Franks. An immense preparation was made for it by the slaughter of horses, cattle, and sheep, and the provision of other

[1] al-khuyūl al-mahallīya, but it would seem that mahallī in this instance has some technical meaning, other than " local " A.S. (p. 105) reads al-jabalīya, "mountain horses."

requirements, the like of which had never been seen, and which absorbed a large proportion of the taxes.[1] He also distributed a great number of Arab stallions, horses and mules, as well as a surpassing quantity of robes of honour, various kinds of brocade and other stuffs, and golden dishes. It was a great day of finery and pomp. It happened that a company of Turkmens from foreign parts, finding the troops off their guard in their preoccupation with and participation in the banquet, made a raid upon the Banū Usāma and other Arabs, and drove off their animals. When word of this arrived, a considerable detachment of the victorious 'askar was sent out in pursuit of them, and they overtook the Turkmens, and recovered from them all that they had seized, which was then restored to its owners.

The king Nūr al-Dīn (may God exalt him) thereafter determined to proceed to the city of Harrān, in order to besiege it and recover it from his brother Nusrat al-Dīn, on account of the advantage which he saw to lie in this measure. He set out with the victorious 'askar on 1st Latter Jumādā (19th June), and when he encamped before it and surrounded it, there took place a series of negotiations, proposals, resistances, and engagements, until at length it was agreed to grant an amnesty to those who were in it. The city was surrendered on Saturday, 23rd Latter Jumādā (11th July), and its affairs were put in order, and benevolent consideration was shown towards its inhabitants.

---

[1] *qāma bijumlatin kabīratin mina'l-gharāmati* ; *gharāmah* here can hardly mean " indemnity," and the phrase may perhaps be translated more generally " cost a great deal of expense."

It was then delivered to the high amīr and *isfahsallar* Zain al-Dīn as a military fief, and its control and defence were entrusted to him.

A.H. 555

(12th January to 30th December, 1160)

The first day of this year was Tuesday [12th January].

On the eve of Friday, ———[1] of Safar of this year died the amīr Mujāhid al-Dīn Buzān b. Māmīn, one of the principal amīrs of the Kurds, and of high consideration in the kingdom (God's mercy upon him), reputed for bravery, gallantry and liberality, assiduous in expending gifts and alms, handsome of face, and of a cheerful countenance when accosted. He was borne from his house at the Gardens Gate to the mosque for the prayer, and thence to the College called by his name, where he was buried the same day. There was not one but wept for him and sorrowed at his loss, because of his generous actions and praiseworthy qualities.[2]

[1] Date omitted in the text ; Safar began on 11th February.
[2] Ibn al-Qalānisī himself died on the 7th of the following month, corresponding to 18 March, 1160.

INDEXES

Index I

NAMES OF PERSONS, ETC.[1]

Index II

NAMES OF PLACES

Index III

CONTEMPORARY WESTERN FORMS AND TRANSCRIPTIONS OF NAMES OCCURRING IN THE DAMASCUS CHRONICLE

[1] Note on the pronunciation of Arabic names :

The golden rule in the pronunciation of Arabic names is to scan them by the rules of Latin verse ; linger a little on every " long " syllable, i.e., syllables containing either a long vowel or a vowel followed by two consonants, and pass lightly over the rest. By the English reader the consonants may be pronounced as in English, the vowels as in Italian (though *a* varies between the sounds in ' can,' ' dart ' and ' pall ' according to the consonants in its vicinity). The main stress never falls on the last syllable unless it contains a long vowel followed by a consonant or ends with two consonants ; otherwise it falls on the long syllable which is nearest to the end of the word ; if all the syllables (or all but the last) are short, it falls on the first syllable of the word. Examples (the accent sign ' preceding the stressed syllable) :—
Rud'wān, Nūrad'dīn, Ba'la'bakk, Īl'ghāzī, Mara'qīya, Mu'hammad, 'Majdal, 'Bursuqī, Ta'rābulus, 'Jabala.

INDEX I

NAMES OF PERSONS, ETC.

361

INDEX II

NAMES OF PLACES

INDEX III

CONTEMPORARY WESTERN FORMS AND TRANSCRIPTIONS OF NAMES OCCURRING IN THE DAMASCUS CHRONICLE